GREEK ISLAND LIFE

View of the harbour and village, Anafi, summer 1966

Greek Island Life

✳

Fieldwork on Anafi

Margaret E. Kenna

PSK
ublishing

Sean Kingston Publishing
www.seankingston.co.uk
Canon Pyon

Second edition published in 2017 by
Sean Kingston Publishing
www.seankingston.co.uk
Canon Pyon

British Library Cataloguing in Publication Data
A catalogue record for this book is available from the British Library.

The moral rights of the author have been asserted.

Printed by Lightning Source

ISBN 978-1-907774-86-7

CONTENTS

ILLUSTRATIONS

ACKNOWLEDGEMENTS

The various pieces of research on which this book is based were partly funded by the following bodies: the doctoral research in 1966/67 was financed by a Department of Education graduate studentship and by a grant from the Committee for Mediterranean Studies set up between the London School of Economics and the School of Oriental and African Studies, London, and the University of Kent at Canterbury. The three months' fieldwork in 1973 was supported by a grant from the Social Anthropology Committee of the Social Sciences Research Council (ref HR2445/2). The research carried out in 1987/88 depended on a grant from the Social Affairs Committee of the Economic and Social Research Council (ref GOO 232341) which allowed me to take nine months' unsalaried leave, after which University College of Swansea (as it was then) granted me three months' sabbatical leave. The Research Support Fund at Swansea helped me to make several return visits to Greece and also gave me a special grant to finance the copying of the archive of glass and celluloid negatives showing the lives of the political exiles in the 1930s. To all these bodies I am extremely grateful.

The quotation from Bob Dylan's 'Ballad of a Thin Man' in Chapter Nine is Copyright © 1965 by Warner Bros. Inc.; renewed 1993 by Special Rider Music. All rights reserved, reprinted by permission of Special Rider Music.

I dedicate this book to the memories of two people whose influence I continue to feel: my mother, Margery Kenna, née Guest (1902–1975), and Thanasis Vafiadhis (1907–1975).

NOTE ON TRANSLITERATION

In transliterating Greek, I have used the system currently (2001) recommended by the *Journal of Modern Greek Studies*. This suggests that well-known people and places should be given in the customary English form (Athens not Athina, Cavafy not Kavafis), so readers may find some inconsistencies.

α	a		χ	kh before a, o, u, consonants
β	v			and after s
γ	gh before a, o, u,			h before i, e (except after s)
	consonants		ψ	ps
	y before i, e		ω	o
δ	dh		αι	e
ε	e		γγ	ng
ζ	z		γκ	g initially
η	i			ng medially
θ	th		γχ	nkh
ι	i		αϊ	aï
κ	k		ει	i
λ	l		ευ	ef before voiceless consonants
μ	m			ev before vowels, voiced
ν	n			consonants
ξ	ks		μπ	b initially
ο	o			mb medially
π	p		οι	i
ρ	r		οϊ	oï
σ, ς	s		ου	u
τ	t		οϋ	oï
υ	i		ωϊ	oï
φ	f			

PREFACE TO THE SECOND EDITION OF *GREEK ISLAND LIFE*

This second edition of *Greek Island Life* marks a half-century since I first arrived to carry out research on the Cycladic island of Anafi. The first edition was given the provisional title 'Far From God', a phrase the villagers used about the island to describe their sense of isolation from the rest of Greece during the 1960s, and, indeed, before that. The full phrase was 'far from God and a hundred years behind the rest of the world'. However, the publisher insisted on a title which was more 'keyword-friendly'. If that original title had been accepted, I would have been able to show the reader very easily in Chapter 9 – even more so now in Chapter 10 – how much the island has changed in fifty years; although, after the tourist season (May to September), the ferry schedule is often still problematic, erratic and frequently curtailed until Eastertime of the following year.

The new material in this edition consists of this Preface and an additional chapter (Chapter 10) which continues the account of my involvement with the island and with migrants from the end of Chapter 9, the final section of which describes a visit to Anafi in the late 1990s. Previously unpublished photos illustrate Chapter 10. A few minor errors in the original text have been corrected.

In writing a new final chapter, I decided to continue the practice of using contemporary materials. In the first edition this was planned to allow the reader to share the experience of finding out information, puzzling over its significance, and trying to fit it into some kind of framework. I did this in the main part of the book by basing the chapters on letters written to my parents while researching on the island and in Athens, on reports to my doctoral-thesis supervisor, excerpts from my personal diary, and from the fieldnotes I wrote every evening. Chapter 10 contains material more or less contemporary with the events described, mostly excerpts from letters to family and friends in the first decade of the twenty-first century, but also from fieldnotes, with some interpolated comments to clarify details. In addition to letters and fieldnotes I have also added excerpts from reports sent to grant-awarding bodies (the Economic and Social Research Council, Leverhulme). Readers who are interested in finding out more can go to the relevant websites,[1] as well

---

1   www.researchcatalogue.esrc.ac.uk/grants/RES-000-22-1641/read;
     www.leverhulme.ac.uk/sites/default/files/imported_pdfs/eliciting%20
     memories-%20%20photos%20of%20long-term%20fieldwork%20in%20greec%20
     (kenna).pdf

as to academia.edu, where most of my publications have been uploaded. The letters, notes and reports cannot help but be different in character from those first writings in the sixties, when I felt very confused and unable to understand the social life and cultural underpinnings of the islanders' life. Thirty-five and forty years later I was much more familiar with the island, with islanders and migrants, and with Greece. There was still much more to learn, but I was better able to make sense of what I was seeing and hearing. Fifty years later I am still learning.

INTRODUCTION[1]

✳

This book gives a picture of one particular year in the life of a community on a small Greek island in the mid-1960s. I first went there in May 1966 as a twenty-four year old unmarried postgraduate student to collect material for a doctoral thesis in social anthropology. So began a relationship with people and a place which is absolutely central to my life, both personal and professional. The initial topic of the thesis was 'inter-island links', and the intention was that I would start by studying a small Cycladic island (Sikinos), move after a few months to a large neighbouring island (Ios), and then to the island which was the centre of the Cyclades as an administrative unit (Siros). This method of collecting information by living in a community, watching what people do and listening to what they say, is known in anthropology as fieldwork. As things turned out, I spent less than a week on Sikinos, moved to another small island in the Cyclades, and stayed there for sixteen months. What happened during that time forms the subject matter of this book. I eventually abandoned the original thesis topic and began instead to trace the interconnections between the pattern of naming children, their rights to family property, and their obligations to carry out rituals for the souls of those from whom they had inherited. I left in August 1967, and began to write a doctoral thesis which was eventually presented in 1971. Just as the focus of that thesis differed from the original intention, so this book is very different from the one I might have written soon after leaving Greece or after the thesis was presented. One reason for the difference is that now I have a further thirty years' knowledge of the island and its migrant community in Athens to draw on, The island

1   To the 2001 edition.

has changed, I have changed, and social anthropology has changed in the intervening years.

In September 1973, having been married for three years, I visited the island again, very briefly, after several months in Athens, making a more thorough study of the migrant community and their Migrants' Association than I had been able to carry out during the first fieldwork. I made another short visit during Easter 1983, accompanied by my husband and four-year old son. That visit provided me with material to make a research proposal for a 'twenty years after' follow-up study and a full year's fieldwork followed, divided between the island and Athens, from the summer of 1987 to July 1988. I visited the island most recently in March 1998, after a gap of ten years.

As a result of this long association with the same place, and with many of the same people, I am able to draw on knowledge of both personal destinies and wider processes. For example: a woman who is described ploughing in January 1967, I know to have died in childbirth ten years later. In the summer of 1988 one of her daughters described attempts to carry the fatally haemorrhaging woman by stretcher to a steamer diverted on its journey from Crete to Piraeus to get her to hospital. The baby to whom she had given birth died a few days after the mother. By 1988 there was a helicopter landing pad on an area of flat ground outside the village and any emergency medical case could be swiftly flown to hospital. Another example: in March 1967, a brief note in my fieldwork diary records that my next-door neighbour's little boy brought me a loaf of bread; I went with him to watch his parents shearing sheep in 1973. He grew to manhood, married, and in 1986 was blown to pieces when a dynamite charge exploded prematurely as he was out fishing with his father. In 1987 I went to the village cemetery with my neighbour and watched her sprinkle fresh water on the two graves. A few years later still, the son's young widow had remarried, an event almost unthinkable in the sixties; as unthinkable as the fact that marriages could also end in divorce, a word which occurred occasionally when women I talked to in the nineties brought me up to date with their family news. A third example: during the early summer of 1966, island men's conversations in the village coffee shops concerned radio reports that the quota of Greek migrant workers to Germany was being restricted. This would have direct consequences for their seasonal migration to Athens to work as building labourers, as there would be greater competition for such jobs. Following the Colonels' coup in April 1967, many previous building restrictions were lifted. Members of the Athenian migrant community, together with seasonal migrants from the island, made money out of this building boom, and later invested it in the development of island tourism. One long sandy beach on the island's south coast, deserted in the sixties except for a few migrant families in August, was, by the 1980s, marked by tents and bamboo shelters housing European holiday-makers from May onwards, and the hillslopes facing the sea were dotted with migrants' holiday cottages, rooms to rent, a restaurant and a fast-food café where souvenir t-shirts and postcards can be bought. Recession and inflation during the '70s, and the effects of government policies on communications, had helped turn the migrant community in Athens from investment in the construction of suburban blocks of flats to the tourist development of their place of origin.

My wider knowledge goes further back in time, too. I now know much more about the life of the political exiles on the island in the 1930s, the commune they established there, their relationships with islanders, and the long-term effects on the islanders' view of themselves of having their island used as a place of exile. My interest in this aspect of the history of the island developed to the extent that I have written a book about the social organisation of exile in Greece (Kenna 2001). Contacts with archaeologists, and with historians specialising in the period of Venetian rule in the Cyclades have expanded my knowledge of the long-term history of the island.

This book is also different from what I might once have written because I can take advantage of new directions in the writing of my professional discipline, social anthropology. Reflexivity, the critical and conscious acknowledgement of the anthropologist both in the field and in the text, suggests that I should now reflect on what helped and what hindered me in my research. Such things as my age, gender and upbringing affected my approach to the islanders and their views of me, some of which I did not discover until months or years later. I can look critically, too, at the different ways in which I wrote about my findings: in letters to my parents, in my personal diary, in fieldnotes, in monthly reports to my supervisor, and, later, in my thesis and publications. Through these, I can trace the way in which I found out about and began to see the connections between the topics which eventually formed the focus of my thesis: the pattern of naming children, their rights to shares of the family estate, and their obligations to carry out a cycle of rituals to ensure the fate of the souls of those from whom they inherited. I can also pick out elements which became of importance in later studies: the role of urban migrants in relation to resident islanders; conflicts within the Migrants' Association between long-established pre-war migrants, mostly in white-collar clerical jobs, and the more affluent post-war migrants who were making money in the building trade. I can trace early indications of tourism, and compare differences over decades in the cult of the island's patron saint.

In writing this book, I have drawn on a number of sources: a bundle of over 75 letters written to my parents, my own personal diaries, hundreds of photographs, nearly 500 pages of fieldnotes, and published and unpublished documents of various kinds (a transcript of the island's population register, annual agricultural reports, travel books, memoirs in English and in Greek). The detail and tone of the letters may perhaps surprise some readers; they were written by an only child to parents who were highly involved in the research. My father, an Australian clinical psychologist who had once studied anthropology as part of his graduate programme at an American university, sent me a stream of references and photocopies; my mother, who as a young bride had lived for six months in the Gilbert and Ellice Islands in the Pacific with her first husband, had later been a court reporter in Australia and was a pioneer voluntary worker in the Family Planning Association. There was almost nothing I could not write to them about (although I did not tell them until later about the theft of a camera, and a serious road accident on the drive to Greece).

My concern throughout this book is to write about the island, the islanders and the migrants, but in doing so I cannot help but write myself into the text, as 'I' constantly appear in letters, fieldnotes, and reports. What I hope to do is to help the reader to share the experience of doing fieldwork. By commenting on what I wrote in the early part of my fieldwork in the light of what I found out later, I do not want to mimic the irritating 'little did I know then' of a voice-over technique, but rather to help the reader follow the process of making sense of fieldwork material and to understand how experience shaped the direction which the research took. In the text, square brackets are used to add clarification, correction or comment.

So far, in this introduction, I have not given the name of the island: Anafi, the most south-easterly of the Cyclades. This is because questions of anonymity and the use of pseudonyms are of critical concern to anyone who carries out anthropological and sociological research. Questions of this kind often affect journalists and reporters who wish on some occasions to name the sources they quote and at other times to conceal and protect them; some of those interviewed or questioned are eager to be named, others refuse. Guides to fieldwork and research deal extensively with problems of 'informed consent'. Islanders, and members of the Migrants' Association, have repeatedly urged me to use the island's name in my writings, but may not be aware of the consequences. If, for example, even a few readers decide to go and visit the island, would this be any more (or less) serious a consequence than the visits of casual island-hoppers? Can informed consent really be given for me to print names of places and people, when many of the passages in which these names occur involve my own misconceptions, or the reporting of rumours, gossip, and speculation? What are the implications for the widowed mother whose son is mentioned earlier, of a public statement that both her husband and son were killed carrying out an illegal, although all too common practice? How will the now adult children of women who discussed their use of various contraceptive devices with me, react? In addition to passages whose sensitive nature is immediately obvious, there may be other sections whose additional significance is not yet clear to me, but plain to an islander or to a Greek reader.

Why not use pseudonyms? If I use a pseudonym for the place, I cannot refer to sources which name it; if I try to conceal identities by mixing actual names and surnames, I still confront the problem of dealing with those in particular positions: when referring to the village secretary, or the brothers who ran an olive press, it will be obvious to those familiar with the island who is meant. A number of islanders and migrants know enough English to be able to read this book. Recognising that this text is as much for them as it is for anyone else, my decision has been to use actual names or identifying occupations except in cases where embarrassment or worse might result.

Another problem is that of personal names. Because of the island pattern of naming children after their grandparents, and after other relatives, there is a fairly small pool of names on the island. So common was it in the sixties to be named Maria, or Nikos, that people with unique names such as Ariadhni, Lemonia, or Khristos were regarded as quite exceptional. I recognise that this will be a problem for readers just as it was for me. Islanders usually refer to each other by first name, often qualified by a personal or family nickname, or by their occupation, but these nicknames are not usually used as terms of address, as they often commemorate embarrassing events or traits. In my notes I identified people by their relationship with people I already knew ('Niko postman's brother') or by physical features ('Yianni bulbous-nose') or other characteristics ('Flora short-sleeves'). Is it reasonable to suppose that readers will remember people named in this way? One device to cope with this difficulty might be to use a reference list of characters such as appears in translations of Russian novels, but the idea was discarded as too cumbrous.

The plan of this book is a mixture of chronological and thematic presentation. The first chapter is arranged chronologically, using my letters and fieldnotes in sequence to recount the circumstances which brought me to Anafi in mid-May 1966 and giving a picture of the first seven weeks of fieldwork, with comments and explanations in square brackets. One way of continuing would be to go on in this way, showing how my knowledge of the island grew over the next sixteen months, and how all the different kinds of information which I recorded began to make different kinds of sense. However, I have decided to present the reader with information about everyday life, work and leisure in the next two chapters, focusing on summer and autumn activities in Chapter Two and on the winter and spring of 1967 in Chapter Three. This will set the scene for material on naming and kinship in Chapter Four. At this point I move outside Anafi, collecting together all the information about my visits elsewhere: to the neighbouring island of Santorini, to Athens, to Mani, and to Turkey (Chapter Five). I then return to the island-based material again in Chapter Six, which concerns religion and ritual, particularly the cycle of memorial services for the souls of the dead which, I argued in my thesis, linked the pattern of naming to rights of inheritance. In Chapter Seven I move away from the 'ethnographic present', and from a preoccupation with my own fieldnotes and letters, to discuss the history of Anafi, as known to its inhabitants, and as viewed by others.

In the penultimate chapter (Chapter Eight) I revert to the chronological mode of presenting material concerned with a number of different topics. This chapter deals with the events of Easter 1967, the time when what has subsequently been named 'the Colonels' coup' took place, resulting in seven years of dictatorial rule by a military junta. By that time I had been living on Anafi for almost a year, knew nearly everybody, and had been entrusted with the village register through which I could accurately name people and trace relationships, and my fieldnotes were long and detailed. My recording of the reactions on Anafi to the news of the coup, and of the attempts of everyone, including myself, to find out what other people thought was going on, is interwoven in the notes with descriptions of the preparations for Easter, as well as with references to what I knew to be the typical events and activities of the annual economic cycle.

In Chapter Nine, I attempt to draw all the thematic and chronological threads together and say something about the island and its migrants from the sixties to the nineties. In presenting the material in this way, I hope to produce a book that will be of interest to other social anthropologists or to those who want to know what it is like to carry out anthropological research. I also want to offer something which can be read by anyone who wants to know about Greece, by giving an idea of what certain parts of Greece were like in the '60s, and what the Greece of today seems like to someone with that prior experience.

I will end this introduction by sketching in the background to my arrival in Greece in the spring of 1966. In April of that year, a few weeks after my twenty-fourth birthday, I left Canterbury with a fellow postgraduate student, Mick Lineton, his wife Nancy, and their two children, Tom, then aged four, and Ben who was eighteen months. (My visits to their fieldwork site in the southern part of the Greek mainland are described in Chapter Five.) We travelled in a second-hand left-hand drive Volkswagen micro-bus which Mick had bought not long before we set off, and which he and I (as co-driver) were still getting used to driving.

State Studentships paid our tuition fees and provided a quarterly sum for living expenses, I received £500 a year, a sum on which it was possible to live adequately, although not luxuriously. A newly established Mediterranean

Research Committee had given each of us a small grant to cover the additional expenses of fieldwork. Mick and I had travelled to Greece together by train in the summer of 1965, before the move to Canterbury, to get an idea of what research would entail and to make a final choice of fieldwork sites. Taking preliminary inspiration from Patrick Leigh Fermor's book *Mani*, Mick wanted to carry out research there on depopulation and urban migration. Even more than other parts of Greece, Mani had experienced massive depopulation; there was nothing there, Mick had told me, but olive trees and crumbling stone towers. By the end of the summer, he finally selected an inland village called Mina, but had made no arrangements for a place where he, Nancy and the boys might live once they reached it. The assumption was that with so much depopulation there must be a house they could rent.

While we were in Athens, using the recently established Social Sciences Centre on the edge of Kolonaki Square as an academic base, we met and made friends with an American postgraduate, Susanna Hoffman, who was intending to carry out fieldwork on the volcanic island of Santorini (Thira); our paths crossed again in Christmas 1966, when she arrived in Greece (see Chapter Five) to begin her research.

Early in those summer weeks of 1965, a Greek friend took me to a tavern in the Plaka, in Panos Street, looking up at the Acropolis and opposite a Turkish mosque, at one corner of the site where the Tower of the Winds had been preserved. Although called the Taverna Kea after the island where its proprietor, Yiannis Pulakis, originated, the taverna was known to most of its customers as the Taverna Pulakis. There were four rooms on the first floor to rent, and a hole-in-the-ground toilet in a shower room. Some of the rooms faced onto a balcony which looked away from the Acropolis, along the long straight street called Athinas which ran into Omonia Square. The balcony also had a tap, and travellers could do their washing and hang it out to dry there. The Taverna Pulakis became a base that summer, as we travelled around separately, and returned occasionally to Athens to collect our mail from American Express just off Sintagma Square. It also became a base during our fieldwork year.

While Mick travelled around Mani, I visited several Cycladic islands and some in the Dodecanese, and had chosen to start fieldwork on a small island called Sikinos, near Ios. Ios was just becoming popular as a holiday place for Europeans and Britons. The intention stated in my subsequent research proposal was that I would start off on Sikinos, and then move on to Ios, noting not only the physical connections between the islands by steamer and small boat, but also the economic and social interconnections such as inter-island marriages. Part of the rationale for my topic was that there was no study as yet of a Greek island community. The only anthropological publications in

English about Greece at that time were John Campbell's book *Honour, Family and Patronage*, about a transhumant shepherding people, the Sarakatsani, in northern Greece, and Ernestine Friedl's account in *Vasilika* of a mainland agricultural village. I had originally wanted to carry out a study of a fishing community to add another kind of subsistence economy to those already described. My experiences in the summer of 1965 had convinced me that it would be impossible for a woman to carry out a study of fishermen, but an island study still seemed feasible.

From the moment our respective research topics had been approved, Mick and I had been reading everything we could find about Greece, and about our respective fieldwork areas. I had been attending Modern Greek classes in London, and could speak tourist Greek of a moderate kind; having taken Ancient Greek as one of my A-level subjects, I was probably better at reading Greek than speaking it. However, once I was immersed in a totally Greek-speaking environment among island villagers, I fairly soon picked up local dialect words and local pronunciation, as did Mick and Nancy in Mani. Athenian Greeks were puzzled, and wondered where we had learnt to speak like this. One Greek friend asked me not to speak Greek to her parents until they knew me better: 'They'll never believe you're from a university with that accent.'

The drive to Greece took over a week, via Germany and Yugoslavia. It was during the drive through Yugoslavia that my camera disappeared when we stopped for coffee near Rijeka. Attempts to report the theft (and to claim on the insurance) were of no avail, and I had to replace the camera once we arrived in Athens. The unexpected extra expense adversely affected my first quarter's budget. A few days after the camera had been stolen, during a purgatory of bumps on the mountain roads leading to Skopje, the microbus sheered off the steep camber and turned over in a field. We all sat for a moment, upside down, and climbed out of the windows. The left-hand side of the windscreen was broken, and a loose pot of jam had smashed, but no-one was hurt. A lorry driver helped us turn the van the right way up and we drove on to Skopje. I didn't tell my parents anything about these incidents at the time. On 23 April, Saint George's Day, we entered Greece.

After several days at the Taverna Pulakis while the microbus was fixed, the Linetons set off for Mani, and I waited for the weekly boat to Sikinos. I was able to leave my trunk at the tavern, so was not too heavily laden when I set off for the island. Having travelled there the previous summer I was prepared for the tedious twenty-four hour voyage by steamer followed by a long, slow, uphill donkey-ride from the harbour to the village on the opposite coast, and was anticipating a warm welcome from the widow from whom I had rented a room, and to whom I had written saying I was coming to stay for several months. What I was not expecting was that my exhaustion from travelling, and anxiety about starting fieldwork, would be entirely overshadowed by a situation which nearly prompted me to turn round, go home, and choose another career.

Figure 1   Map of Greece showing Anafi

CHAPTER ONE

'A fieldworker with no field'

Sikinos and Anafi, May 1966

✳

Up to the point when I set off for Sikinos I had not written any fieldnotes, as I considered I was not yet carrying out fieldwork. The first fieldnotes in my notebook were written mostly in English. I can remember hearing Greek sentences, being able to distinguish the words, but failing to comprehend what they meant. A few names and words in my notebook were taken down in Greek, but later when I came to type them up, I either transliterated them or translated them into English. Occasionally I left a space in the typescript to insert a handwritten Greek word or phrase. Without really thinking of the implications, I went on using this system with all my fieldnotes. I gradually began to realise that this had been an extremely bad error of judgment, as the original Greek wording of conversations and remarks tended to be lost.

I do not recall this technical problem, of how to write fieldnotes in the local language, and one's own observations and commentary in one's own language, and then type them, being addressed at all during the postgraduate fieldwork training year. The problem would not have arisen for my supervisor when he was in Turkey, as English orthography could be used both in handwriting and typing, and it had clearly not come up with students he was supervising in Italy and Spain.

I was writing a personal diary, but cannot now refer to it for a picture of those early days in Greece. The diary was stolen later in the year, along with some books and clothes, from the Taverna Pulakis. I started another diary, and some excerpts from it are used later on. When I reached Sikinos I began writing fieldnotes in a mixture of self-consciousness and confusion. The reasons will become clear from the letter I wrote to my parents two days after my arrival on the island.

LETTER 6, SIKINOS, FRIDAY 13 MAY 1966

I think this is approximately the same spot on the path from harbour to hill village from which I wrote to you last year when I was choosing my fieldwork site. And enclosed are some flowers from the hillside.

This is however a letter of not-such-good news. I will not dwell on it much, in case I start feeling sorry for myself, and I need all the resilience and confidence I can muster. I arrived on Sikinos after a 22 hour journey from Athens, on Wednesday. When I got here, I found another anthropologist, a Frenchwoman called Erica, who is working on social change from the point of view of the penetration and influence of mass media – radio, newspapers – and of ideas about the outside world (from nearby islands, to Greece itself, and foreign parts), from letters and visits from internal and external migrants. Of course this means the basis of the same sort of community study analysis of social structure which I intended to do, although the final bias of the thesis would be different. So here I am, a fieldworker without a field, an anthropologist with no anthropi. It would be very difficult for me to stay as those people I got to know here last year are now rather antipathetic towards the other anthropologist, and I might get used in a schismatic struggle, or be an object of antagonism.

I'm writing this later, on Saturday, after having a long talk yesterday afternoon with a kind of local magistrate and notary, the irinodhikis, in which he told me all about the island of Anafi, east of Santorini, which is very like Sikinos, with one village above the harbour. There are about 350 people: farmers, shepherds and fishermen. He said that the Anafiots are a bit 'wild', aghrii, they don't talk very much, and are rather reserved. The men go as migrants to Athens, and some are sailors. Anafi is the turning round point of the steamer on a route from Piraeus to some of the smaller Cycladic islands, it calls there every Wednesday. It is three hours by caïque from Santorini which has a boat six times a week to Piraeus.

So I am leaving here on Tuesday night for Anafi which he has prepared for my arrival, by phoning so that there will be a small boat ready to take a person (instead of just supplies) when the steamer arrives, and by giving me letters of introduction to the mayor and schoolteacher. He says that he usually stays with a cafenion owner would cooks for him, so maybe I could do the same. This man, Thanasis, is a former political exile who married an Anafiot woman and has links with the island community through her. So I'm more or less – more really! – committed to Anafi, and I think that unless it's triple star awful I should stay there.

The fieldnotes which follow were written soon after I reached Anafi from Sikinos. They say nothing about my arrival on Anafi, or accommodation and food. Both of these had been greatly facilitated by the notary who had phoned ahead to make sure that there were donkeys waiting to transport me and my luggage to the village, and that the one-time exile café-proprietor was expecting me. On the steamer I met a young woman, Thetis, from the Byzantine Museum in Athens, who was travelling around the islands to compile a list of Byzantine antiquities and ikons. Her first stop was to be Anafi, and she was later to go on to Sikinos, Folegandros, and other small islands in the Cyclades. After climbing down a ladder from the steamer, to jump into a small dinghy, and lurch up and down as our luggage was handed down after us, we were rowed ashore to a ruined jetty, the result of the Santorini earthquake ten years earlier. We shared the donkeys which had been sent down to meet me, and decided to stay together in a room which had been prepared for me below the exile's café. This room became my own lodging for the next sixteen months. I will describe it, and the neighbourhood, in more detail later.

FIELDNOTES, ANAFI, WEDNESDAY 18 MAY 1966

The harbour on the south coast of the island is called Ayios Nikolaos [Saint Nicholas, who is the patron saint of sailors and sea-travellers in Greece]; there is a concrete shed where people wait for the steamer and where the fishermen store their nets; there are two new-looking concrete houses (not used at present) plus a chapel. Three fishing boats were moored and about seven dinghies, some with flare lights. The largest caïque belonging to an Anafiot is named *Panayia* [the Greek Orthodox Christian name for the Virgin Mary, meaning the All Holy One], and has a sail patched with sacks once containing flour from America: there is a pair of clasped hands and 'gift of' on one part and 'the peoples of America not to be resold' on another. [Presumably made out of post-war aid food supply bags.]

The road up to the village is at first very broken and then improves. On either side I could see overgrown hill terraces. The policeman on the quay, Mikhalis, is from Crete. He is one of two constables, *khorofilakes,* and there is a senior policeman, an *astinomos*; when we walked back up to the village, he carried a string of fish and chatted amiably to the muleteers (a husband and wife he addressed as Kostis and Katina [their surname was Nikolis]). They told me they had a baby daughter, Popi [Kalliopi], a son Andhreas, and a girl, Ioanna, at school. The other donkeyman is called Nikos Khalaris; he said his wife has the same name as me, Margarita.

The village president, *proedhros*, Mikhalis Ghavallas, on whom we called to show Thetis's letter of introduction from the Byzantine Museum, and my own, from the Social Sciences Centre, says that the island has a few lemon trees, a few orange and mandarins (and almonds, too, judging by the spoon sweets served [candied fruit in syrup, served on a tiny glass saucer, to mark the arrival of a guest]. I noticed dogs, cats, pigs, donkeys and hens in the village; there are said to be sheep, goats, cows and partridges. There are two ruined windmills on the ridge, facing west, towards Santorini, and others on the other ridge facing east above the path to the harbour.

FIELDNOTES, ANAFI, THURSDAY 19 MAY 1966

Thetis says that two of the churches in the village are privately owned. One has a Russian ikon. The church is named 'the Falling Asleep of the Mother of God', *Kimisis tis Theotoku*, the Greek Orthodox name for the Feast of the Assumption, on 15 August. Apparently this festival is always celebrated here, rather than in the main village church. The Kimisis church belongs to the family of a seventy-year old widow whose grandfather built it. The other privately owned church, Ayios Kharalambos, belongs to the wife of an elderly man I've seen in the cafés who is said to have been a policeman here long ago.

East of the schoolhouse seems to be the poorer part of the village. The road is unpaved, clothes are dried on bushes rather than on clothes lines; not many houses seemed to have courtyards. The houses are not so freshly painted as in the main part of the village. At the edge of the village on this side is the shell of a church being built by the *proedhros* in memory of a son who was killed on military service, in Cyprus I think; I should check the names on the war memorial. Also two more ruined windmills. The proedhros's money is said to have come from his father who had a café in Cairo. Further east, about five minutes' walk from the village, is the cemetery with the chapel of Ayios Markos, Saint Mark.

LETTER 7, ANAFI, TUESDAY 24 MAY 1966

My first week has been lovely as I met a Greek archaeologist called Thetis (the name of the mother of Achilles, I think) on the boat from Sikinos to Anafi. She is from the Byzantine Museum in Athens and has come to list all the ikons in the churches of Anafi, Folegandros, Sikinos, and Kimolos. So I've accompanied her – mostly by donkey – to all the island churches, which means I've seen nearly the whole island. There are terraces of barley, wheat, figs, vines and gardens by the few streams or springs which run down to the sea in the folds of the hills. There are a few scattered homesteads outside the one village which is walled by cactus, on the top of a steep, rocky, hillside above the tiny harbour. I've clambered up and down mountains (and sat on several prickly bushes), joggled over rocks and steep hillsides and rocked and splashed over clear, deep blue water to the monastery of Panayia Kalamiotissa [the Virgin of the Reed, the Anafiots' patron saint], where the island priest, a monk-less Abbot, spends half his week with his golden wine, white horse and black dog.

The houses in the village have arched roofs because of the earth tremors from volcanic Santorini, so the village seems as if it is all churches. They're nearly all painted white, with pots of carnations and geraniums and vine arbours in their courtyards, and their own water cisterns (bang goes the idea of collecting gossip at the village well!). Thetis and I were immediately taken over by the youngest but more senior policeman [named Nikos, often referred to in my notes as the astinomos], a Cretan (as Thetis is) who has shown great kindness and thoughtfulness. He brings us hot milk every night, and has also given us honey, shoe polish, and as a crowning touch, pink toilet paper! He comes with us on our expeditions, sometimes with one of the other policemen, Mikhalis. [Mikhalis was a married man with a son at the village school; I became quite friendly with his wife Khristina. Much later on, he and I had an altercation outside one of the cafés in January 1967 which is reported in Chapter 3.] We've had a meal with the village president, and a few of the children are daring to say hello to me now, so I feel that my initiation has been very much smoothed over for me, a compensation for a false start.

A few days ago, outside a church on a lonely rock by the sea [Ayios Antonios] the air seemed to grow opaque and the day dulled and chilled. When I looked up, the silhouette of the moon was passing across the sun (an eclipse, as I discovered later, looking at my diary), and a slantways beam of light hit the sea by the rocks and made it gleam like a mirror. The water was so clear I could see the seaweed on the rocks, and the sand. The water was the most delicate pale green-blue, the rocks red, with purple and grey bushes scattered up the mountain side.

There were no noteworthy ikons in the church for Thetis to record, but a wonderful wall painting, splashed with whitewash: the Presentation in the Temple – Simeon leaning forward tenderly, but stiffly, with an iron grey beard, Joseph with two doves in his hand, and Mary, staring out with great tragic eyes, the curve of her robe around the tiny baby. [In 1992, with the help of an Anafiot migrant's daughter who worked in the photo-archive in the Benaki Museum in Athens, I was able to obtain a copy of a detailed description and evaluation of this fresco, with speculations as to the total iconographic scheme of wall-paintings into which it had once fitted.]

At night, from the village, the flare lights of the fishing boats are strung out across the water. Between Anafi and Crete – 60 kms away – are two tiny, uninhabited islands and a larger one, also deserted. At night their shapes are just discernible, at dusk they catch the rays of the setting sun, and glow pink, seeming to float in the sky. From the village square one looks across into the setting sun, and towards Santorini. The main church, the war memorial, and two ruined windmills make three sides of the square, the fourth side is made up *of houses, and by the 'main' street (I can touch the walls of the houses on either side with my arms stretched out).*

I don't know much about the Greek political situation, although Thetis told me the present (post-Papandreou) government are staving off elections on the pretence that they'll give rise to riots, but really because they fear that Papandreou will be elected with a huge majority. Nearly all Greeks, said Thetis, see Queen Frederika as the main cause of this situation and they hope that King Constantine's Danish wife, Anne-Marie, may develop a strong enough character to balance Frederika's influence on the King. The sort of history which is written from the point of view of personality seems designed for Greece.

Letter 8, Anafi, Sunday 29 May 1966

Here I sit after a long stint in church from quarter to eight until after nine. The 'liturgy', as the equivalent of mass is called, starts at 6:30am but nearly everyone goes at the third and last bell; today being Pentecost [fifty days after Easter; the festival which celebrates the descent of the Holy Spirit on the Apostles], there were three extra readings. Everyone went down on their knees for these, babies howling, boys scuffling, old ladies groaning, old men clinging on to the side stalls. Through the side door, I caught a glimpse of blinding white wall, cactus, and the sea beyond, heat haze hiding the horizon line.

Thetis left for Folegandros in the dark on Wednesday morning. The walk back up hill in the dawn after seeing her off was so beautiful, the houses were standing on the ridge like irregular teeth above a cactus beard. Since then, I've been trying to evolve a pattern for myself which gives me time for studying Greek, writing fieldnotes, washing (this takes some time, but I'm getting quite skilful with a rope and bucket) and conquering my shyness to go out and walk round and be stared at and talk to people. I really do think that it is terribly hard (especially with my upbringing!) to do nothing. Just to sit and watch people, swatting flies, smiling, and trying to understand conversations.

But yesterday afternoon was a major breakthrough for me; some of the little girls have got to know me and not be shy, and begin to talk slowly to me and tell me who people are. In exchange I give them English 'lessons', really just giving them the names of things. And some older girls have got friendly and I am going swimming with them next week. As evening fell it was a really good feeling to be sitting there with a little girl on my knee shouting 'good evening' in reply to the people I know now who greeted me. Later on I sat out on the police station balcony while the three policeman who are all from Crete danced to a Cretan song from a transistor radio. My supervisor will no doubt point out that policemen are outsiders to the community and that I should be careful not to align myself with them too closely.

I'm also beginning to get a picture of the various social rankings here. The village president Mikhalis Ghavallas, who comes from a family which had made money in Egypt, has a daughter named Stella, married to the school teacher, another Nikos. The president's family name is on holy pictures in the monastery church, and the main street and square have plaques up with the family name, so he's obviously an important person! I also know the postman, yet another Nikos, a returned islander. He isn't a postman in the sense that he simply delivers letters and parcels, but is in charge of the village post office, and the one telephone from which calls can be made. [As he told me much later, Nikos knew more about most islanders' business and secrets than the police and the priest put together, but like a priest, he had the duty of his office to preserve those secrets. He never betrayed any of these confidences to me, while doing his best to help me with my study of the island.]

I've also met the Abbot of the monastery who is the son of a previous village priest, and I've bought a few things from a shop run by a widow called Maria who keeps one of the two groceries. A married couple keep the other grocery, nearer to where I'm living. Then there are Kiriakos and Maria who run the café opposite Thanasis's place, and a childless married woman, Adhriana, who runs a tiny one-roomed café next to the Kiriakos café. There doesn't seem to be competition involved as most of her customers seem to be young shepherd boys who sit for hours with their 'submarines', glasses of water with a scoop of vanilla-flavoured sweet stuff on a spoon. I was told that this woman does sewing and ironing too, if I needed laundry done. I also know the two donkeymen [Kostis Nikolis; Nikos Khalaris], and their families – so that's a start out of 400, in my first fortnight.

On Sunday afternoon there was the Greek equivalent of school sports day in the square. The women and small children sat on the church steps and on benches around its walls. Men, trying to look blasé, sat in ones and twos on the low walls on the other side of the square, where the ground slopes downwards with the houses one above the other. The upper classes (postman, the priest, president, his wife, the three policemen and one of their wives – if you see what I mean – plus the schoolmaster's wife and the anthropologist) sat in the shade by the war memorial. There were gymnastic exercises, obstacle races and finally dancing, first to the schoolmaster's accordion and then to a little boy's homemade wooden whistle, and then, when he headed the line for a circular line dance, to the lute and clarinet played by older men.

Yesterday, being the feast of the Holy Spirit, was another holiday. The schoolmaster and his wife Stella (the village president's daughter), and the president himself, the school mistress (a dumpy pale girl from Samos who told me she had a brother in Sweden studying chemistry), two of the policemen and I, joined by the priest, went to the President's garden at a place called Ayio

Yianni, Saint John, an hour's walk from the village. The chief purpose was to examine a sarcophagus outside the church, just above the garden, for Thetis. It was carved on all sides (a sphinx; two griffins; wrestling cherubs; a warrior with a winged horse, probably Bellerephon and Pegasus). I drew a sketch of it and the schoolmaster measured it. Then we went down again to have lunch under the trees. The President's garden had a fantastic irrigation system for its terraces. He is a shrewd and forceful man and is clearly one of the most monied villagers. I wonder whether he sells his garden produce within or outside the island.

When we got back to the village I was immediately invited to go to a christening, so in dusty shoes and with sweaty face I followed a crowd of children to the church where, as the sun was setting, the priest censed the metal font, blessed the oil and water, breathed on it, anointed the child and then immersed her. It was a fantastic ritual with everything in threes: promises, blessings, censings, crossings, immersings. I was asked to the house of the child's parents (her father was at the christening, but the godmother plays the chief role) where we were given almonds in honey, and ouzo, and the godmother pinned little ribbons with medallions on us all.

Babies are swaddled here, they are wrapped in crepe bandages on top of movement-restricting long dresses. When the child was undressed and redressed at this baptism it seemed to have very many layers of clothes. But at about nine months old the babies' older sisters bundle them around the streets, playing with them and teaching them to walk, etc. Fathers seem to pay more attention to sons but most men will take the time to pinch a cheek or pat a bottom. I've noticed the terrible teasing that goes on, holding things away from small children, and whipping them up into a rage, or tears, while the parents don't intervene. Campbell in his book on the Sarakatsani suggests this teaches children only to trust their most intimate family and kin, but I've noticed that it is family members who are often the worst teasers. They tease animals too – telling a dog to chase a cat and then hitting it for causing an uproar.

Negotiations are in progress about a house for me to rent; it would need to be painted and furnished. There is one room with a kitchen, and use of an untenanted pigsty next door for a lavatory.

As things turned out, I did not move after all, but continued to live, until August 1967, in the room where Thetis and I had stayed, which I rented from Thanasis Vafiadhis. It was part of a complex of three linked buildings on the slope overlooking the harbour; the highest up the slope, on the south side of the village's main street, was the café. I did not know then, but the café itself, a barrel-vaulted room, entered from the street, was rented from his wife's uncle (her mother's brother, Mikhalis Kollidhas, one-time chairman of the Anafiot Migrants' Association). The next building, whose roof formed the base of the café terrace above, was entered from a courtyard lower down the slope. This building was the property of Margarita Vafiadhu, Thanasis's wife, inherited from her mother, who had been drowned when a dinghy capsized off the south coast of the island in the early 1930s when Margarita was in her early teens. Margarita's father had re-married, and she was sent to live with relatives in Athens. Thanasis lived in this section, but Margarita was living and working in Athens with their three children. The third building, linked by a common wall to the one above it, was on a lower 'step' down the slope, and had its own self-contained courtyard entered by a lockable gate. This section was my home for the next sixteen months.

Below it, on a lower step again, were outbuildings including a grape-pressing floor, *patitiri*. My courtyard room was also part of Margarita's dowry house, and this was the room I rented for an agreed sum of 200 drachmas per month, about £3 at that time. It had an uninterrupted view down the steep zigzag path to the harbour, and southwards towards Crete. To the left, in the distance, was Mount Kalamos. The house next door, to the east, was the home of Eleftheria Kollidha, her husband Antonis, and their three sons, the eldest of whom was severely mentally handicapped, and partly physically handicapped. From the terrace outside Thanasis's café, I could look down into the courtyard of Eleftheria's house. Eleftheria first called me Margarita, and soon 'neighbour', *yitonissa*. Thanasis cooked a meal for me most evenings. I ate in his café, initially watched by a large crowd of curious children who commented on the way I used my knife and fork, and nudged each other whenever I made a comment to myself in English. Thanasis knew a few words, and echoed my approval of his cooking when I said 'very good' or 'delicious', but if I said anything he didn't understand he would comment 'she's swearing at us', *mas vrisi*, an implication I found curious. Until I bought myself a little bottled gas two-ring cooker on a visit to Santorini, I depended on him for breakfast as well.

Over the next few months I pieced together Thanasis's links to other Anafiots through his wife. Her father was Iakovos Russos, nicknamed *aspros*, Iakovos the White (or fair) to distinguish him from a first cousin, also named Iakovos, and nicknamed *mavros*, Black (or dark). Dark Iakovos was still alive and living in the village but Fair Iakovos had died. His second wife, the village midwife, had produced a son, Tzortzis (Margarita's half-brother), now married and living in Athens. Tzortzis and his wife Popi were to play an important part later on in the touristic development of the island. The widowed midwife, Evangelia, was living at the eastern end of the village.

Letter 9, Anafi, Saturday 4 June 1966

You asked me in your last letter whether there was a 'directing principle'; here on Anafi, water is the directing principle – because it hasn't rained, the cisterns are failing, water has to be brought into the village from springs outside, the harvest isn't very good, so there won't be enough grain for a year's worth of flour to make bread until next year's harvest, there won't be many grapes, and so on and so on. The sheep and goats are giving birth to lighter, weaker, young, and these won't have very good grass to feed on. Those villagers – like the president – who have springs in their vegetable gardens and irrigation systems, are fine, other men are going to have to go to Athens when the harvest is over to earn enough money to buy in food. They'll return for the winter planting and hope for a better year.

We had rain on Saturday and I could hear the water dripping down into the cistern, and could almost feel it being sucked down into the earth – but it's too late now for the crops...

Letter 11, Anafi, Tuesday 21 June 1966

I've been asked if we have the same phases of the moon in England. When I tried to explain about tides there was blank disbelief as of course the Mediterranean doesn't have them. I'm reading 'Emma' at the moment, quite an antidote to harvesting with sickles. As I came back from watching the harvest, the sun threw my shadow onto a rock and the silhouette was just like a figure from an ancient vase – mainly because of the huge flat brimmed sun hat I'd been lent and the staff in my hand. My donkey riding style might not be quite Badminton standard but I'm getting quite adept at balancing on the wooden framed saddles and clicking my tongue to urge the animal forward.

Letter 12, Anafi, Monday 27 June 1966

There has been a post office strike in Greece, and although the island postman sent off our letters, none came for us on last week's boat. A fortnight without mail has driven me to desperate measures, like starting on a village plan and beginning to write up all the information I've got on the Cyclades and Anafi for my first-of-the-month report to my supervisor [the agreement was that I was always to write him a report on the first of each month]. The village plan got off to a splendid start on a wild windy afternoon. My skirt went whirling above my head and pages ripped out of my notebook, and there was a crowd of little girls so tightly wedged around me that my elbows were jammed against my sides. Still, I sketched in all the houses on the main street from the school to the main square, that is from end to end; and marked where side paths lead off up hill and down, to other groups of houses, so I can now fill in the gaps until I've got the whole village down. I tried to label each building with information from the little girls: shed, pigsty, shop, café. There are disused buildings, churches, and houses shut up while the occupants are in Athens, or spending the summer in other houses outside the village and near their fields. I completed a harbour plan (a few houses and all the boatsheds) one day last week, and have even got a few kinship charts among my fieldnotes, so I feel like a real anthropologist.

Several weeks later I had still not heard from my supervisor whether or not the change of fieldwork site would be acceptable, but I decided to stay, and to make a start on getting to know the village and the villagers. By this time I had begun to learn the names of quite a number of people and could recognise others. I will conclude this chapter by giving examples of the kind of fieldnotes I was now writing. In line with the terms of my project, to investigate inter-island, and island-mainland links, I was noting how many people were travelling to and from the island, and trying to identify them. Although most arrivals and departures were by the regular steamer, Anafi was also linked to other islands by occasional commercial *kaïkia* (caïques, small sailing boats, usually with diesel engines). These were sometimes specially chartered or ran a regular weekly service only in the summer months, when the grocers and café proprietors ordered supplies. Fishermen and sponge-divers also visited the island. I tried to find out exactly what goods were being imported and exported. This supposedly focal topic hardly formed any part of the doctoral thesis which eventually resulted from the research. The fieldnotes are jottings, from which some sense might be extracted at a later time.

FIELDNOTES, ANAFI, WEDNESDAY 29 JUNE 1966

Boat day: Vasilis the policemen, who also acts as harbour-master, on duty. Patiniotis, one of the grocers, came down for a consignment of tomatoes and to take beehives to Mega Potamos [Big River, the name of a beach further along the south coast of the island near the Monastery, and of the area of land above the beach. One of his brothers, a shepherd, lived there]. He also took some long posts – scaffolding, for rebuilding a house there. These arrived on the steamer together with doors, bed frames, etc., probably for migrants' summer houses.

Tied up in the harbour were sponge fishermen from Simi, sorting and threading sponges and also fishermen from Vatika [on the eastern-most peninsula of the Peloponnese.] They had a fridge full of lemonade and orangeade. They shared their lunch with Nikos the astinomos and Manolis the fisherman's wife's father [a good example of how I had to identify people before I knew their names. This man turned out to be called Antonis Ghavallas, nicknamed *meraklis*, a word used to refer to a connoisseur and ironically applied to him, as his occasional public drunkenness was considered over-indulgent.]

Yiannis Dhamigos, one of the café proprietors, sells ticket for the Tipaldos line steamer. He told me that he has a record of all those leaving with names on the ticket stubs.

This was an important discovery, particularly as I was later allowed to look at several years' worth of ticket stubs recording the names and destinations of passengers. An analysis of these enabled me to show that the overwhelmingly important links for the island, in terms of passengers' destinations, were not with neighbouring islands, but with the mainland. Of more than one thousand steamer passengers over three years, 83% travelled to Piraeus (the port of Athens), 8% to Thira (the large neighbouring island, also known as Santorini) and the rest to Siros, Naxos, Paros, and other much smaller islands on the steamer's route. On later visits to Athens, to get a perspective on mainland-island links from the other end, I tried to get hold of figures for passengers to Anafi from the various steamer companies which went there. I was told that no figures were available.

As I later noted, departures were so few in the 60s, and there was so much time for buying a ticket, that all the stubs were endorsed with the names of the travellers, and I could chart comings and goings of particular individuals. The largest numbers were urban-based migrants leaving at the end of their summer holidays, usually just after the island's patron saint's festival on 8th September at the Monastery at the foot of Mount Kalamos. I also noted the tendency for reasonably well-off elderly islanders to leave in October and November to spend the winter in Athens with their children. A very few stubs, instead of being marked with a Greek name, had the comment *turistas*, a tourist, and on one was written *enas lordhos*, a lord, meaning an Englishman. Twenty years later there were so many people travelling in the summer that annotated ticket stubs, as a source of information about travellers, no longer existed.

Five people left on the weekly steamer, including the schoolmistress who had been at the sports day, accompanied by lots of little girls to farewell her.

[The schoolmistress had been teaching the youngest children in the village primary school; she had been lodging with widow Maria who kept the grocery, an astute choice for both of them to preserve their reputations, as later gossip about widows and unmarried women on their own later revealed to me. She did not return at the end of the summer holidays and for the rest of my time on the island the remaining schoolteacher, Nikos Ladhikos, had to teach all the classes himself.]

Seven people arrived, including the proedhros and his wife and their two nieces from Athens; also Manolis *Takhidhromos*, a woman with a summer house in the village (a relative of Kiria Adhriana), and Nikos the astinomos from a short trip to Santorini presumably on police business. The Takhidhromos's sacks are marked with his initials, EPA; there were also two heifers with his initials on their flanks.

This last mentioned traveller deserves more extensive comment. I had already begun to realise that he had a particularly important role in linking the island residents with the migrant community in Athens. Manolis *Takhidhromos* had the formal name Emmanuel Petru Arvanitis, which accounts for the initials on the sacks and on the heifers' flanks. In his case, the epithet *takhidhromos* could not simply be translated as 'postman'. Manolis was constantly on the move between Anafi and Athens, travelling on the steamer nearly every week. When on the island, he lived in a small house up on the kastro rock, next to a crowded room which acted as both a store-house and as a dry-goods grocery. His sister Maria was married to Tzortzis Russos, son of Dark Iakovos, and he sometimes had meals with them. He would deliver what he had brought from Athens, and collect further commissions for his next visit to the city (for which he charged 10% of the value of the transaction). As I found out in March and April the next year, in the period just before Easter his main activity was taking boxes packed with island-made cheeses to the city. These cheeses were made by island shepherds whose herds of sheep and goats grazed hillsides and abandoned hill-terraces; an agreed weight of cheese was paid to the owner of the land as a form of rent. If the owner lived in Athens, the cheeses had to be sent there. Manolis would also take live animals to Athens for sale or slaughter, and bring new stock to the island. He stayed in Athens for a week with his wife and children executing commissions for islanders, getting spare parts for machinery, for example, renewing prescriptions, taking baskets of island produce from anxious mothers to migrant children, as well as buying things for his store. He also collected baskets and parcels of urban goods to be delivered to island relatives.

I hoped to carry out further research on the role of the *takhidhromos* to find out whether this important linking role was exclusive to Anafi, or, as I suspected, a well-established one between isolated communities and urban centres, although I had never seen it referred to elsewhere. When I made a short study of the migrant community in 1973, the research plan included a male research assistant who would accompany Manolis on several of his weekly trips, but the scheme foundered.

FIELDNOTES, ANAFI, THURSDAY 30 JUNE 1966

Feast of St Apostolli so I take sweets to Kiria Margarita's son Apostollos, named after an uncle in Athens, and to the younger son of Nikos postman (named after his mother's father).

Figure 2   *'Men meet in cafeneions': Barba Tassos (L) and Iakovos Mavros (R)*

Found out that the postman's family are holding an ?aspris? [added later: *esperino*, evening service similar to Vespers] because tomorrow is the feast-day of Saints Kosmas and Damian, *Ayii Anayiri* [literally 'the holy silverless ones', meaning that they did not ask for payment] who are *iatri tu kosmu*, patron saints of anyone with medical problems. This is for their elder son Manolis, who broke his wrist at secondary school on Santorini. [Nikos had received a telephone call about the accident and went across by caïque to bring him home.]

The saints' chapel was up on the Kastro hillside. The bell was rung and people came from the cafenion. The congregation numbered about five men and ten women including Stella and her mother. Five round sweet loaves were brought in a basket. Stella told me it is called *artos*, and came from Athens [presumably a commission brought by Manolis Takhidhromos on the steamer the previous day]. Three candles were arranged in a tripod and stood on top. They were censed and breathed on by the the Abbot, who also doubles as village priest. Manolis, with his arm in plaster, stood inside the sanctuary and was censed as well. Then the artos was cut up and shared out between all present.

Stella took me to see a house being built for her and Nikos. She said that the Abbot had built the arch in the sitting-room wall; ten years ago he worked as a builder before becoming a priest. The house has the only pedestal toilet I've seen in the village so far, and also a shower. There are water tanks on the flat roof for the kitchen and bathroom taps. I suppose water is pumped up into them from the cistern in the courtyard.

Thanasis says that here even first cousins marry each other. This is against canon law, but he says everyone is inter-related anyway. The brother of Maria Antoniadhis the dressmaker, Tzortzis Russos, son of Dark Iakovos, was talking to Thanasis in the café, and Thanasis told me afterwards that Tzortzis couldn't understand in the least why I'm here and that he was trying to explain. I wonder what exactly he told him?

The doctor was in Kiriakos and Maria's café this morning and ordered coffees for everyone there. When I made a remark about cost he replied: 'I am a rich man, to me this is nothing'. Do they feel patronised? The doctor mentioned to me that Kiriakos (busy mending floor boards in the new room of the café) is leader of the village opposition; it suddenly occurs to me that none of the Proedhros's family patronises his café, and if Nikos the astinomos takes Stella and Nikos for coffee they go to Dhamigos's café. I should watch to notice any other non-attenders. [I later found out that Kiriakos's café was associated with left-wing political sympathisers, and Yiannis Dhamigos's with right-wing views. Most adult married men in the village patronised one or other of these cafés. The other two cafés catered for the extreme ends of the age spectrum: Thanasis's café was mainly patronised by old men, to whom he read the newspapers and for whom he would write letters; Kiria Adhriana's by much younger, unmarried men, and by shepherd boys.]

An interesting point about names came to my attention today, Nikos astinomos was telling me the surname of one of the little girls who is particularly friendly towards me, Zoï, and he referred to her father's surname as 'Birbilis' but she said he was Khalaris, and thus I found out the former is a *paratsukli*, a nickname.

LETTER 13, ANAFI, FRIDAY 1 JULY 1966

I've wondering about the scruples and worries I have about my behaviour here. I really hate intruding in people's affairs, observing quarrels and scenes, and watching behaviour (like people clowning about) which just embarrasses me. I'd much rather walk away...

Last night was cloudy and with a strong, warm wind. The moon is nearly full, so the reflections of the hurrying clouds made pale islands on the surface of the sea. Earlier, at sunset, a little cloud got caught up in the peak of Mount Kalamos at the eastern end of the island, and it looked like a patch of snow on its slope turning pink and gold as the sun went down. Because of the lack of electricity here and dependence on torches to move about at night, I've become very conscious of the phases of the moon.

*Which reminds me: my rhapsodies about the beauty of the evening sky brought an unexpected result: I was asked the English for moon (*fengari* in Greek) and when I said it the men laughed and the children sniggered. The word* muni *appears to mean the equivalent of 'cunt', so I'm now surrounded by crowds of horrid little boys asking me innocently the English for 'sun, stars, – and moon?' and then shrieking with laughter. Although a word of 'shame' (the little girls avoid asking me that word now in their English lessons) it does not seem to reflect badly on me, in fact some of the married women had quite a joke with me about it – at the same time as telling me to be careful about using it.*

I also found out something interesting because of a discrepancy in a surname given me by two different people when I was trying to work out kinship relationships in a particular family. The reason why so many people have the same name is because men name their first born son after their father, so if Kostas Sighallas senior has two sons who name their sons after him, there are bound to be two more males with the name Kostas Sighallas. So people invent paratsuklia, nicknames, to differentiate the two grandsons. I feel like sending my supervisor a telegram like Zorba's 'have found wonderful green stone, come at once'. I'm also beginning to recognize people's voices – men shouting 'naaaa' at their donkeys, and women calling children, and little girls giggling down the road.... Whenever I feel besieged by demands on me, I think at least I'm not isolated and rejected.

REPORT TO SUPERVISOR, JULY 1966

This is my sixth week on Anafi, and as I am going to Athens next week for my visa [necessary for any foreigner intending to stay in Greece for more than three months] and to do some library work. I shall be in Athens for a fortnight, visiting the Statistical Office for population figures, and looking up all the references in Greek which I could not find in London.

At the moment the grain is being harvested by hand, threshed by donkey, and ground by machine. The owner of one of the two flour milling machines also owns the fishing caïque which conveys passengers to the steamer, makes trips to Santorini, and provides most of the fish for the village. He is said to take 'half' the flour as payment, but this seems rather exorbitant. As far as shares of the fishing go, he takes one share for himself, and one for the caïque, the other two fishermen (one is his younger brother) take a share each.

The harvest is poor this year because of little rain in March and April, hence men are going to Athens to look for work. Most have relatives there already; the young boys join older siblings and get jobs through them and their friends [in 1973 I made a preliminary study of the 'hiring café' in the Athenian suburbs which migrants frequented, and where they picked up jobs]. I was told that the men will probably work on building sites or do very low status jobs like cleaning out the barrels in Athenian and Piraeus tavernas for the new vintage. A lot of the sheep and goats will have to be slaughtered or sent to Athens because of the lack of grazing. The island's other export, honey, seems likely to be in short supply this year, as the flowers have been so few. The cisterns are failing now, and water has to be brought up into the village from springs and streams outside.

I have completed a plan of the harbour and have begun a plan of the village. It lies on a roughly east-west axis along a ridge above the harbour on the south coast of the island, but the houses curve around the sides of the surmounting rock with its ruined Venetian citadel. The path up from the harbour is paved to a half-way point where funds gave out. I have heard whispers of a hot scandal spread by the village president's enemies of misappropriation of funds. The harbour path joins the main street of the village. This street slopes up the sides of the hill, with occasional flights of steps, and ends in the square, which looks west to Santorini and the sunset. Houses in different areas seem to form small neighbourhoods whose womenfolk have constant daily contact.

Men meet in the cafenions. These face each other, two by two, across the main street. Two are kept by married couples, and are the most frequented; a third is run by a former political exile. The fourth is kept by an elderly widow who goes down to the harbour every week to run a cafenion in the harbour shelter for arriving and departing steamer passengers. Boys and young men whose fathers' presence in the main cafés makes it impossible for them to go there, patronise these other cafés, as do very old men.

Houses at the harbour and in the village are being got ready now for their summer tenants; they are being freshly whitewashed and their roofs mended. A new house by the harbour had its roof put on yesterday and the workmen were paid in the evening in one of the main cafés [Yiannis Dhamigos's]. The proprietor was foreman on the site, and kept a record of days worked, and by whom, and he and the housebuilder consulted this record while they were arranging the wages. These ranged from 55 to 80 drachmas per day according to the type of work. How the workmen were selected, or whether they offered themselves, is not clear. Some of them just worked odd days in between harvesting their own fields and acting as wage-labourers on other people's fields...

The barber brings his equipment into one of the main cafés on Saturdays and Sundays. Relatives, workmen, or friends going to fields nearby take supplies to those who live outside the village (like a lame man at Klisidhi, an area of garden land behind a beach next to the harbour). If a villager goes to work fields which are many hours distant, he will stay overnight in a small hut on the site.

The main street also contains two grocery shops, one run by a widow who says she has to keep it to pay for her sons' education (one is at High School on Santorini, another at Technical School in Athens), the other by a married couple. The husband makes occasional journeys to Athens for stock. I was told that this grocery sells contraceptives; men usually wait until the husband is serving, but women will buy from him, or from his wife...

There is one hardware and clothing shop which mostly sells plastic shoes.... I go to church every Sunday and have kept note of numbers... You'll understand, I hope, how difficult it is to make generalisations so soon. However, I have got a few ideas on how to organise the material which makes it easier to ask the right questions. I want to make a household survey later on, but at the rate I'm going I will have done it all by informal visits before I set out on a questionnaire!

What worries me at the moment is the absence of a Problem, or a co-ordinating theme. But I keep telling myself, I've only been here six weeks after all. Six weeks without English has done wonders for my Greek...

CHAPTER TWO

'Olive trees looking like brides'

Summer and autumn 1966

✳

In the next two chapters, although I will follow on chronologically from the previous one, I pick out and link together all the material concerning the economic life of the island: the agricultural cycle, seasonal and permanent migration, fishing, livestock rearing, and so on. The main topics covered, in order of presentation, are the autumn olive harvest and winter ploughing and sowing (in this chapter), and animal husbandry, particularly milking and cheese-making, and livestock sales in the spring (in the next chapter).

I was told quite early on in my 1966 fieldwork that, according to a government survey of the island (later confirmed by reference to figures published by the Greek National Statistical Service), only about one-eighth of the island's area (totalling roughly fifteen square miles; about forty square kilometres) was used for agriculture. About half its total area was used for livestock raising: grazing for an estimated 2,500 sheep and goats. The remaining area was considered too steep and rocky for any kind of productive activity. The information given to me in 1966 used the old measure of how much land could be ploughed in a day, the *stremma*, a quarter of an acre or one-tenth of a hectare (very roughly, a stremma is equivalent in area to six tennis courts or half a football field).

In a rough headcount and census which I carried out, I estimated that there were about 400 residents on the island, living in 125 households, most of which were in the village. If land was evenly distributed (which it was not) each household would have had 30 stremmata (three hectares, about eight acres) of agricultural land and just over 50 stremmata (five hectares, about 12 acres) of grazing land. In fact, some people had no land of their own, others had holdings as small as two stremmata, and only five people on the island held totals of agricultural and/or grazing land of more than 100 stremmata.

What would such holdings mean in terms of yields? Did any households achieve the aim of self-sufficiency which had been expressed to me as: enough fields to make bread from our own flour, enough trees to have oil from our own olives? An answer was worked out by inference. The characteristic hill terraces of the island were planted in a three year cycle; barley the first year, wheat the second, and in the third (fallow) year, a catch-crop of beans and dry cucumbers. A family with hill terraces in different parts of the island at different stages of this rotation cycle would be able to harvest all three types of crop. I worked out that the typical household (man, woman, several children) would need at least 400 kilos of bread per year and 60 kilos of olive oil. To get enough grain to make bread (and leave enough seed to sow for another harvest) and enough olives for that amount of oil, a family would require between 30 and 50 stremmata of farming land and at least 40 olive trees. In addition, the family would require additional farming land to produce fodder crops for donkeys, mules and draught cattle.

Taking farmers as the norm (which seemed, on the face of it, a sensible thing to do; of the ninety active males in the island population, sixty defined themselves as farmers), I wondered how those without land could become self-sufficient. Thinking about this later, I realised that self-sufficiency did not only result from ownership of or access to land and to olive trees. For example, the fishermen brothers, Antonis and Manolis, had no fields and would not inherit any from their father, Barba Kostas, who made a little money by playing the goatskin bagpipes for parties and spent long gruelling hours in the summer hauling water by donkey from a distant spring to the village for cigarette money. Neither brother had married a woman with a dowry which included fields and olive groves. When I had asked about their land-holdings I was told 'their fields are the sea'; they made their living from fishing rather than farming. Instead of fields which grew grain, they owned a flour mill which gave them 10% of the flour they milled for their customers.

Some of the excerpts in this chapter make reference to other ways of finding food, or gaining an income. For example, I was surprised to find quite a lot of 'foraging', on the island: the collecting of many different kinds of wild greens, *khorta*, in the early spring after rain, the gathering of wild herbs such as oregano, *righani*, and expeditions to find delicacies such as wild capers and caper leaves to be preserved in brine for winter salads. In addition, women picked wild autumn crocuses, and dried their stamens to produce that most costly of all spices, saffron, for domestic use and for sale. Women also added to family income in a variety of ways: Maria, the wife of a café proprietor, made dresses and did alterations and repairs with a treadle sewing machine; another woman had a knitting machine; the village secretary's wife had a loom and made rag rugs. Men tended to be more interested in the hunting, trapping, and shooting of small wild animals such as rabbits and birds, particularly partridges, larks, thrushes, all of which tend to be found outside the village. This is why shotguns were kept in the huts near their fields. When the Colonels' coup took place in April 1967 and all arms had to be handed in to the police, many village men had to make long journeys to collect their guns from distant field-cottages. Men's specialist income-generating occupations ranged from playing musical instruments at parties and weddings to the making of stiff-brimmed harvesting hats from palm fibre.

In my thesis I summarised the main events of the farming, shepherding and fishing year in a three-column table, running from October through to the following September, so that the reader could see what was happening in any particular month by reading across the table, and could follow each occupational year separately by reading down. To represent the cycle of economic activities on Anafi for these chapters, I have adapted a diagrammatic scheme worked out by other scholars (Bourdieu and further developed by Greger, see bibliography) using the upper and lower halves of a circle, joined in a wave shape, so that the cycle is seen to flow through historical time as well as to repeat itself. The long wave shape can be further arched and segmented so as to show the seasons, to incorporate important religious days, and to record the types of social activity characteristic of particular seasons. In line with this approach, the account in these two chapters will also refer to everyday leisure activities, such as women's evening visiting and men's patronage of particular cafés, and will also discuss the adaptation of resident islanders to the requirements of their holidaying migrant relatives, and to the very few tourists who were finding their way to the island. Inevitably, my notes about farming and shepherding also include information and speculation about such topics as half-shares tenancies, day-labouring for cash or kind, and land-ownership; topics which will be developed in Chapter Four, on kinship, naming and inheritance.

My account of the economic cycle starts in late July when harvesting was continuing, the first men were leaving for summer seasonal work in Athens, and the first summer visitors were arriving. I returned to Anafi after the fortnight's visit to Athens mentioned in the July report to my supervisor with which the previous chapter ends.

FIELDNOTES, ANAFI, WEDNESDAY 20 JULY 1966

The steamer arrived at 4am. Many passengers are islanders' relatives coming for holidays. They all brought provisions, by the sack and trunk-full. Patiniotis the grocer left for Naxos. I'm told grocery stocks are very low; no matches

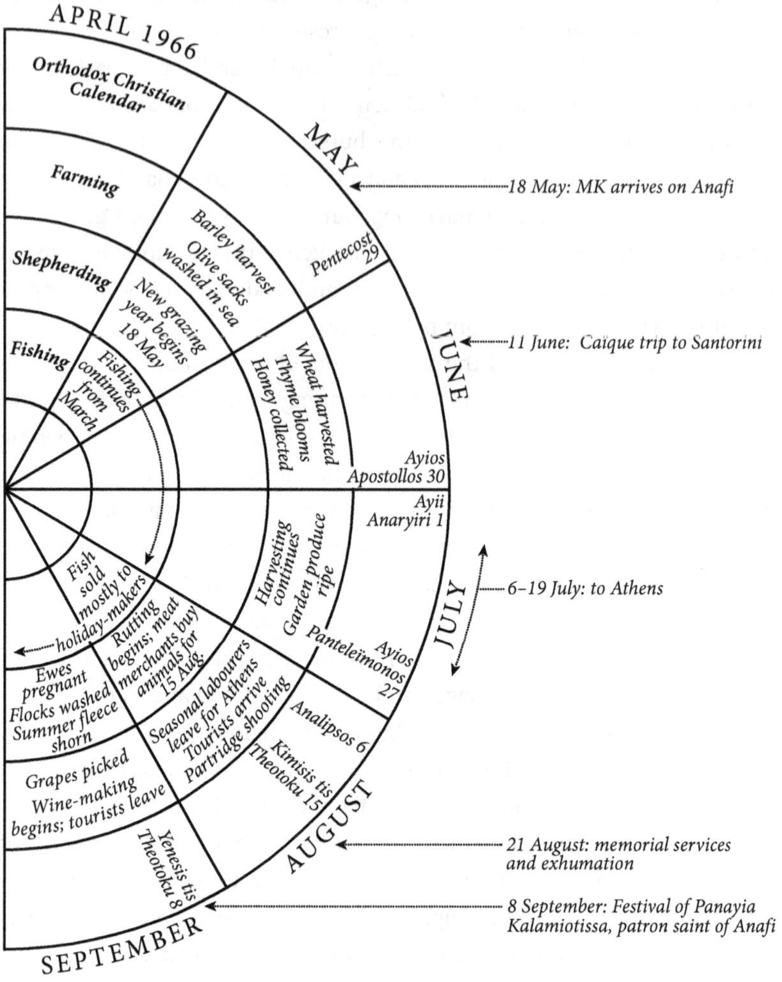

Figure 3a   The annual cycle in historical time

or fly-spray. Because of so many summer visitors? A Danish tourist who said his name is Ole, an astronomy student, is staying in the village guest-house, *ksenona*.

LETTER 16, ANAFI, THURSDAY 21 JULY 1966
Anafi is full of summer visitors now: migrant women with small children and teenagers on school holiday, to be joined by husbands and fathers later. The atmosphere is quite different from earlier in the year, there are women in the cafenions, even bikinis on the beach. I must be careful to cut down on the extent of my involvement in holiday fun, rather than strictly work-type, activities.

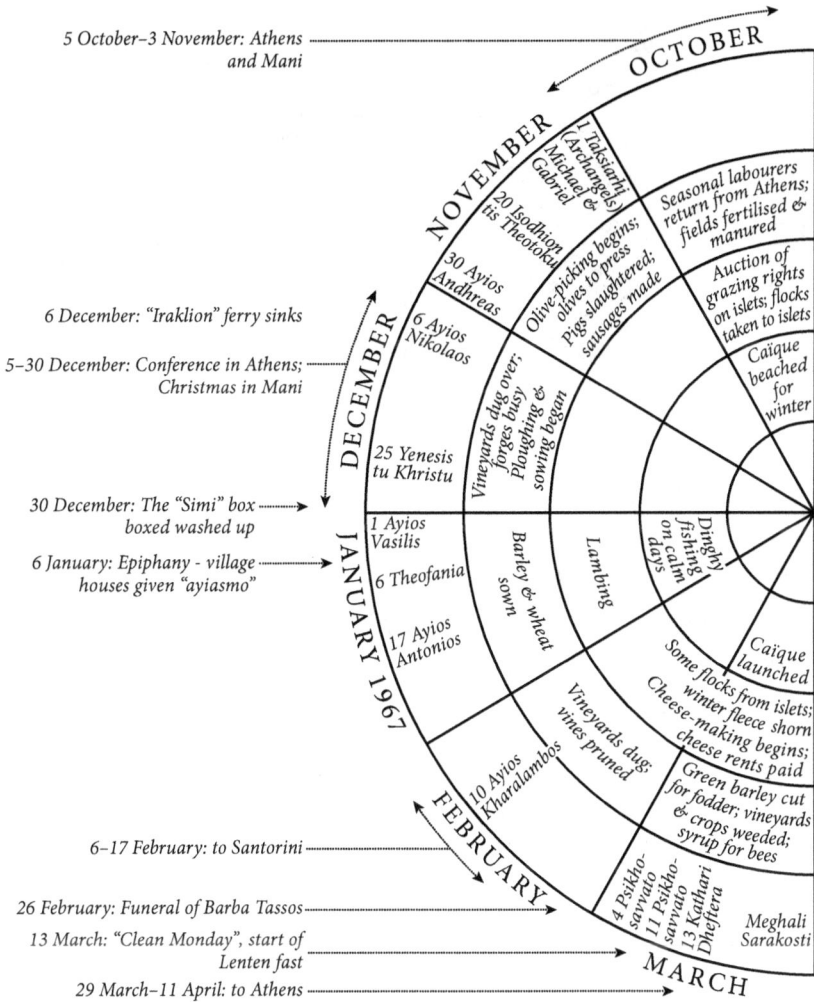

5 October–3 November: Athens
            and Mani

6 December: "Iraklion" ferry sinks

5–30 December: Conference in Athens;
            Christmas in Mani

30 December: The "Simi" box
            boxed washed up

6 January: Epiphany - village
            houses given "ayiasmo"

6–17 February: to Santorini

26 February: Funeral of Barba Tassos

13 March: "Clean Monday", start of
            Lenten fast

29 March–11 April: to Athens

Figure 3b   The annual cycle in historical time (continued)

Otherwise the summer will drift away in a haze of bathing-parties and English lessons.

FIELDNOTES, ANAFI, THURSDAY 21 JULY 1966

Down to the harbour, many more small boats and motor boats than usual. Dhamighos's son fishing; Anna Arvaniti the wife of Makarios, who is secretary of the Anafiot Migrants' Association, is staying with her two children in a boat-house as their holiday home. Margarita [known as Rita, the elder daughter of a migrant Anafiot nicknamed *Foksakis* because of his penchant for the foxtrot] was wearing a bikini for swimming and sunbathing and this was known in the village by evening.

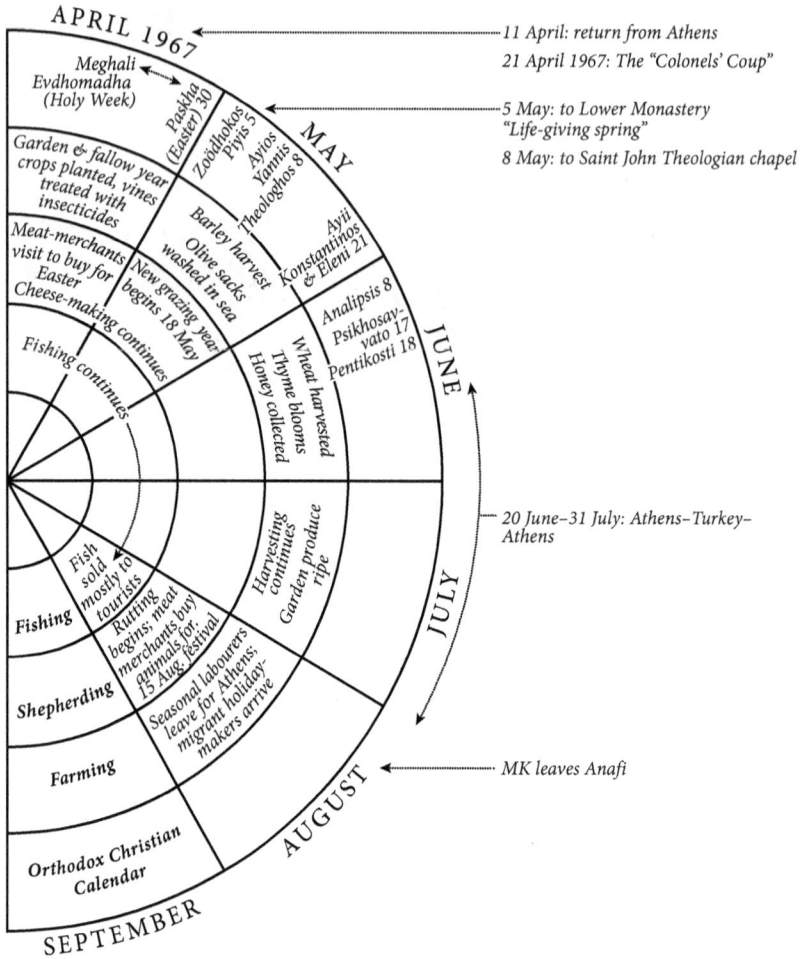

Figure 3c   The annual cycle in historical time (continued)

Ole says the blankets in the *ksenona* are full of fleas. I told him that the meat-merchants who come to buy livestock in August and before Easter are the only people to stay there usually. He has to fetch water from the house behind the schoolteacher's new house, as there is no water in the cistern of the guesthouse.

Manolis the fishermen was mending nets again, he gave me a piece for an amulet, *filakto* [as protection from the Evil Eye]. He told me that the caïque and the little boat belong to his brother Antonis; the other crew consists of a third brother, Nikolaos, and Merkuris, a weather-beaten old fisherman from Rhodes. The three of them are, like himself, just workers, *erghates*, for Antonis. Nikolaos is unmarried and referred to by everybody as stupid or 'touched', *palavos*. The shares go: one to Manolis, one to Merkuris, one to

Antonis, one to Nikoloas, one to the caïque (i.e. Antonis gets an additional share).

One of the boatmen has a list of arrivals which he ticks for their ten drachma fares. He was going around to collect what was owed, and insisted that Ole had not paid; Ole said that he had given ten drachmas to a man at the harbour who had asked for it but could not now say who it was. He refused to pay again and there was quite an argument, which I tried to resolve by saying that I would pay the ten drachmas; both the boatman and Ole would not allow me to do so.

FIELDNOTES, ANAFI, SATURDAY 23 JULY 1966

Nikolaos Ghavallas and his wife Marika (he arrived on the same steamer) are now staying in the village. They are having a boat-house built at Ayios Nikolaos, just below the path down from the village. They told me they live in Makriyianni, just below the Acropolis. [I visited them during one of my visits to Athens in 1967 and again seven years later when I was carrying out research among the urban migrants.]

Nikos the astinomos is living in the schoolteacher's boathouse for free, he told me (which means that most of the summer visitors must rent them). This is only possible because there is a telephone down at the harbour, below the biggest of the summer houses, so he can be contacted from the police-station. The Proedhros was at work on his new boat. He and his wife Maria are staying in Stella's house at the harbour.

Nikos Khalaris the donkeyman was working down on the harbour on Mr Peter's house [my neighbour Eleftheria's brother, Petros Allafuzos]. Yiannis Dhamighos the café proprietor is supervising. Nikos told me that Dhamighos's baby grandson (his only son's son), Yianni (his namesake), will be baptised in August so I should soon be able to see a christening.

Mr Peter has a boatshed built into his new house, with a motor-boat in it named 'Aghapia', after his mother (because he hasn't any children, he said)... [I didn't understand the significance of this, boat named as child, at the time, but see Chapter Four. Eleftheria gave birth to a daughter, her first, after three sons, in February 1968 and named her Aghapia after her and Peter's mother.]

FIELDNOTES, ANAFI, WEDNESDAY 27 JULY 1966

The caïque which Patiniotis had chartered from Naxos arrived, with all the supplies his grocery had run out of: cement, bottled gas, biscuits, fly spray, matches, melons, etc., etc. Streams of donkeys were going up to the village from the harbour all afternoon.

LETTER 18, ANAFI, TUESDAY 9 AUGUST 1966

The Summer, and Silly, Season has really hit Anafi. On the most recent boat there arrived the three nephews of the widow Adhriana (her sister's children); she's the very old woman who keeps the smallest cafenion. They brought with them a battery record player and a cardboard box full of Greek pop records. Yesterday the harbour waiting shed was reverberating with the noise, interspersed with one of them strumming on a guitar. Manolis was mending his nets and his brother Antonis was trying to sleep and swearing into the cement bags. Today the sound is booming out from Adhriana's house in the village. Their father is from Kalamata. [I did not know then that the man, Ilias Tzakalis, who danced the kalamatianos, *had been an exile on Anafi in the 1930s. He is mentioned in the published memoirs of Kostas Birkas.]*

The water in Kiria Margarita's cistern has run out and I saw her and her husband, Nikos the donkeyman, yesterday morning standing on the roof of Kiriakos's café fixing pieces of plastic hose and metal piping together to get water from the cistern of a house higher up the hill. How am I going to find out whose cistern (probably that of a migrant relative?- it certainly wasn't a philanthropic act – nobody gives or lends water from their household cistern).

The village dressmaker, Kiria Maria, whose husband is leader of the village opposition party and keeps the café 'Cyprus' opposite Mr Vafiadhis' café, is making me a dress; I enclose a scrap of the material. [Having a dress made meant that when I went to Maria's house for fittings, I had the opportunity to talk to her more privately than in the cafenion.]

The island fishermen (Antonis, Manolis and Merkuris) are said to be selling the best of their catch to the summer visitors at twice the normal price and then bringing the rest round to people's back doors at the ordinary price. There was a great shortage of fish for yesterday (Feast of the Transfiguration), the one day in the fortnight's fast leading up to the Dormition of the Virgin in about a week's time [a festival perhaps better known to Western Europeans as the Assumption of the Virgin] when fish can be eaten.

Your comments about migration have set me thinking. There seem to me to be two kinds: for summer jobs by older men, and for full-time jobs by younger ones. Some of these are as young as twelve, having just left school. The second sort becomes in time the phenomenon of a migrant in Athens with old island parents to whom summer visits are made. When I think how slowly I'm getting to know things here, and how comparatively simple they are, and how mediocre it will all be, I'm astounded at my perseverance.

Lately I've been noticing the key-mania here – people are always locking up drawers and cupboards and doors. Both men and women have bunches and chains of keys, even children lock up carefully – even if they then hide the key in an obvious place, like over the lintel. I can see the sense in securing outhouse doors which animals could push open and eat grain and stores, but the locking up of drawers and cupboards (such as the cigarette cupboard in a cafenion) every single time, seems to smack of obsession. Another aspect of this might be the wrapping up of things carried publicly in newspapers or cloths. This isn't for hygiene but for privacy. No-one likes anyone else knowing what they're up to.

I'm going down to the harbour now for a swim and a read of Redfield's book on peasant communities. He cheers me up because what he says seems to fit so well with what's going on here.

FIELDNOTES, ANAFI, FRIDAY 12 AUGUST 1966

Mikhalis the policeman told me that the *aghrofilakas* (fieldguard; an official position with a small salary) here is Yiannis Kollidhas, he is chosen by the proedhros and his council, usually one suitable candidate emerges for choice. He makes sure people's flocks don't stray into fields and cause damage, *zimia*.

FIELDNOTES, ANAFI, SATURDAY 13 AUGUST 1966

Mr Vafiadhis told me that Papakhristos bought 30 kilos of fish yesterday, thus depriving all the village. [Dhimitris Papakhristos had built as a holiday home a large concrete house down at the harbour; it had a windmill generator on the roof. He had married a woman from an island family, whose dowry included two houses in the main street of the village rented out as cafés. Kiriakos and Maria ran the two-roomed left-wing café, Adhriana kept the small one-roomed café patronised by young shepherd boys and unmarried men.]

LETTER 19, ANAFI, TUESDAY 16 AUGUST 1966

The steamer company ticket seller here, Yiannis Dhamighos, who runs the café next door to Thanasis's, told me that he has kept all the record books of the names of those he has sold tickets to. This means I can get details of all those leaving Anafi by the steamer; although it won't be so easy to find the corresponding details from the Athens end, particularly as three different steamer companies have handled Anafi in the past four years. Anyway, I spent yesterday morning copying out the names of people leaving for this year and the numbers for 1964 and 1965. By far the greatest number of people go to the mainland which makes my idea of studying the links between Anafi and Santorini look a bit sick. I was beginning to think anyway that the contact was mainly administrative. Although some sorts of supplies are sent, there is not a great flow of goods across. So now I'm going to look at all Anafi's links with the outside world, keeping the island very much at the centre of the study and not shifting the focus of interest to look at Anafi from the Santorini end...

As mentioned in the previous chapter, I was later able to collect totals for passengers leaving Anafi for other destinations which confirmed the impression that Anafi's primary contacts were with the mainland and that the majority of passengers from Anafi were either Anafiot residents going to Athens for a variety of purposes including the search for urban employment, or migrant Anafiots settled in Athens returning after visits to the island for a variety of reasons including religious festivals and summer holidays. I had no luck in collecting figures from the Piraeus end in an attempt to double-check the numbers. In 1988, when I was studying the rapid tourism development of Anafi, I was able to collect figures from one of the two steamer companies running boats to Anafi and from the Statistical Service of the Greek Merchant Navy. In the period between April and September 1987 at least 4,000 people came to the island, bringing with them 45 cars, 25 lorries and 150 motor-bikes, scooters and other small-wheeled vehicles – despite the lack of any properly-surfaced motor road. The average number of weekly arrivals in the summer season in the '80s was almost as great as the annual totals twenty years earlier.

And now, why this sudden activity on my part? At long last I've had a letter from my supervisor: 'Dear Margaret, I expect you are by now used to my neglect. Many thanks for your letters and the sad story of your change of location which all seems to have worked out for the best.' He tells me not to worry about the 'absence of overriding theoretical problems of world-shaking import' but to look in detail at the interaction of Anafi with the outside world. He asks how long I intend to stay here before I move on to Santorini, but I think now I will keep my base here and make trips to Santorini and Siros, and possibly Naxos, and finally to the Anafiots in Athens. He says Evans-Pritchard's letters to him in Turkey were totally useless and therefore doesn't know what to say to me except: 'don't worry, you cannot miss; go on gathering data, trying to make a pattern. It always comes right in the end.' My instant reaction, to begin more positive work, proves to me how subconsciously worried I've been. So now I've had my spoonful of reassurance I'm up and doing like crazy.

FIELDNOTES, ANAFI, THURSDAY 18 AUGUST 1966

One of the summer visitors, Petros Khalaris, was treating workmen to coffee in Mr V's café in the evening. I think they had been repairing his olive-press [see Chapter Eight, Fieldnotes, 26 April 1967]. Marulidhi's father (Yiorghos Pelekis) was in the café too, saying he has a sick goat which he doesn't know whether to kill or not. Mr V says the islanders don't treat their animals with any medicines or herbs. He also said he was intending to go to one of his fields [actually his wife's field] tomorrow, for the first time in a year. Also to look at his bees – there will be no honey because there are no flowers because there's been no rain.

Barba Kosta, the father of the three fishermen brothers, brought his goatskin bagpipes, *tsabuna*, into Adhriana's café. The man with the fat finger, Manolis Birbilis, one of the Khalaris brothers who are all known by their father's nickname, played the drum and two other men sang. I think one of the summer visitors paid them to do this. Kostis Nikolis said that he and his wife Katina are going out to Vayia tomorrow (to pick grapes?). Barba Kosta told me that he did the water-carrying from the spring at Vidha, below the village, to those households with empty cisterns for 'cigarette money'.

FIELDNOTES, ANAFI, FRIDAY 19 AUGUST 1966

Mr V said his fields had nothing – he brought back some grapes back for the chickens to eat and they wouldn't touch them. [This turned out to be a bit of an exaggeration. I went to help pick grapes and later watched the wine-making.]

A yacht, *kutero*, with tall slender masts came into the harbour about 6pm; someone said they were French tourists. Others said it was the millionaire Ghulandhris who sails round the islands in the summer. People came out of their houses to look at it.

Widow Maria with the grocery says she is leaving Anafi to live in Athens where she has two married sisters, and will probably work in a shop. She will shut up the grocery; two of her sons will go to school on Santorini as usual.

LETTER 21, ANAFI, TUESDAY 30 AUGUST 1966

Mr V's elder daughter Rula arrived on Wednesday's steamer. She is a hairdresser, and has already cut Kiria Maria's hair and done a perm for one of the village girls who wanted me to photograph her in her curlicued newness. At first I said that my stocks of film were for 'my studies' and then felt very mean, so took a photo of her by one of the few trees in the village, just outside my courtyard gate. But I might run out of film before my next trip to Santorini or Athens. [From migrant holiday-makers like Rula, island girls had the opportunity to find out about urban life and fashion, and Rula made a little extra money during her holidays.]

I had a good talk with Mr V one evening in which I explained to him the mechanical analogy of society. He replied 'yes, and the machine of Anafi works without oil'. We have some really deep chats sometimes, about evolution and religion and human institutions. The more I know of him (Mr V) the more he fascinates me. He has obviously read widely, often conceals his knowledge from me to see how much I know, and surveys the islanders with an ironic, almost Olympian, detachment.

September Report To Supervisor

I am beginning to get a picture of the variety of reasons for leaving the island: girls going to Athens to learn dressmaking (where they learn to use electric sewing machines, so that they can work in garment factories), boys to be water-boys and junior waiters in cafés and restaurants, men going to building jobs, women with their youngest children visiting relatives in Athens and taking the opportunity to bring back clothes, provisions and new furniture, summer visitors returning to their jobs... One point which emerged immediately was the lack of contact with Santorini, and next Wednesday I am going over there for a preliminary investigation to see how much Anafi is dependent on her larger neighbour for more than administration. [See Chapter Five] It already seems that the opportunities are not taken to import fruit and vegetables and other supplies from Santorini; main contacts are definitely with Athens.

These ideas are further reinforced by an examination of the village register, which I was recently entrusted with. A minimal percentage of Anafiots go to other islands, the others are all in Athens, and from the notes made when they decide to change deme (i.e. voting registration), it appears there are two main areas of the Athens suburbs where they go, Ano Dhafni and Iliupoli.

October Report To Supervisor

If supplies were sent to Anafi from Santorini, having been sent there from Athens, with import costs, the suppliers add again to the cost, hence some supplies from Santorini are more expensive than imports direct from Athens. So Anafi's contacts are directed towards the mainland. Those with relatives in Athens receive baskets and parcels of fruit, vegetables, white bread, shoes, and clothing. Links with Santorini are less regular. For one thing, the steamer route alternates, one week coming to Anafi from Santorini but not calling there on the return, and the next week getting to Anafi earlier and going on to Santorini; so that if someone is ill, there is only a fifty-fifty chance of them being able to get to hospital on Santorini. Most people would prefer the big city anyway, where they have migrant relatives to visit and with whom they could recuperate.

Many of the same surnames occur in both islands: Allafuzos, Arvanitis, Dhamighos, Khalaris, Sighallas. There are no recent relationships between the families, however, and from the village register I can discover only a very few instances of marriages between the two islands. A few people from Santorini come over for the festival at the Monastery in early September.

Administratively, Anafi is linked to Santorini, in a way which implies close contacts, but these are mainly on paper. Farmers' subsidies from the Agricultural Bank are sent across, and an agricultural advisor makes infrequent visits; pensions are also sent from Santorini. Police supervision from there is backed up by surprise visits from the Chief of Police, who comes over by caïque.

LETTER 25, ANAFI, FRIDAY 23 SEPTEMBER 1966

The grape treading has begun... the donkeys bring boxes and baskets of grapes in from the fields, and these are thrown into the treading pit, and laid out to dry on terraces and roofs. I'm going tomorrow to Mr V's fields to see the grapes being cut by his workmen.

I'm now typing by the light of my new paraffin lamp brought back from Santorini, which will make quite an efficient heater too for the winter... I also bought a bottled gas two-ring burner for cooking when Mr V goes to Athens in the winter.

FIELDNOTES, ANAFI, SATURDAY 24 SEPTEMBER 1966

Went with Manolis 'Birbilis' [Khalaris] on his second trip to Lefka where Margarita Vafiadhu's fields are, next to those of Maria (Arvaniti), wife of Tzorzis Russos (son of Dark Iakovos and therefore a distant cousin of Margarita), and near the church of St John the Baptist where the bones of the Arvanitis parents are. There are gardens around a sort of concrete pond which he called a *sterna*; lemon trees, flowers, tomato beds, etc.

Tzortzis, who was working there, said that as he and Margarita V are cousins, he wasn't getting a share of the wine or the grapes as payment. On our return Mr V got a basket of grapes ready to send down to the harbour to an 'uncle' of Margarita's.

Tzortzis showed me the chapel; when we came out he went and kissed the tomb (*ostiofilakion*, bone depository) of his wife's parents. Tzortzis and I cut grapes, filling the boxes and finally spreading the remainder out on the ground to be packed on a return journey. 25 boxes in all.

FIELDNOTES, ANAFI, MONDAY 26 SEPTEMBER 1966

Katina Nikoli was treading her own grapes in Mr V's *patitiri* (grape-treading pit). Her fields are at Vayia and at Lefka beside his [i.e. his wife Margarita's]. The grapes were packed in boxes, then she tipped them out, trod them (in gumboots), put them in a basket with a heavy stone to squeeze overnight; the drain was strained by a twig. All the skins and stalks will be heated up and distilled to make *tsikudhia*, a clear spirit, extremely strong. Katina's husband is in Athens until the end of October working as a building labourer, *ikodhomos*.

Mr V said that stills for home-distilled spirits for domestic use only were allowed by the law, but the *tsikudhia* could not be sold. However, he can sell me some of the wine he made 'to keep me company' over the winter.

[The Agricultural Report for the island for 1966 said that 102 stremmata of agricultural land were used for growing grapes. 3,800 kilos of grapes were produced for wine-making and 2,000 kilos of wine had been made; 2,000 kilos of table grapes had been produced. If these figures are correct, Anafi produced enough wine for each household to have 16 kilos per year.]

LETTER 26, ANAFI, THURSDAY 29 SEPTEMBER 1966

My recent visit to Santorini unsettled me more than invigorated mostly because I found mostly negative evidence, and I know now one needs TIME dealing with Greek officials. They tell you what they think you want to know, or, fob you off with the answer that's easiest for them to give you, so you need really to know the answers before you ask the questions. [For example, while on Santorini I visited the Agricultural Bank to try to get information about the Agricultural Cooperative on Anafi. I was told that there were no figures for Anafi there, they were held in Athens. Later, on a visit to Athens I met an official of the Agricultural Bank who said that figures for transactions such as fertiliser were indeed held at the branch on Santorini and he gave me a letter of authorization to the manager there to show me the records.]

This typing is abominable because I sliced my finger when cutting a bunch of grapes from Mr V's fields. It's healing, but typing is impeded by a plaster which keeps sticking on the keys.

A German mathematics student called Alexander has been here the past week, he has travelled in India and Afghanistan, and been to several of the smaller Cycladic islands. He says that each island tends to have its individual characteristics, its own feel. Not so much in its economy but in its inhabitants. For instance, he said he had never met people as unfriendly and unhospitable as the Anafiots. He was always asked (elsewhere) to people's homes, invited to weddings and christenings, asked where he would stay, and accommodation found for him. This despite him being German. The unfriendliness was shown him here before his nationality was known. So it seems that Mr V is right in his views of Anafi 'running without oil.' Mr V and I have had more long talks while I'm eating my supper in his café, and I become more and more impressed with his range of knowledge. He talked Einstein and general principles of Pure Maths with the German student and can follow me on Fossil Man and the Neolithic Revolution. He takes a perverse delight in teasing the Anafiots who say the Turks aren't human beings because they're not baptised, explaining that their religion isn't the same but that they are just as devotedly religious in their own way as the Greeks.

Mr V made quince compote, and gave me a plateful, partly because I helped collect the quinces when I was cutting the grapes which are responsible for this disastrous typing; and partly because I helped carry the crates of grapes, now collected up from the terrace, with great slaughter of hornets and stinging blackbeetles, down to his winemaking vat.

I decided to give myself a bit of a break by going to the Monastery to make a 'squeeze' of the altar dedicated to Apollo. Do you remember me mentioning the archaeologist from the American School of Classical Studies, Richard McNeal, who said the altar inscription is as yet unrecorded? I went off in the caïque with Manolis and his dog (he went partridge shooting). The stone in question was spattered with whitewash and hendroppings. I washed it (I had brought a nail brush and a sponge) measured it and described it in great detail, then got out the squeeze paper, wet it and pressed it against the letters, pressing it down to get out the air-bubbles and wrinkles. Each time, however, as it began to dry, the wind whirled the paper off the letters. One version blew away and another fell into the puddle of water around the stone. The inscription is: ΥΠΕΡ ΤΟΥ ΥΙΟΥ ΑΡΙΣΤΟΓΕΝΕΥΣ ΑΠΟΛΛΩΝΙ ΑΣΓΕΛΑΤΑΙ, 'To Apollo Asgelatas, on behalf of (my) son Aristogenes'. I had as audience Eleni Ghavalla, second wife of lame Dhimitri, (whom I got to know early in September when she washing dishes at the Monastery feast). I worked about three hours in the sun and she fried an egg for me and brought me some cheese. I went back into the Monastery to return a water bucket and found the Abbot there, eating a plate of tiny fried fish, wearing an old pair of trousers, with his hair straggling down his back. I apologised for wearing trousers, and he for not wearing his robes!

FIELDNOTES, ANAFI, SUNDAY 2 OCTOBER 1966

Mitsos Nikolis (nephew of Barba Tassos) and the Abbot were drinking on Mr V's terrace – joined by gap-toothed Nikolaos 'Birbilis', Zoï Khalari's uncle, and another old man. Mitsos said Barba Tassos had been seized by the Devil and become a miser. He owns four rented-out houses in Athens but watches every drachma. The Abbot appeared to agree with all this.

Yiorghos and Anezini Khalaris (Zoï's parents) are building an extra room where their hen run used to be, opposite their front door, 'because all the children are growing up'. (Probably for the use of their older children now working in Athens to stay in when on holiday).

LETTER 26 CONTINUED, MONDAY 3 OCTOBER 1966

Yesterday evening, the Abbot, and one of the Athenian Anafiots, sat outside Mr V's café, on the terrace which is the roof of my room, and drank beer. The Athenian's uncle is a widower referred to as Barba Tassos, and everyone says he's a miser – he's very short of sight and breath. The old man nearly had apoplexy to see the plates of cheese and sardines and the bottles of beer being carried out onto the terrace. So of course they started to play up to him, rolling bottles across the terrace and calling for more... And when I went out this morning the old man was in the café, counting the empty beer bottles on the shelf in horror at the expense. The point of this is what was said about him. I made some comment that it was unfair to tease him, but his nephew said that he was a bad man, 'seized by the Devil', as was clear by his miserliness, the fact that he never went to church, and by the fact that he had no joy out of his money. The Abbot approved of all this – no admonitions of Christian charity. I just wondered if this sort of deliberate teasing was really a social affirmation of the culturally valued characteristics. On one example it's difficult to say.

I went to buy some Anafiot honey to take to Mick and Nancy when I visit them in Mani next week. This involved the purchase of a container which was weighed at the grocery, then I was taken to the house of the woman who still had some honey in quantity (I recognised her as someone whose baby's christening I'd been to). [In my notes thereafter I always called her 'honey Anna'; her eldest son, only ten years old in 1966, was village secretary during my fieldwork in 1987–88 and still held the position in 1998]. I sat in her house while she went to the outhouse for the honey. There was a large tin bath on the table, full of grapes for jam-making, and the baby was in an old wooden cradle with a lace curtain over it to keep off the flies. Then I took the filled container back to the grocery to be weighed and a price calculated.

Of course now everyone knows I'm going to Athens and on to Mani, I've got numerous commissions... as well as a spate of photograph taking before I go so that I can get the film developed in Athens. In some strange way these demands infuriate me – I know that they are useful for my work – in that it makes contacts for me in Athens, and I have a photographic record of families, however horribly and formally posed – but it's being treated as a public convenience that annoys me – keeping me hanging about in the sun while they all go and change into their Sunday clothes, and assuming I have unlimited film to use on them... I can't reach a balance between being obliging and being a doormat.

Yesterday was a very hot and summery day, but in the evening a sea-wet air rose up to the village, and today has been just like an English washing day, cloudy, sultry, grey, with large but short-lasting drops of rain... Mr V keeps plying me with quince compote – this time because I'm to take a basket of goodies to his wife... One thing I will have to do soon in Athens is to go to a dentist ... several fillings have fallen out.

I left the island on 3 October, to collect that quarter's instalment of my grant from Athens and to visit the Linetons in Mani, and arrived back on 4 November. An account of my visit to Mani is given in Chapter Five.

NOVEMBER REPORT TO SUPERVISOR
It seems to me that I have more than enough to do on Anafi alone, so I do not intend to move on to another island, but rather to extend the study of the island, as I indicated previously, to its relations with its neighbours, and particularly

with the mainland. It is this Athenian end of the study which is both vague in outline and intent. So my major query is whether to stay on after the official fieldwork year is up, that is, after the Greek Easter on 30 April next year, to concentrate on the Athenian end of the study, or whether to return to England, and come back later on, but I am worried about the finances.

I have a rough picture of movement to and from the island, starting in late June to early July after the harvest when young men and those with young families go off for three months' work, usually on building sites in Athens. A little after this begins the influx of summer visitors building up to a climax just before the island's patron saint's festival at the Monastery on 8 September, and leaving rapidly after it. At roughly the same time the men begin to return, although the greatest proportion come back at the end of October. A few elderly people leave to spend the winter in Athens after their grape and olive harvests. During the winter only the Takhidhromos travels to and fro. In the spring, about March, the old people return, and those who work all year in Athens try to return for Easter.

From conversations with Mick, I began to see some comparisons between his fieldwork village and Anafi which set me asking further questions about the island. Anafi is a more isolated and more stratified community and its other features seem to follow from these two factors. The isolation of the island means that the inhabitants are unused to visitors other than their own relatives, and hence the apparent lack of the supposedly Greek characteristic of hospitality, particularly in the form of 'treating' strangers in the cafenions. As it is usually the high status islanders – the village president, the doctor, summer visitors – who offer drinks to others, it seems that islanders may regard such behaviour on their part towards strangers as a sort of patronising gesture, out of keeping with their own idea of their place in the status hierarchy.

At the moment I have no very clear criteria for differentiating these strata; there is a broad occupational basis, with the few white-collar workers (the post office clerk, the policemen) seemingly in a different category from the farmers, the few fishermen, and the shepherds. However, there are marked differences among these latter occupations. The village president, though by definition a farmer, merely supervises his workmen, and himself improves an irrigation scheme in his gardens; one of the fishermen owns a flour mill, which he works with his two fishermen brothers; the other flour mill is owned by a café proprietor. Those who possess fields and gardens which generally provide sufficient for a family's needs, may often employ labourers from among those with few fields and little property of their own. These men, who for various reasons do not go to Athens for summer work, do labouring jobs on the island, helping in the building of summer holiday houses by the harbour, assisting in the grape harvest those families who have no younger members to do these tasks. I want to find out why the poorest island families do not move away, perhaps because they have no family or personal contacts on the mainland, and to find out why they are poor – little or unproductive land, no remittances from Athens, very large or very small family size... In your letter you told me to look for a pattern. I don't think I've found it yet.

In fact, if I trace back in the letters and fieldnotes with hindsight, I had already found, without realising it, elements of what might be put together as 'the pattern'. I later conceptualised this pattern as one of structural principles linking the system of naming children with their rights to family property and their obligations to carry out various religious rituals. Part of the pattern was to link stage in the domestic cycle with inheritance: a married man whose parents were still alive and active, and whose wife had a dowry consisting of a house and a few olive trees but not enough for self-sufficiency, was forced to find work as an agricultural labourer on the island, and a seasonal building worker in Athens, until such time as he inherited his share of the family estate.

FIELDNOTES, ANAFI, SATURDAY 5 NOVEMBER 1966

When I went into Kiriakos' cafenion I asked about notices pinned up in the café about the annual auction of community-held land, the *dhimoprasia*. Those who wanted to rent the uninhabited offshore islets from the community made tenders and these are the people who got them:

    a)   Pakhia [the largest of the islands off the south coast, its name means 'Fat']: Yiannis Arvanitis 3,200 dracs p.a.

    b)   Ftena [two small islands nearest the south coast, their name means 'Narrow', they are the islands which Apollo is said to have put his feet on when he revealed Anafi to Jason and the Argonauts, see Chapter Seven]: Manolis Kollidhas 250 p.a.

    c)   Makria [the most distant of the islands, its name means 'Far']: Antonis Kollidhas 600 p.a. (Eleftheria's husband)

Kiriakos said that they will wait until it rains to take the animals across there by caïque, and leave them on their own to give birth in caves. They will go every 2–3 months to see them.

I collected estimates of the olive harvest and yield of oil from various people. Maria, Kiriakos's wife, said they got 44 okas from their trees (4 go to the press) [an oka was a measure of weight still used in the '60s in country places and now superceded; it equalled 1.28 kilos; the Antoniadis's olive trees thus produced about 56 kilos of oil, allowing the couple at least one kilo of oil per week for the coming year]. Mr V reckons he filled 11 tins (*tenekedhes*, old paraffin tins) with olives. [Later I was told that a tin held 25 kilos of olives. Eleven tins of olives, totalling 275 kilos of fruit, could yield at least 46 kilos of oil]. Tzortzis Russos [son of Dark Iakovos] said he would rather have 50 okas of oil than 300 and all the trouble, while Mr V said wouldn't he prefer to see his olive trees looking like *nifes* (i.e. brides)?

When much later I was given access to the annual agricultural reports, I found that Anafi supposedly had 15,000 olive trees giving a yield of 20 to 50 kilos of fruit each, depending on the area in which the trees grow, and on the amount of rain. Olive trees have a two year cycle: good crops come in alternate years, the difference being between two and four times as much as in the lean year. The ratio of olives to oil was reckoned at three to six kilos of fruit to one kilo of oil, but in a rainless year there could be a disastrously poor yield. I was told in the late '80s that an average year's yield for the island was 22,000 kilos of oil (an average of 176 kilos per household, about 3 kilos per week for domestic use), not much more than one and a half kilos of oil per tree.

LETTER 32, ANAFI, THURSDAY 10 NOVEMBER 1966

What a feast of letters to return to after my return from Mani! No-one died while I was away and two babies were born. It still hasn't rained here although there have been flooded streets in Athens... Most of the cisterns are empty (not ours yet, thank goodness, and Mr V won't let anyone have any water, except from the upper cistern which isn't drinking water) and people are asking why God won't rain ... 'Are we murderers, or thieves to be punished like this?'

At the moment the chief task is picking the olives and pressing them for oil in the donkey-powered presses. It really should rain about ten days before the picking and then the ground under the trees can be ploughed for fodder crops. There is now a weekly caïque from Santorini, on Mondays, which will bring orders such as fresh fruit and vegetables, and take passengers. Mr V had set up my Petrogaz stove while I was away, so now each morning, I put on a pan of water as well as the briki *(tin container for Turkish coffee, although I use it for hot water for tea or Nescafé) and can have a proper wash. I went down with Mr V to watch the olive picking.*

In the account which follows, I have combined the description in the letter with the more detailed version in my fieldnotes.

The olives were on Margarita V's land on the terraces below the village. Five women were there: one was the mother of Marulidhi Sighalla (wife of Manolis the fisherman). Mr V gave them crème de menthe liqueur, menta, *and sweets. He pruned each tree as they picked. They had started from the topmost terrace and were working down towards the road. They spread sacks under the trees and then stripped the branches of olives, together with leaves. Mr V says that trees that are carefully picked bear every year. There were piles of fertiliser*

Figure 4 *The last day of olive-picking: Thanasis Vafiadhis inspects the crop*

on each terrace, covered with soil and stones, to be spread when it rains. He imported about 650 drachmas' worth of fertiliser from the Agricultural Bank last year, and pays a workman to do three lots of digging (at 50 drachmas per day). The first digging is for 5 days, the second and third three days each, 550 drachmas total.

The picking women are those who have no olives of their own. Each day the number and personnel may change. Usually they work for an oka of oil (about one and a quarter kilos) per day, but they might take some of the olive leavings for pig food, or some other form of payment in kind. After picking each tree clean, the sacks with olives lying on them were cleaned, leaves thrown away, and dropped olives picked up.

I went on to the olive press to watch the oil being extracted. Two of the island's four presses are in use this year. The olives are crushed first on a circular platform, by a donkey pulling round a marble wheel. Then they are put inside pieces of sacking and put into the press. After the first pressing, the sacking envelopes are taken out, opened, the olives stirred round and boiling water poured on, and then there's a second pressing. The oil from the first pressing, and oil and boiling water from later pressings, runs into a wooden trough, skafi, at the foot of the press. They used a conch shell to scoop the layer of oil off the water, and to pour it into a measuring can. Every tenth can was poured into the olive-presser's own jar, a very simple way of taking 10%. The water was heated in great boilers, and poured into the sacks with gourd scoops. When the screw on the press had been wound down by hand, a pole was fitted into it, horizontally, and attached to an upright pole by a rope. As we turned the upright pole round like a turnstile, by sticks pushed into its sides, the rope wound round it pulling the bar across and tightening the screw.

From the last of the oil, soap is made. Olives suffer from a disease called ghanghos *which turns them white. Mr V described a salt filtering process which he uses but the islanders don't. They 'wash' the oil to get impurities out of it. They all say they make* lukumadhes, *rather like doughnuts, at this time and fry them in the new oil.*

The Agricultural Report for the island for 1967 listed 7,500 kilos of 'olives for oil-making', whereas a separate report on oil production gave the total amount of oil produced from the village's three olive presses as 7,700 kilos for 1966–67 (an average of 62 kilos of oil per household). The apparent discrepancy might be explained by saying that the figure for olives was for those picked in the autumn and winter of 1967 only, whereas the figure for oil referred to oil pressed from all the olives picked in the autumn and winter season of 1966–67. Such problems are common for researchers working with locally produced statistics.

Personal Diary, Anafi, Thursday 10 November 1966

A haze of sights and sounds in Antonis's olive-press: the smoke and steam from the fire and the boiling water, the gloom of a building with a few grimy windows, the noise of the donkey's hooves, the man's feet and his whistle, the popping, crunching sounds of the olives crushed by the marble wheels, the groaning creaks of the pole and the rope as the screw was wound down, the trickling of the oil into the huge covered trough.

In the evening you plunge out of the night into the light and warmth of the cafenions with their half-doors closed. From inside, looking out, there's a face framed in the doorway, the hand fumbling with the bar on the inside; the person outside looks at those within, deciding whom to greet, whom to sit with. Manolis the Takhidhromos came in to get his hair cut, and Lambros the barber hopped around his great frame on the small chair, snipping and combing with great seriousness.

Letter 32 Continued

They slaughtered pigs while I was away in Mani, and the courtyards are strung with coils of sausages. Things have been fine this week since I've been back; I really feel now as if I'm beginning to get established. Now I can ask questions and wander about without feeling shy and paranoid. ...I'm thinking of coordinating the study of the island with an investigation of the islanders in Athens. An understanding of the island depends on seeing its links with the outside. So after Easter I want to have arranged a questionnaire to give to the Anafiots in Athens, to see what made them leave, if they intend to go back, what will be done about their property on Anafi, etc. Is it better to come home and then come out again for the Athenian part of the study or is it better to stay out here and get the whole thing safely finished before I come home?

Letter 33, Anafi, Wednesday 16 November 1966

There is going to be another post office strike tomorrow so I must write very hurriedly to get this to you on Friday's boat. I have begun questioning in a more regular way – not so much a questionnaire as an aide-mémoire – and I keep a running notebook as I am no longer embarassed about writing things down in front of people. I try to make it clear that I am writing down Greek words rather than information and when I ask questions which might be of personal import I make sure no one else is overhearing. Mr V has been planting onions and new flower seeds and instructing me how to look after the cat, and his bees, while he's away. When it rained the women went out to gather autumn crocuses; they use the stamens as dye; especially for New Year bread. [I found out later that they also sell the saffron to the meat merchants.]

LETTER 34, ANAFI, SATURDAY 19 NOVEMBER 1966

This morning I went for a walk outside the village to see them ploughing the hill terraces. Pananos, the brother of the man who has one of the olive presses (Manolis Arvanitis), was ploughing with two donkeys, and further up the hill another man was using two cows. They sprinkled manure or a white fertiliser on the ground first, then the seed, and then ploughed, the wife or another man following behind with a mattock. Near the terrace were the cows' two calves, wearing strips of cloth stuck with prickles to prevent them taking milk from their mothers.

It was marvellous up there, feeling the wind, and watching the soil turning over. Being so high up, with a view of the sea, reminded me of that Bruegel painting of the Fall of Icarus; it has a peasant ploughing in the foreground, a masted ship at sea and a tiny pair of legs disappearing into the waves. Further down the hillside was Maria i trelli, *'the mad woman', shouting to herself, knitting, wearing a white kerchief and white gloves. One of the women told me that Maria is popularly thought to have gone mad when the man she loved married someone else. [When I got hold of the village register I found out that he had married one of her sisters.]*

The steamer had to go to a harbour on the sheltered western side of the island, as the winds are coming from Crete, south-south-west. I went up to the square and watched the line of donkeys coming up over the hills and up the path to the village. I could make out the fat figure of Manolis the Takhidhromos in his patched pullover, Antonis the fisherman holding his shoes in one hand, donkeys laden with long pipes, shining water cans, laden baskets with sewn covers (usually pieces of cloth with an Athenian address on one side and the Anafi one on the other so that people can send things back and forth).

I've now asked seven people my list of questions about dowry, fields, and relatives in Athens. It only takes about ten minutes and is very simple. I decided not to make it an elaborate questionnaire type thing, so I just ask, after saying that everything I write down is just for my study and won't be told to anyone else, things like 'Is your house rented or bought, or part of your dowry? Where are your fields, which of them are your dowry and which are your husband's inheritance from his father?'. It seems that the house is essential for a woman's dowry, but not necessarily fields. And if fields are part of the dowry the most important are grain fields 'for bread' and then if possible, a little of everything else, olives, vineyards, gardens.

When I called on one woman she was listening to an episode of a morning serial on the radio, and as it mumbled away in the background I realized that it was a Greek adaptation of 'Jane Eyre'. I exclaimed that I knew the story and she asked me to tell her a bit she'd missed when she went out olive-picking.

Unfortunately, I spoiled the story for her by mentioning the mad woman in the attic, adding 'Kirios Rochester's wife'!

LETTER 35, ANAFI, WEDNESDAY 22 NOVEMBER 1966
Yesterday and today have been calm, almost summer-like days, warm enough to sit outside, but mild enough for walking to be a pleasure. I went yesterday with Nikos Ludharos the post-office man out to the land-holding that Nikos said a childless man had given him in exchange for holding a memorial service for him when he died; he didn't have any relatives to do it for him.

[This piece of information was crucially important, although I didn't realise it at the time. The usual pattern was for children to bear the expenses of funeral and memorial services for their parents, in reciprocation for the parents' providing them with a share of the family estate: a dowry house for daughters, fields for sons. Childless people who didn't trust their relatives to fulfil such obligations looked around for someone whom they could rely on. Nikos was obviously such a man.]

We went out at midday and walked inland for about an hour until we heard the shouts of Yiannis Ghavallas, the boatman with only four fingers on one hand (people say he shot his thumb off in an accident), as he ploughed with his two cows, another man digging up the furrows behind him, and his son taking over from time to time. [Later fieldnotes record that on the hillside opposite to this holding were old mineworkings: calamine, used in galvanising processes, and ochre. Nikos Ludharos told me that some of his paternal relatives had worked in them when young. They closed in about 1920.]

Yiannis four-finger's brother is married to Niko's sister so they addressed each other as brother-in-law, bazanakis. *It was a lovely afternoon, the first time here I've been so sharply reminded of the qualities of an English autumn. There was that faint tang in the air, a promise of winter, and more than that, a nostalgia, an atmosphere of waiting and thinking. Working with Nikos's wife, helping her paint the rusted metal supports of the vine arbour, was Elizabeth Rinaki, youngest daughter of the retired Cretan policeman who married an island woman.*

Elizabeth took me to see pottery beehives, nearly three feet high, narrow, with a band of clay pressed with finger marks around the neck. These are laid on their sides, almost buried by stones and brambles on a hill-slope. Nikos said that there used to be a potter, Andhreas Kollidhas, who used to live outside the village, at Vayia, where there are clay deposits. He made these beehives, and also different sized jars for water and oil. He died only a few years ago, but his widow lives in the village. Most of their children were migrants to Athens, but there is one daughter still on the island; she is married to Nikos' brother Yiannis. The majority of beehives used now are the ordinary wooden sort, brought from

Athens. Mr V has three old pottery hives in his wine shed where the treading
pit is. After photographing the beehives, I photographed the ploughing and then
walked back to the village in the late afternoon sunshine, picking wild crocuses
from among the brambles.

On Monday it was the feast of the Presentation of the Virgin (Isodhion tis
Theotoku), and after church there was a procession around the village with the
ikons. Quite a number of men didn't do any work (because there really wasn't
much to do, or out of respect for the festival?) so the cafenions were full most
of the day. Because it was so calm the caïque had been out and we had fish for
lunch. In the late afternoon another caïque came over from Santorini bringing
fodder for the proedhros's flocks from the Agricultural Bank (he's the only man
who ordered it, everyone else is waiting for rain) and also bringing Patiniotis the
grocer back from Naxos with sacks of potatoes and cement.

I've also been to see the forge, where new metal tips are put on the
ploughshares; I was told that the coal comes from a Piraeus importer –
sometimes from Cardiff, sometimes from Germany. A father-in-law (Andhreas
Sighallas) and son-in-law (Russetos Kollidhas) have a forge near the castro.
Nikos Ludharos's brother, Yiannis, has the other forge (their father's), out near
one of the olive presses.

Mr V and I were like a couple of old age pensioners when the strong wind
was blowing. My leg started to play up [I had had polio as a small child in
Australia] and the circulation seemed to slow down. So we were both sitting
in the cafenion rubbing our legs and groaning. He sends you his best wishes.
Mikhalis the Cretan policeman says I am to tell you I am only a medium good
pupil at Tavli (even though I've beaten him twice!) but that I am to send you
his very best wishes.

LETTER 36, ANAFI, SATURDAY 26 NOVEMBER 1966
On Friday, 2nd December, Mr V leaves. I go to Athens a week later for two
weeks [to attend the Mediterraneanists' Conference at the Athens Hilton], I
hope to return on the boat leaving Piraeus 22nd December, arriving back here
on the 23rd for Christmas.

This was all my parents knew at this stage about my travel plans. On 6
December, a steamer from Crete, the 'Iraklion', sank in bad weather, near the
island of Falkonera. Among those lost, it was reported, was one Briton. Until
they received a letter from me, postmarked Athens, my parents thought that
I might have been on that steamer. After the Mediterraneanists' conference
I intended to return to Anafi, but the weekly steamer was cancelled due to
continuing bad weather, and in response to public worries in the aftermath

of the 'Iraklion' tragedy. I spent Christmas in Mani with the Linetons, and returned to Anafi on 28 December in time for the New Year celebrations.

CHAPTER THREE

'God has rained gold'

Winter, spring and summer 1967

I arrived back on Anafi at the very end of December 1966. Mr Vafiadhis stayed in Athens until after Easter 1967 (and the Colonels' coup on 21 April, see Chapter Eight). So, from late December onwards, I had to cook for myself, and no longer had the excuse of eating my evening meal in his café to be in the cafenion area at the busiest time. I now had to make more of an effort to be in places where I could hear daily gossip. These winter months were the loneliest and bleakest of my fieldwork.

This chapter deals mainly with livestock, particularly sheep and goats; with milking, cheese-making and the sale of animals for export and slaughter. Some of the letters and fieldnotes for April 1967, concerning the build-up to Easter, which involved the use of milk and cheese products in cooking, and attempts to obtain a lamb or kid as the main part of the Easter-day meal, have been omitted from this chapter and can be found in Chapter Eight, which deals with Easter and the Colonels' coup.

FIELDNOTES, ANAFI, FRIDAY 30 DECEMBER 1966
Back earlier than expected as the boat arrived at 7:30 am, contrary to its timetable, immediately after Siros, Paros and Naxos. A light showed from the village. Manolis said later they had been waiting on the harbour since 3am and were ready to go to Prassa 'because of the waves'. [Prassa is an inlet on the north-west coast, used when winds at the harbour were contrary].

Manolis was using a motorized dinghy; his brother Antonis Sighallas and two others were in a larger rowboat. They went backwards and forwards three times, bringing many baskets, and taking the doctor's wife to the steamer (she had visited him while I was away). The village secretary's daughter also returned, she had been in Athens to help her sister Kalliopi with her first baby, a boy. She was welcomed by her mother, father's mother, and father's sister (widow Maria).

From this point on in my fieldnotes, I began to make a daily record of who visited which cafenion, assuming that patronage was linked to political sympathies. I will give a sample of the kind of entry I made.

In Dhamighos's café: village secretary, Rinakis, and two others playing cards, three watching. Young Pelekis and Lambros talking, Yiannis Sirighos the whitewasher and an elderly Arvanitis at one table. Aghrofilakas with astinomos [Nikos the policeman] and Pananos at another. Yiannis Ghavallas and Markakis, Anastasios Kollidhas next to him. Barba Tassos alone. In Kiriakos's café: Nikos Khalaris, Tzortzis Russos.

LETTER 44, ANAFI, SUNDAY 1 JANUARY 1967
The BIG NEWS is that it has been raining since I left and HARD. Everything is sodden, my cistern is nearly full, and when it threatens to overflow into the kitchen I shall have to climb up onto the roof and block up the pipe from the terrace and roof into the cistern chute. Mr V's vegetable garden is a riot of green; the village street is muddy and running like a stream. I did some washing and it all got soaked so I strung up a line inside and lit the paraffin stove and was reminded of my London bed-sit days.

LETTER 45, ANAFI, SATURDAY 7 JANUARY 1967
There is a force 9 wind tonight; I have just finished writing up my 20th 'interview'; I received a lovely telegram from you, it read:

HARRY NEW YEAR THINKING OF YOY LONE DADMYM...

Nikos postman's attempt to transliterate the telephoned message into English orthography produced some splendidly apt errors.

The wind is insinuating itself through every crack (and there are many) in the door and through the ill fitting window panes. I've used up all my Weekly Guardians stuffing up the crannies. Luckily it isn't a cold wind but very strong, so I sit with my paraffin stove on and my paraffin lamp throws off a lot of heat. All steamers are confined to harbour so of course we won't get a weekly boat and probably the Monday caïque won't dare come across. So – stranded.

This fieldwork is not going to turn out THE GREAT WORK ON A GREEK ISLAND. It isn't being dramatic to say I might decide not to present a thesis. I don't think I have enough material or enough ideas. Perhaps this sounds rather despairing – it isn't really; I am having a super time: people are being much kinder now I am on my own. On New Year's Eve a group of men with the island bagpipes came to sing the St Basil's Day song to me and I tape-recorded them. Then the next night my cistern overflowed after a torrent of rain. Water poured over the edge of the well-doors and into the kitchen, and from the other side, soaked the bedroom wall. I put on my oilskin mac and sou'wester, took my lantern, found that the path was flooded, and walked up to the village street on top of the wall; then knocked on the door of the postman Nikos Ludharos. I shouted 'help help' like Piglet in Winnie-the-Pooh, and he came out and waded down the path, climbed on the roof and found the hole where the rainwater runs down into the cistern and blocked it up. Meanwhile I swept out the flood, made myself a hot water bottle and went back to bed! The story was great village gossip for days.

PERSONAL DIARY, ANAFI, THURSDAY 10 JANUARY 1967

I went into Yiannis Dhamighos's café where he found me the receipt book of aktimon ['landless ones', people to whom ex-Monastery lands were redistributed, those with little or no land-holdings of their own]. I went to get him the metal spiral from one of my notebooks for his machine (to act as a temporary spare-part for the flour-mill), and found him rolling out the water jar made by the island potter for me to photograph and draw – it has been whitewashed and is decorated with applied rings of clay in wavy lines. Mikhalis the policeman made rude faces in the background… then Yiannis Sirighos took me to his house to show me similar jars and beehives which I photographed and measured. He put on a bee-keeper's fencing-visor-like mask and showed me how swarms were dropped into the clay hives. His storehouse was very tidy, and he took great care not to mess it up. His niece, a young widow, came to watch and accompanied me to the house where I had sweet cake and some cinnamon-flavoured distilled grape-spirit, tsipuro, two glasses because I 'came on two legs'. The house was also scrupulously tidy, with crochet-edged white covers over the wooden chests and side-tables.

LETTER 46, ANAFI, SATURDAY 14 JANUARY 1967

I sat up until 3am last night piecing together bits of my village plan undertaken on various days since last June. Yesterday afternoon I tried to fill in a blank area and came to a part of the village I'd never been in before, with lots of ruins and shut-up houses. Rather eerie and drab, and with a stark poverty shown by the old clothes on the washing lines and unpainted gates and doors. Then I traced bits of different maps and put them together and tried to get a better idea of the shape of the village but being composed of houses one on top of the other up a hillside and also curved round its contour lines, makes it almost impossible to

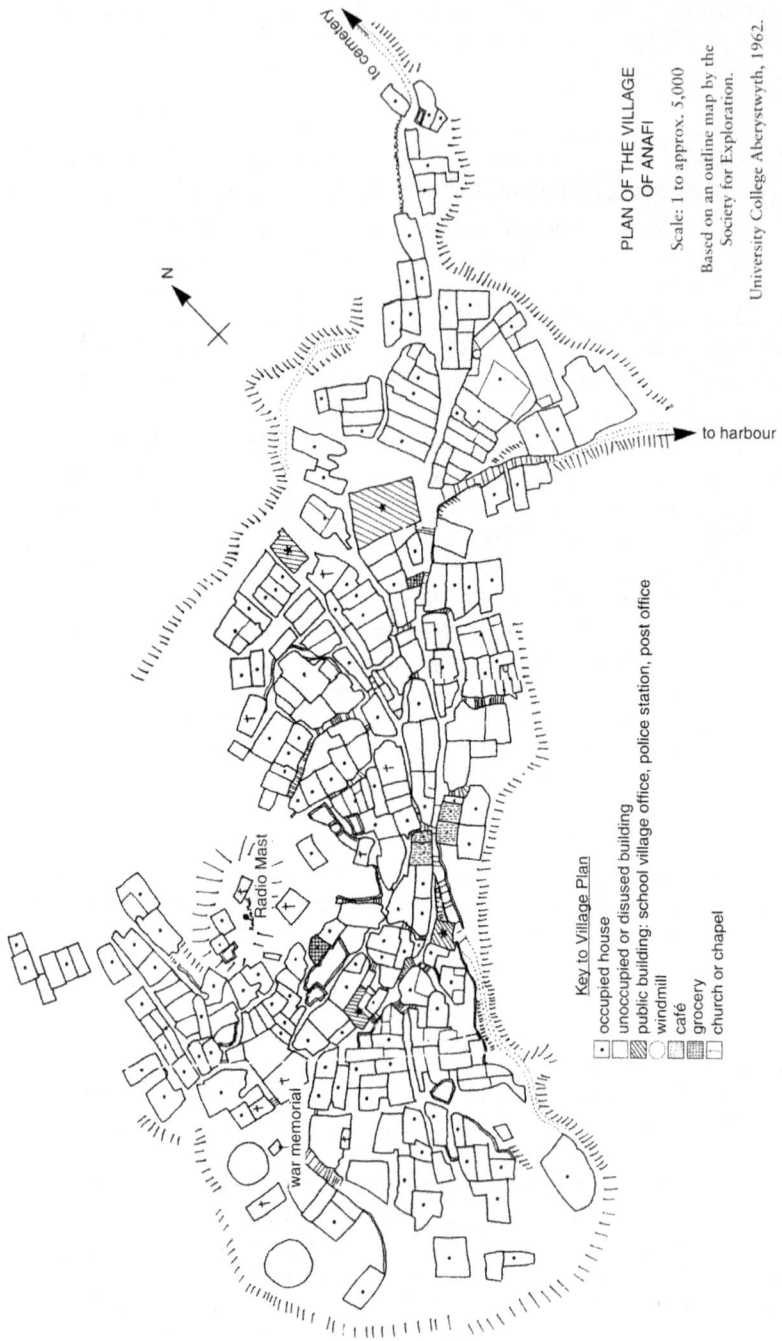

N

to cemetery

PLAN OF THE VILLAGE
OF ANAFI

Scale: 1 to approx. 5,000

Based on an outline map by the
Society for Exploration.

University College Aberystwyth, 1962.

to harbour

Radio Mast

war memorial

Key to Village Plan

occupied house
unoccupied or disused building
public building: school village office, police station, post office
windmill
café
grocery
church or chapel

Figure 5   The final version of the village plan

represent it on a piece of paper. I mapped the village main street as long ago as June but the little winding streets up to the ruins of the Venetian fort are terribly difficult to do. Some of my photographs are a great help and I think I shall take more.

The remark that I found a part of the village which I had never seen before, after living on the island for seven months, links up with a comment made to me by a woman when I told her that I had been in a particular part of the village that day. She said that she hadn't been in that area for over forty years, since she had played there as a child. She had no kin or other connections in that neighbourhood, *yitonia*, so there was no call for her ever to set foot there. Similarly, there were parts of the island where some Anafiots had never been, or had not been for years. Unless they had family lands in that area, there would be no reason to go there. Younger men might roam all over the island on partridge-shooting expeditions, but older men (apart from the the field guard, *aghrofilakas*) tended to be familiar only with strictly defined localities. For example, in May 1967 I went to the chapel of Ayios Yiannis Theologhos with 'Granny Glasses' (Marusi Ghavalla) and with Patiniotis the grocer, partly for him to estimate how much whitewash would be needed to repaint it. He said that it was the first time in his life that he had been to that part of the island. He was then in his early fifties.

LETTER 47, ANAFI, SUNDAY 22 JANUARY 1967

I had supper with the Proedhros last night. They had killed a pig the day before and there were great wooden troughs full of meat to make sausages and his wife was cooking pieces of fat to make 'butter', vutero, i.e. lard. No wonder they can't understand the English eating bread and butter and jam! Their daughter Stella and her husband the schoolteacher came in, also Nikolaos, the workman at the Proedhros's garden, and his wife Kalliopi, a very jolly woman who is said to have inherited the power of the Evil Eye from her father. It was a nice evening.

    And I bet in a thousand years you won't guess what I've been learning to do. I'm spinning wool. I've teased out a fringe-like piece cut from the sheep's coat, pushed it into a stick which goes under my left armpit, with my left hand I pull out the threads, and with my right, spin them round the spindle. Just like 'the moonspinners' [my mother had sent me the Mary Stewart novel of the same title]. I'm very bad at it. Tonight was my first attempt: the wool goes thin and breaks or else thickens into a huge lump. And it tickles my nose. I found out, you see, that the village barber makes the special crochet-hook ended knitting needles used by the island women – they sling the wool around their necks, or else have it running through a safety pin on the left shoulder (or a blue bead – for the Evil Eye – held on by a metal clasp) and use the left hand to put the wool round the needle – what we would call Continental style knitting. They say the way I knit is how women knit 'in Athens' so I have learnt the island method and thus will join the evening gatherings with something in my hands.

Remember I told you that when I was making a plan of the village someone told me that some 'students' had done the same thing several years ago? Well, their address was in a drawer in one of the cafés; they were students belonging to the Expedition Society who came here from the University of Aberystwyth. [I was later sent a copy of their properly measured-out village map, and used it as a basis for my own; see Figure 5, page 58.]

The village plan is suddenly beginning to fit together and I hope to get a first draft finished this week, and then, if and when I see the Aberystwyth 1962 village plan I can compare it and see how many people have left or changed the use of buildings since then.....love from your spinning, atropaic, daughter.

LETTER 48, ANAFI, 26 JANUARY 1967

So many lovely things by Tuesday's post: your tape, your parcel and a letter from my supervisor! It was marked 'Express' but took three weeks to get here. Among his apologies he said he was very interested in my material, which he thought would make a very good book, and was particularly interested in the house-as-a-dowry pattern which is similar to that in Italy where one of his other students did research. He also wanted a summary of my financial position to show to the Committee and said 'since your first grant was so modest the case for giving you some more is very strong indeed given only that I can find a source. In view of the potential financial difficulties it seems to me that you would be wiser to pack up in the middle of April and come home. If humanly possible we will send you back for a brief period before finally submitting. Lengthening the research period will create further problems of keeping you alive while writing up, so do not count on more fieldwork at this stage.'

As you know, I intend to stay at least until Easter here (April 30th) and as my money is holding out well, I then intend to do a brief survey in the various suburbs of Athens before returning. I honestly think it is best to stay out here as long as I can, because I don't foresee a return trip soon and I want to have as much material as possible to work on. So what I need to do is have a good hard think: what do I need to find out to tie Anafi and the Anafiots-in-Athens together? I need to have a fairly coherent account of life on Anafi; what people do here, the summer migration of men for work in Athens, the point where families migrate en masse (the poor, or not-so poor? those with jobs to go to? etc., etc.) and the Athenian end must be a very generalised picture of the summer migrants, the recent full-time migrants and the established ones. So of necessity, I am having to put a frame round all this cluttered and unequal data – what theory cannot provide, a time limit and finances will!

It got very cold after I returned from the celebrations at the chapel of Ayios Antonios [see Chapter Six], but the last few days it has been quite hot during the day, hot enough to sit outside the cafenions in the sunshine, and hot enough to puff and sweat as I tramp round the village, climbing up steep paths and onto walls and roofs to complete the village plan. I do a little section at a time and then sellotape it to what I've already completed; the patchwork of different coloured biro and felt-pen corrections stretches along the sofa. As I tramp around I come upon women baking, or washing, or sifting grain, cutting up greens, knitting or crochetting, men digging foundations for a new stable, mending a broken down wall, making a well cover at the forge. It is quite a good excuse for getting the flavour of daily life in the village. I am getting quite a dab hand at spinning, and the thread is much less bumpy and uneven than at first....

I found out yesterday evening that the grocer, Patiniotis, has a big credit book, and the accounts have to be paid up at Easter (after the meat merchants have bought sheep and goats for the Paschal dinners on Ios, Santorini, I conjecture). His father came to Anafi (from Amorgos) to plant tobacco, and had six women working for him then. Patiniotis is the second son; he married during the Occupation, and they worked someone else's fields for halfshares then as neither of them had land of their own...

One afternoon the hardware shop man, Vinzenzos, was drinking tea and he suddenly asked me about my research and volunteered the information that all those who had left Anafi had gone to Athens except one who had gone to Germany. Those who stayed behind were those who weren't strong enough for tough building work in Athens or those who had no relatives there who could start them off with somewhere to live or those who had enough here to live comfortably on without chancing the competitive and more expensive life of the city, and those who were too poor to leave.

FEBRUARY REPORT TO SUPERVISOR

I have been working on the shepherding system here. Shepherds look after other people's animals in return for half the young, and half the wool of the two shearings per year. The wool is sold only on Anafi. Rent for pastures grazed is reckoned in cheese, and paid during Lent.

In my December report I made a tentative effort to outline for you the 'fields to eldest son because he has his father's father's name' and 'house to eldest daughter because she has her mother's mother's name' pattern. Friedl says 'in Vasilika [her fieldwork village, near Delphi] there is neither an explicit nor an implicit pattern of giving daughters only dower property and sons only patrilineally inherited land', so the Anafi material offers a contrast to this. I am continuing to collect material.

FIELDNOTES, ANAFI, SATURDAY 4 FEBRUARY 1967

I went up the rocky slope by the school – the midwife, *mami* [Evangelia Russu, Margarita Vafiadhu's stepmother], Pliti Peleki, and Marulidhi were making soap from olive oil sludge in a great cauldron; one of the olive presses is close by. Do they have a right to the sludge from their own olive pressing? Or do they buy it from the press?

On my return [from an interview for my household survey], Rembelia and Anezini were sitting on R's balcony cleaning grain. R said she had washed hers and was sun-drying it. It is harvested, threshed, tossed (chaff for animal fodder), put in sacks, brought to village (or left in storehouse), washed (if wanted), picked over in a sieve, milled, sieved again... The sequence is *therismo*, harvest, *alonisma*, threshing, *liknisma*, which I think means sieving, *tsuvali*, literally 'sack', storage, *koskinisma*, another kind of sieving once it is ground into flour. [This account leaves out taking the grain to a flour-mill for it to be ground; maybe, knowing my incessant questions, the women did not want to initiate a string of queries about the millers' percentages.]

Lots of fishing boats out near the islets. Some of the crew were up in the village talking to the Nikos the astinomos today in the morning.

LETTER 49, ANAFI, SUNDAY 5 FEBRUARY 1967

Now that I am busy twirling my spindle and whirling the crochet hook, I have entrée to the evening gossip sessions, and can pretend to be very busy, while listening hard to the uninhibited conversation. The current topic is really fantastic: someone is said to have put a stick of dynamite down the exhaust-fume chimney of the flour mill, and when it started working next morning, there was an explosion. However a metal bar had prevented the charge slipping down the pipe into the mill-room, so that only the chimney and stones on the roof blew off, all over the square and down into the village. No-one was hurt at all (one explanation is that the mill is next to the village church). Anyway, speculation is rife as to who-dun-it, but I haven't heard any names mentioned as yet, no-one seems able to think who it could be. This morning in church, the other flour-mill owner, Dhamighos, (who has the café next door to Mr V's and is the steamer company ticket seller) made an announcement at the end of the Service that he had heard gossip that he might have done it out of spite, and swore on the ikon that he hadn't, burst into tears and rushed out of the church. People seemed to think he had been a little dramatic about it all; he is elderly and putting the charge into the chimney involved climbing up a wall and over a roof, which he is unlikely to have been nimble enough to manage.

FIELDNOTES, ANAFI, THURSDAY 23 FEBRUARY 1967

[I had gone over to Santorini for a fortnight to help Susanna get established in her fieldwork village there; she had been let down by a Greek research assistant at the last minute. See Chapter Five. I returned to Anafi by caïque, not by the weekly steamer].

The man who got onto the caïque at the harbour on Anafi as I disembarked was said to come from Meghalo Khorio on Santorini. He had come on February 7 and stayed two weeks; he is a *ghanuzis*, a tinker (*ghanotis* is the more usual word I was told) and had come for the first time in three and a half years, but is known here. He came to fix pots and pans, particularly those in which cheese will be made in about three weeks time, in the field cottages. He worked in Adhriana's house. Margarita Dhamighu told me in the evening that Barba Konstantin will make his cheese in the old house beside the harbour path – it belongs to Thanasi (i.e. to Margarita). They make a sweet called *melitera*, cheese and sugar in pastry. It suddenly occurred to me that there are periods of glut at which obligations are repaid (shortbread-like sweet cakes, *kurabies*, at New Year, sausages and meat in November, cheeses in Lent, etc.)

FIELDNOTES, ANAFI, SATURDAY 25 FEBRUARY 1967

Up at nine. Did some writing-up, then to the post-office, rang up Susanna, asked Nikos the postman to help me name people in my photos. Kalliopi the deaf girl came in [daughter of Markakis, Markos Dhamighos]. I went to see her mother Irini and asked my household survey questions. She said that Anafiots live *krifa apo to Theo*, hidden from God, a phrase I have heard many times before, together with *makria ap' to Theo*, far from God. She was very cagey about the lands they held but at least I learnt about her husband's role, together with Vinzenzos and Patiniotis, as middle-men between shepherds and customers in the sale of meat within the island. She told me that now they are killing kids and lambs because they need to milk the mothers. Otherwise the questions went well.

Shopped at Patiniotis's grocery; the gossip is that Barba Tassos is ill and cannot recognise anybody. Went out at three to see Proedhros's wife, she was boiling up kids' heads. She told me that they had bought meat from Patiniotis. She confirmed that Vinzenzos, Patiniotis, and Markakis were the intermediaries between shepherds and customers. If a shepherd sells a whole flock he may give them at one all-inclusive price; others sell individual beasts. The Santorinian meat-merchants take the animals away live.

I left about four. Came down to write until five, had tea in Kiriakos's café, Yiorghakis Birbilis was there with his little daughter Katerina. Vinzenzos was also there. Astinomos came in and played cards with Merkuris. A group of men, including Manolis Birbilis, rode past the café singing. They had finished work on Manolis's vineyard (probably spring pruning). Note that Yiorghakis hadn't gone to help his brother.

Later, I went to see Marulidhi, Manolis the fisherman's wife. She told me that Barba Tassos had died. Another visitor to her house mentioned that the men who had passed the café were having a party and that Rinakis had said that it wasn't suitable as someone had just died. Answer: We had arranged to enjoy ourselves tonight, why couldn't he have waited until tomorrow to die?

LETTER 54, ANAFI, FRIDAY 3 MARCH 1967

A terrific windy day, shutters creaking, powdery whitewash falling, dust and fluff blowing under the door, the postcards fluttering on their sellotape attachments, my windcheater on the line dancing madly, looping the loop and twining itself around the rope. The first pinks, some lovely, white, waxy freezias, and tiny purple starry flowers are blooming in the old paraffin-tin garden.

I made syrup for the bees just as Mr V had instructed me, and stirred the heavy, rather dirty sugar round and round until it melted, and then poured it out into the flat trays with their bridges of tiny sticks for the bees to sit on while they suck up the mixture. I am fearless with my paraffin pressure lamp now, and last night attempted by its light a culinary feat known as cauliflower cheese à la nécessité, made with a gift of cauliflower, and a sauce of soup-cube, tinned milk and Primula cheese. I boiled up some potatoes and had the whole delicious mixture with luncheon meat. Pudding of sliced apple with lemon juice and sugar.

LETTER 55, ANAFI, SATURDAY 11 MARCH 1967

I am suffering terribly from my bottom right wisdom tooth and from a stiff neck. The discomfort is almost worse than pain because with pain you can just go away and take aspirin and go to bed but I don't feel justified in doing that and so I have been drifting around the village in a haze of aspirin and brandy. Women have been baking lovely soft-cheese and honey-filled cakes and bread dyed with crocus stamens for this, the last Sunday before Lent begins. Again I have a kilo of kid's meat for my own celebrations; and on Monday (with which Lent begins here), I may go out to one of the islets with some of the shepherds to cut fleece and bring some of the animals back to land. That Monday – Clean Monday it is called – is traditionally a day for outings. There will be no school, and people are planning to go down to the sea if it is a fine day, and gather winkles off the rocks, and fry fish. There's supposed to be no meat eaten after Sunday and fish only on feast days; fasting here means no meat, fish, eggs, milk, oil... no wonder they used to die during Lent!

I have had my first gift of fresh milk from a shepherd's wife... Anyway the milk was lovely. I had some of it hot with brandy for my tooth, and the rest I made into crème caramels. And the proedhros' wife gave me some soft cheese and yellow bread. Susanna reports from Santorini she is getting so much milk from villagers that she could take baths in it like Cleopatra.

I feel a bit like the young reporter Durrell describes in the Alexandria Quartet. He was always on edge in case he might be missing a story, so he used to hurry out of a café or party he was at to take a walk round the block to quell his conviction that something else more important was happening that he was missing. That exactly describes me. When I sit in the cafenion, I think: I should have gone evening visiting tonight, and taken my spindle, there'll probably be masqueraders and gossip about such-and-such that happened today. And when I'm evening visiting I think: I wish I was having a quiet coffee in the cafenion before going down to hear the news, type up the day's report and read another chapter of Graham Greene in Mexico. Never satisfied.

I wonder whether my preoccupation with events is because I really haven't as yet got to the structural level which underlies them? Once I can see the different pulls of kinship, neighbourhood, kumbaria [wedding sponsorship], godparenthood, etc., then I can see these themes in different events as they occur, but at the moment I am still hoping that I may see in a happening some indication of the structure under it. Do you see what I mean? Should I be so obsessed with trying to keep track of everything, when I know that my most significant discoveries have usually come by chance? And how does one put oneself in the way of chance? I don't fancy sitting on a wall all day watching the world go by and waiting for chance to give me the anthropological scoop of a lifetime.

I've been helping the village secretary's wife wind the threads for the warp of her loom. She had nails hammered into the floor of her mother's house (the old granny is a neighbour of mine) and wound the threads from eleven spindles strung on a ladder-like frame across the doorway, up and down the room, zig-zagging them round the nails. Then she looped the long snake of threads into a plait-like crochet chain-stitch with her hand as the crochet hook, and carried it back to her house. There she and her daughter (the one I came back from Athens with) and I undid the plait and straightened and pulled out the threads which were being wound onto a thick horizontal pole and from which they stretched the length of the loom to the front, where the shuttle went across... It is funny to hear the verb klotho *[to spin], as it is to hear skin called* epidhermidha *as if everyone here had a highly technical knowledge...*

FIELDNOTES, ANAFI, SUNDAY 19 MARCH 1967

Dark Iakovos was in Kiriakos's café and told me that he had been a very successful man in Athens but that his money had been 'eaten up' during the time of the Occupation. He had bought pigs to sell and been to Amorgos on a sail boat. He had lived in Makriyianni and worked in a shop there. He said he remembered a time when the present Abbot's father was priest and the Abbot never went to church at all. He adopted a very conspiratorial tone to talk to me.

Later I went in to the Dhamighos's café and was called out by Manolis Birbilis who said I was wanted at Rinakis's. Presuming it was so that I could see the cheeses being paid as rent for grazing land, I went and got my camera. At their house Andhreas Kollidhas, Lemonia's husband, had brought a crate of cheeses, which was weighed, then the cheeses were taken out, the crate and rush baskets weighed, and the cheeses' weight worked out.

In the account which follows, all the terms were carefully written in Greek, with pencilled-in dictionary definitions to clarify their meaning.

Andhreas told me that the animals are taken inside the *mandhra*, sheep-pen (literally 'wall') to be milked into an *armektra*, milking pail, made of pottery. The milk is strained through a cloth into the *kazani*, cauldron, cooking-pot. *Maiyia* (*mayia*, yeast, but here obviously meaning rennet) is put in to clot it, made from the stomach of a *pithia*, kid, which must be eight days old, *na kani ikhrisi tu ghalaktos* in order to thicken the milk. When it thickens it is stirred *na skotonume* (to kill, presumably meaning the microbes) with a *tarakti*, wooden rod, and put into the *tirivoli* made of *vurla* (the cheese baskets made of rushes) bought from Nikolas Sighallas *tu Barba Riga* (a nickname distinguishing the unmarried brother of Lambros the barber from a number of other men also named Nikolaos Sighallas). New cheesebaskets are bought each year, costing about 60 drachmas for four. In about one and a half hours the baskets are *strayiksi*, drained). For *vrasti* (literally 'boiled', a kind of cheese], the *tsirros* is heated and sea water or salt put in. The proportions are five okas of whey to one of milk.

I remember that on one occasion when I mentioned in one of the cafés that I was going down to the harbour for a swim the next day, I was later asked if I would fill a bottle with sea water while there and bring it back up to the village on my return for cheese making.

The relationship between the owner of the grazing land and the shepherd is denoted in the term *kollighas*: 'he is my *kollighas*' is used by either

Figure 6   Weighing the cheese-rent: Vasiliki with Andhreas the shepherd

party about the other (so the dictionary definition 'share-cropper' can't be correct here, because such a term could not be employed by both parties). *Paktomataris* is used for the owner of the land, *paktos* meaning cheese, so presumably 'receiver of the cheese rent'? Some land is grazed only in summer (i.e. after harvest of fields) from 6 August to 26 October (from the feast of the Transfiguration to Ayios Dhimitrios's day), although if the planting is delayed by drought, the grazing is extended. After all the cheese rent is brought, the agreement about continuing the arrangement is made (or not), but the actual date of the new arrangement beginning is 18 May. Decisions about giving animals to be grazed by the shepherd are also made around 18 May. Andhreas said the animals and the wool are shared half and half with the owner. If it is an odd number of animals, the value of one of them is reckoned in money, and whoever takes the animal pays the other man half the value. The owner usually shears his own goats. In old days the hair used to be made into ropes, but now the hair is sold to Patiniotis and the shepherds make their ropes out of *kanavi*, hemp. In the past two or three years the island women who have looms have begun to use goat hair for rugs. They first saw goat-hair capes when the political exiles came. An occasional caïque may come with pottery jars and seek goat hair to buy.

The Agricultural Report for 1967 said that there were 1,000 sheep and 1,700 goats on the island; 27,000 kilos of hard cheese were produced; and 4,000 kilos of *mizithra* (soft cheese). The report also claimed that during the year 480 lambs were slaughtered, and 750 kids; about 200 lambs were sold and about 150 kids.

LETTER 56, ANAFI, TUESDAY 21 MARCH 1967

One afternoon recently I sat out in the sunny courtyard with an old woman who was peeling onions and potatoes. She had done a huge wash as she and her husband had been out at their fields for over a week, weeding the crops, pruning the vineyards, and ploughing the fallow fields. It was very pleasant to sit there and chat, and I asked her about fields and inheritance and she confirmed my idea about funeral rites, and also supported a new idea about the composition of the evening gossip groups. It seems to me these are the women's version of the cafenion, and the house where these groups meet might be an indication of differing statuses between families, which it is hard to find out about. People don't make explicit distinctions among the other villagers although it seems to me obvious that there are differing standards of living and people might tend to keep into roughly corresponding groups. These gossip circles cross-cut the isolation of the family and the close neighbourhood limits. Neighbours and relatives call in, but not kseni, *'strangers,' i.e. those with no kinship or* kumbaria *(wedding sponsor or godparent) links to the family.*

There has been some soft rain and I had to light my paraffin heater one chilly evening. The weather is very changeable.

On Tuesday evening I went visiting and sat in a family kitchen while the mother sorted peas, her mother spun, and her father leaned on his stick and told me about the old days while the two small boys did their homework. The old man told me that when there had been a larger population here some men had owned lots of land, and rented it to others to work – so presumably there was an even greater social differentiation then. And the old lady told me that until a few years ago they used to have silk worms on the mulberries and spun their own silk for export. They wound the thread onto spindles to send away, I don't think they made material. [In 1987, I found examples of Anafiot silk in the Benaki Museum in Athens.]

I'm finishing this letter off after three days of rain and hail, buffeting winds and damp walls. 'God has rained gold' one woman told me...

LETTER 57, ANAFI, THURSDAY 23 MARCH 1967

*... fasting means that people have to eat more greens, more mashed pea soup (*fava*), more beans, instead of milk and meat and fish. And on Wednesdays and Fridays they abstain from olive oil as well. So you might say that it turns the attention to vegetable proteins more. But it seems to me to be mainly women, and married women and widows at most, who observe the Lenten fast in its entirety. The schoolmaster and his wife kept the first week strictly and the Wednesday and Friday of subsequent weeks, although they eat meat and fish on other days, for there is the other question: how do the shepherds get rid of the surplus young male animals before Easter?*

FIELDNOTES, ANAFI, SATURDAY 25 MARCH 1967

I went to get milk from the *proedhrina* (as she is abstaining from it during Lent) and then visited Margarita Khalari. Mattheos, her brother-in-law, *kuniadhos*, was there, having brought cheeses from Margarita's lands. He told me he owed about 400 *okades* of cheese to different land owners. Her husband Nikos was writing down the weight of the cheeses brought and complained that last year Aryirios had cheated him on the weighings – at least he had sent his son (I think he meant that the son rather than the father cheated him, but I got a bit muddled). Rembelia came in with Flora [her daughter]. She mentioned that she and Nikos are first cousins – her father Mattheos Nikolis and his mother, Katerini, were siblings.

On 29 March I caught the steamer to Athens, joined by Susanna when it called at Santorini. In Athens we met up with the Linetons to celebrate Susanna's birthday on the first of April and my 25th birthday the next day. I also met up with Rosalind Horner, a friend from my undergraduate days, who had planned a short holiday in Greece before setting off for her own fieldwork in Burundi. She joined me on Anafi towards the end of her holiday. The excerpts from letters and fieldnotes which end this chapter round off the yearly cycle on Anafi; more detail about Ros's visit can be found in Chapter Eight, which records the major political events of April 1967.

LETTER 62, ANAFI, WEDNESDAY 12 APRIL 1967

It is marvellously warm, but not burning hot yet, so I can sit scantily clad without sweating into a pool of butter like Little Black Sambo's tigers. Yesterday although the air wasn't sparklingly clear, I could see far beyond the most distant islet to the south-east, Zafora, and thought I could see, to the south-west, the outline of Crete thirty miles away, a vague shape above an indistinct but perceptible dividing line between sea and land. All the fig trees have bright bright green buds and sprigs of leaves. I paid off my debts to the grocer, who has promised to bring me some goat meat tomorrow, but secretly, as slaughtering is now against the law. I'm not clear about it and can't ask the policeman in case he realises why I'm asking. The meat merchants are here, six of them, one left by caïque before the steamer came, and one came on the steamer; they are making their buying arrangements, and will leave, to return just before Easter with caïques to transport the animals for slaughter. They seem to be taking their meals in the card-playing room of Kiriakos's cafenion, and probably sleeping in the guest house, but I'm not sure of the details yet. It is so slow finding out the tiniest bit of information. Whenever I ask 'What's the news?' everyone says 'All quiet' and it's just because I noticed the strange man landing with us and later saw the others in the cafenion that I realised that the meat merchants were here.

Among the post waiting for me was the village map from the Geography Department at Aberystwyth – not quite what I expected, as it is only an outline of the different blocks of built-up sites. There is no detail of separate houses, no distinction between courtyard and house etc, just an accurately traced boundary line round the house and walls of each house and shed with a path right round it; so my own work on locating each house and shed wasn't at all wasted, I can fill all that data in, inside the lines this plan gives. [See Figure 5, page 58; the Aberystwyth plan with my additions.]

LETTER 63, ANAFI, SUNDAY 16 APRIL 1967

I've been reading through all my fieldnotes, and writing down queries on unclear points, or ideas to follow up. My friend Nikos the postman has helped me clear up most of the queries, particularly names of people in photos. I found a diagram I made some time ago with the island terms for the winds of different directions, and on checking it with Nikos, found that there is much greater differentiation between the various south to west, to north winds than between the northerlies and easterlies; that is, there are names for northerly, and easterly winds, and then separate names for SSW, SW, WSW, WNW, NW, NNW winds. This could be because the island faces south, and the important subtleties in winds depend on them coming from Crete (SW) or Santorini (W).

New stock, by the way, is brought in through the Agricultural Bank, but the Cooperative's president here [Rinakis] has been eluding me since January and I can't pin him down to a day to talk over the importing of seeds and fertilisers to the island. The meat merchants left by the regular caïque which came on Thursday morning.

LETTER 65, ANAFI, MONDAY 1 MAY 1967

[This was the first letter I'd written after the coup on 21 April. Because of possible censorship I made no reference to political matters.] Rosalind left last Tuesday morning, with moonlight on a spuming sea, breaking over the quay and pouring down the steps from the other side; the little boat bobbed and bounced out to the steamer. At the last minute the Takhidhromos decided to take several animals to Athens, so a shout went up, and the kids and goats were slaughtered on the concrete, blood pouring out of their mouths and washed away by the sea, the bodies still jerking when they were thrown into the dinghy. It was the first time I had ever seen anything killed. Later it all hit me: no sleep, excitement, fear, the sadness of Ros leaving, I burst into floods of tears and felt very lonely and homesick.

I couldn't even sleep, so did all my washing and then went out, which meant standing up to all the comments of: 'so your friend's gone now, you're all on your own again'. So I went for a walk, and had a lovely bonus. I picked lots of flowers and then met a shepherd woman who took me along to watch her milking and making cheese. I sat on a stone inside the high stone walls of the fold, the kids and young goats running nimbly along the top, the older goats balefully chewing with super-critical and supercilious gazes through their half-closed eyes. The sheep sitting in another corner of the fold were much quieter, although more difficult to milk. They are all grazed together and the milk is put in one container. Campbell's Epirot shepherds kept their flocks apart and they were looked after by the opposite sexes: men for sheep, God's animal; and women for goats.

This encounter cheered me up, and by Tuesday evening I was fairly restored to equanimity. It rained that evening and when I went up to the cafenion there was lots of talk about cheeses (for Easter cake-making) and the animals which were to be taken across to Santorini. Those sold to the meat-merchants were being herded outside the village, and were driven across the island early on Thursday morning to be put on a caïque which had put in to a sheltered inlet on the north-east coast. The shepherds had had prior notice by telephone, but from the moment the flock got to the village it was the meat-merchants' responsibility and so hired men drove them to their 'fate-doomed caravel'. While they were still grazing near the village there was the constant clanking and tinkling of bells, and baaas and maaas and squeaks from the kids. I got fleas again from my visit to the fold and had a chilly all-over wash and hair-rinse to get rid of them.

Everyone baked on Thursday, and I went and watched at several houses and had cosy chats with some women. After many hours of church services on Good Friday I wrote fieldnotes till 4am and got up at midday. There was a terrible smell of blood and shit all over the village; people were cleaning the intestines of slaughtered animals to make into a sort of soup, which is eaten after church on Saturday-Sunday night, because of the weak state of the stomach after fasting. My stomach turns to think of eating it! By late afternoon people were putting their roasts in the furnace, and sealing the door with cement, and I thought idly, how symbolic, the lamb in the tomb-like oven, opened up after the Resurrection is announced.

After the midnight Easter service I was asked to go back and eat with the schoolteacher and Stella and we had liver, egg and lemon soup. They had put their roast in a neighbour's oven (lots of neighbourhood cooperation on this) and couldn't get it out yet because he was waiting to open the oven until all the neighbours were assembled.

PERSONAL DIARY, ANAFI, EASTER SUNDAY, 30 APRIL 1967, 2:30 AM

Returning from an Easter meal with Nikos and Stella I thought I saw a shooting star but it continued so regularly across the sky that I decided it must be a satellite. It is very still, almost warm, tonight. A sudden roaring of aeroplanes extinguished the continual sea noises. The moon is directly above the islets; the edge of one of them shows like the silhouette of a battleship. The sea moves very gently eastwards in wrinkly waves, the wind corrugating the sea like breath on custard skin or thick porridge.

LETTER 65, CONTINUED

In the morning little girls were swinging on improvised swings of ropes and sacking, this is traditional but I don't know its significance. In the olden days, I was told, the young girls and married women used to do it to show off the lace on their petticoats, and the boys used to come spying. Disparaging versions of the traditional songs were sung or they teased each other about their sweethearts (all very like fertility rites in The Golden Bough!).

The old widow I call 'Granny Glasses' asked me to go for lunch to share her cold roast, heavily garlic'd. Her son is President of the Anafiot Migrant Society in Athens, and they have lots of land here. I found out, contrary to my 'need for cash' idea that all their land is worked half-shares rather than for wages or rent. But maybe her family doesn't need cash and prefers produce?

I told my problems in getting any details out of the villagers to Nikos the teacher, and he said he would help me to construct a list of areas of Anafi and people's land there. He would be able to tell me whether it was inherited, bought, rented or worked half-shares. They still insist that most people on the island are the same although it is plain that there are differences in quality of clothes, houses, way of living....

It's pouring with rain now, and ten minutes ago I was typing this out on the balcony. I dropped the bucket and its rope into the well this morning and had to fish it out with a long cane with a hook on the end, borrowed from a neighbour. I nearly fell in.

LETTER 67, ANAFI, SUNDAY 14 MAY 1967
Susanna came on the most recent boat for a week's visit. There was a magnificent baking day on Thursday when one of the island women offered to teach me to make cheese cakes – melitera – and of course while mixing and kneading and watching the furnace we gossiped and I learnt lots of things about birth control habits here – coitus interruptus mostly and tablets 'to bring on the period'...

LETTER 68, ANAFI, SATURDAY 20 MAY 1967
It is raining, there are clouds, and the wind has been blowing almost incessantly for over a week. The one time it stopped was on the evening of my anniversary of arrival on Anafi. I sat on my terrace and looked out at the lights of the fishing caïque and a distant ocean liner moving slowly across the horizon behind the distant islets, proving they weren't pasted on the sky. I have been finishing off the village plan, standing on walls and roofs, correcting my own attempts, and trying to fit them into the plan from the 1962 Aberystwyth expedition. Susanna left last Monday on a caïque with 120 sheep and goats, two calves, and a cow which had to be winched on board!

LETTER 69, ANAFI, SUNDAY 28 MAY 1967
Your most recent letter had a very dramatic arrival. The wind was so strong last Tuesday at dawn that no little boats could go out to the steamer and it just hooted and turned round and sailed away with our letters, provisions and passengers. They were all landed on Ios, two islands further on, except for

Mikhalis the policeman who was so sea-sick that when the boat got to Santorini they had to land him there. Because of the wind he couldn't get off at Fira, the main port, but had to be disembarked on the island of Thirasia opposite. The caïque from Ios picked him up the next day and came on to Anafi with post from the steamer. So my letter to you left on that caïque. My post included a huge parcel of courgettes and tomatoes (very pulpy after such a round-about journey) from Susanna, with magazines and a thriller and some packets of crème caramel for using up the milk I get from the Proedhros's wife every evening.

Over the last week I have been trying to work at some sort of economic rating of the village households according to the three categories in the village register. It seems very unsatisfactory and I need a better rating scale and to know what criteria were used. I think the schoolmaster may be the best person to get a fairly accurate subjective evaluation of different people's wealth from.

I have been hunting down the president of the island cooperative; he finally said he'd see me on Sunday, and when I went to his house he wasn't there. Then I found him in the cafenion and as he left I made to follow him, to go and look at the records and ask him about the work of the cooperative: 'I'm too busy' he said. I was furious.

JUNE REPORT TO SUPERVISOR

Things are going well, although there seem to be as many kinds of stonewalling to frustrate attempts to get information, as there are skins on an onion, so that I keep finding that previous data were out of date or incorrect. Recent events have had little direct effect on island life or behaviour; indirectly, there has been caginess in expressing opinions both between villagers and to me, delays and some censorship of mail, and a clear polarisation of clientele between the two main cafés which are run by members of the village council who support opposing political parties.

At the moment I am investigating the economic differences between families: I had hoped to get some reasonably objective data from the records of the flour mills and olive presses but the books are said to have been mislaid or thrown away. [Even in 1988, I could not get hold of such records; however, I was given access to all the copies held in the village secretary's office of the annual Agricultural Report sent each year to the National Statistical Office, and have used the reports for 1966 and 1967 in this and the previous chapter.]

The village register has economic ratings for each family, but these are subjectively determined by the village secretary; I went over this with the schoolteacher who gave me his version. He also listed the island's 'most respected' families, although he refused to discuss families with bad reputations. [In retrospect, I notice the elision here between economic status and 'respect'.]

The most exciting ideas I'm investigating are those which link the naming system, inheritance and dowry, and the funeral and memorial rites. I know that I have mentioned these things separately in previous letters; now I am sure there is a connecting network between them. Understanding each aspect involves an examination of the other two, and the whole construct links past, present and future relationships and ties them to property. I am sure that this will form an important part of my thesis and I am working on all the details.

As for the Athenian part of the study, I am planning to go there at the end of June, and to return to Anafi for the last five or so weeks before I come back to England at the end of August. I have decided to follow up only those things which specifically relate to the island, and not investigate the job network, the various migrant communities and their neighbourhood ties, or the change in family relationships and dowry and inheritance within the migrants. I want to know what is done with migrants' houses and land on the island. From this end I know that many holdings are rented to shepherds for cheese, worked by relatives for half-shares, or workmen are employed. I also want to find out whether the Anafiots in Athens are the only market for island produce. I am hoping to leave with the Takhidhromos (who takes the cheese-rent to Athens, and delivers baskets of eggs and other foodstuffs to relatives, as well as selling honey and eggs) so that I can accompany him on his rounds. [This proved impossible.]

LETTER 70, ANAFI, SUNDAY 4 JUNE 1967

I've had a couple of sessions with the schoolmaster getting a better idea of people's economic differences – but still he made so many people 'medium'. He told me about the people with 'good' economic status, but was very troubled by the thought of giving me the names of those defined as 'bad', so it's as if the economic category also reflects moral status – but his wife gave me a lovely piece of gossip about a murder 20 years ago, involving three men in love with the same woman, now married to Kiriakos, the left-wing café owner.

I was able to validate some of the details of this story twenty years later when examining the Death Register and found the report of the death of a man in a knife fight. Two men had been arguing over Maria (Russu, daughter of Dark Iakovos, later the wife of Kiriakos Antoniadhis). They began to fight, and bystanders (including Kiriakos) stepped in to pull them apart. One man was pulled by both arms; while he was in this position, the other man, who had one hand free, pulled a knife, and stabbed it into his opponent's armpit, causing his death. I was told that the perpetrator was sent to prison for ten years. I am not clear whether the sentence was the customary ten years for a 'crime of honour' or for manslaughter.

LETTER 71, ANAFI, SUNDAY 11 JUNE 1967

I learnt that there is a custom linked to Ascension Day, last Thursday, of the free distribution of the morning milk to anyone who comes and asks. If its withheld, the milk when used for cheese will turn to blood. Some people in the past, I was told, would go and get lots of milk from different shepherds and then make cheese for themselves to last part of the year. I went down to watch, but just as I got near the milking pens, I was called from the village to go back and answer a telephone call at the post office. They said the call was from England so I thought it was you and that something terrible had happened. In fact the call was from [friends of one of my mother's friends who wanted to visit the island]. I was so cross to miss a once-a-year custom. I also had 15 minutes of terrible worry as I pounded uphill in the sticky morning sunshine that it might be a call from you, or about you, or even from some official to advise me to leave because of the Mediterranean and Middle East situation.

LETTER 72, ANAFI, SUNDAY 18 JUNE 1967

I'm sitting on the rocks by a lonely beach, half an hour from the village – midday heat, lapping waves, almost all the landscape bleached of colour by the overhead sun, no shadows to act as contrast. [The English couple who had phoned] are lying on the rocks reading. They arrived by caïque from Santorini on Friday afternoon. I gave them lunch and cups of tea and answered a string of questions and criticisms about my work, the Greek economy and way of thought. They both smoke pipes! I escaped out into the fields to take photos of harvesting and threshing. I spent the morning watching the preparation of kolliva for the evening service on the Eve of Soul Saturday. I saw the whole process of cleaning and boiling the wheat, then censing it and drying it in the sun, and mixing it with sesame, pomegranate and dried grapes.

I got back from my harvesting expedition in time for the evening service after watching Margarita Khalari and her husband Nikos half-pulling, half-cutting the grain with small sickles. Nearby, on 'the marble threshing floor', a man drove two mules and two donkeys round and round over the harvest, holding a large spoon shaped spade for catching their dung.

On 20 June I left Anafi for a fortnight's holiday in Turkey with Susanna, returning to Athens in mid-July to meet my parents who drove from England to visit me. After their visit, I made my last journey back to Anafi.

LETTER 74, ANAFI, WEDNESDAY, 9 AUGUST 1967

I have now got a full and detailed list of all the fields and garden land of the whole island which should be good data to show how the ideal system of bilineal inheritance (houses through lines of women, land through lines of men) is actually carried out. I'm very pleased about that.

I'm not sure what day I'm leaving as it depends on when the wind drops so that the caïque can get across to Santorini, maybe Friday or Saturday or Sunday. The wind dropped yesterday and it was ferociously hot, the light bounced off the white walls and it seemed to sear the eyeballs.

In this and the previous chapter I have presented pieces of the jigsaw from which I eventually built up a picture of the Anafiots' economy. I would never have imagined that it would be possible to summarise all that I had painstakingly collected over the previous sixteen months in a few lines, nor that the island would in the next decades experience an upturn in population and prosperity: 'In the 1960s, the islanders had been trying to maintain a barely sufficient subsistence economy, supported by a few exports (barley, livestock) and by migrants' remittances; in the 1980s, agricultural production had declined while fishing had expanded; government subsidies, agricultural pensions and income from tourist-related enterprises (mainly run by returned migrants) were key features of the economy'.

CHAPTER FOUR

'Because of the name'

Kinship, dowry and inheritance

✳

As I began to get to know people, I also began to find out about the kinship links between them. The first excerpts which are given below, some of which have already been quoted in earlier chapters, are oddments about names and kinship connections, nicknames, and the inheritance of property, to some of which I was later able to add systematic comment as further links became clear. Even more detail was made possible when I was given access to the village register. Some of the people whose names are given will, I hope, be familiar to readers by this point. Most passages are quoted to give examples of the kinds of evidence from which I eventually drew out the pattern of naming to which dowry, inheritance and ritual obligations were linked. My first explicit formulation of these ideas was outlined in Letter 54, written in March 1967. This is quoted toward the end of the chapter on pages 92–3.

One of the themes of everyday life on Anafi which I tried to bring out in my thesis was the see-saw of mutual dependency between kin, neighbours, land-owners, and labourers. At harvest time, kin helped each other to cut, thresh and store wheat and barley. Land-owners with few kinfolk were desperate for labourers, who at other times of the agricultural cycle were themselves desperate for work. At times of high demand for labour, people had to balance their obligations to their kin against the benefits of 'obliging' a land-owner by working when they were sorely needed, so as to be given preferential employment when jobs were scarce. These instances of reciprocal help and preferential labour were described as done as a favour, *khatirikos*. One of the dictionary definitions of this adjective refers to the word *rusfeti*, a word of Turkish origin, often used for political favours carried out to win or reward votes. At first I thought that what made something *khatirikos* on Anafi was that payment in cash was not involved, but gradually I came to realise that whether or not work was done reciprocally, or for wages, the critical element was that in offering labour to a neighbour, the labourer arranged the working days to suit the other's plans, and could then only offer unallocated days to any other potential employer. In my thesis, I went on to comment: 'This latter contractual relationship does not contain the element of obligation because the labourer works the days which suit himself rather than those which suit his employer. It is thus not the payment which distinguishes employment from help, but the recognition that in 'help' there is the obligation to adapt to the needs of others who have established claims to preferential labour'.

FIELDNOTES, ANAFI, THURSDAY 30 JUNE 1966
Feast of St Apostolli so I take sweets to Kiria Margarita's son Apostollos, named after an uncle in Athens and to the younger son of Nikos postman (named after his mother's father).

Nikos the postman's family perfectly exemplified the pattern of naming, although I hadn't at this point realised that it was systematic. Once I had the village register, I was able to find out the names of Nikos's mother and father, and of the father of his wife Zabella. The four children, in order of age, were named: Manolis, after Nikos's father; Efthimia, after her mother Zabella's mother; Irini, after Nikos's mother; Apostollos, after his maternal grandfather. After working for the post-office for twenty-five years, Nikos retired on an occupational pension, still a vigorous middle-aged man, and moved from Anafi to Varkiza, a seaside suburb outside Athens, where I visited him in 1973.

Nikos and Zabella's elder son Manolis (the boy who broke his arm at school on Santorini, for whom his parents gave an *esperino*, described in Chapter Two), and the younger son, Apostollos, both entered DEE (*Dhimosia Epikhirisis Elektrismu*, the Greek Electricity Company) and were posted back on Anafi at the time when power and telephone cables were being installed for the village, harbour, and Klisidhi beach. The man who now ran the post-office was Manolis Ludharos, the son of Nikos's brother Yiannis. Yiannis himself seemed to have given up running his father's smithy, and was now guard of the ancient monuments on the island, *arkheofilakas*.

FIELDNOTES, ANAFI, SATURDAY 23 JULY 1966
Dino [whom I had met in Athens at the Pulakis Taverna] told me he had been a political exile on Anafi for 6 years. He said that Anafi was a matriarchal society with women making decisions about fields and houses.

When Dino described Anafi to me as 'matriarchal' I dismissed his characterisation as simply 'wrong', as I knew that women were not in sole control of property. What I did not understand was that Dino, as a Greek from the mainland, was familiar with another pattern of kinship relations and residence from that on the islands, one in which wives went to live with their husbands and in-laws, and in which the husband's parents' names were given to the first children of each sex to be born to the couple. To him, the Anafiot pattern, in which a newly married couple moved into the bride's dowry house, usually close to her parents, must indeed have seemed matriarchal.

Mr Peter [Allafuzos, brother of my neighbour, Eleftheria] has a boatshed built into his new house [at the harbour] with a motor-boat in it named 'Aghapia', after his mother (because he hasn't any children, he said).

The name of Aghapia eventually 'came out', as the Anafiots put it, when Peter's sister, my neighbour Eleftheria, gave birth to a daughter in February 1968 and named her Aghapia after their mother. Aghapia is now married and has Eleftheria's house as her dowry house. Peter died in November 1966. When I carried out research on tourism on Anafi in 1987–88, I was told that Peter's holiday house at the harbour now belonged to Eleftheria. Eleftheria's husband Antonis was using the boathouse.

FIELDNOTES, ANAFI, SATURDAY 13 AUGUST 1966

Stella [the school-teacher's wife] was kissed by all Adhriana's nephews on their arrival for summer holidays, because, she said, they are her second cousins. The link is through her father's father, Nikolaos Ghavallas; he and Adhriana's mother were siblings.

Adhriana, proprietor of the café patronised by young unmarried men and shepherd boys, was born in 1893. The village register gives her father as Iakovos Russos, and her late husband as Konstantinos Kurebis, said by villagers to have been her third husband, and a former exile. Her mother was born a Ludharu, related in some way to Nikos Ludharos the postman. The boys' mother, Adhriana's sister, was married to a man from Kalamata, Ilias Tzakalis, also a former exile. Maria Antoniadhi (Kiriakos's wife) said that Tzakalis' wife was a cousin of hers, which must mean that Adhriana was also a cousin of hers (Maria's maiden name was Russu). Adhriana had another sister, Marulia, who was married to Marinos Ghavallas, an old man whom I first met when Thetis and I were exploring the island for ikons. Marinos brought roses and other flowers for me each time he came into the village.

Markakis [Markos Dhamigos] has two daughters, the elder one, Kalliopi, named after her mother's mother, is deaf, but not dumb, she makes sounds, uses hand gestures, and is obviously bright (she goes to the village school); the younger daughter is named Flora. Presumably she was not named after her father Markos's mother whose name in the village register is given as Margarita. However, I was told that Flora is the 'same name' as Margarita (because both are names of flowers?), just as Zoï is the 'same name' as Zabetta. I don't understand this. Also, no men's names are said to be 'the same', and to me Tzortzis is the same as Yiorghos, as they are both forms of George. Markakis is brother's son to Yiannis Dhamigos the café proprietor who also owns a flourmill; Yiannis was village president before Mikhalis Ghavallas.

FIELDNOTES, ANAFI, THURSDAY 18 AUGUST 1966

Kiriakos Antoniadhis, proprietor of the 'Cyprus' café, says all his kinship relationships on the island are through his mother, a Sighalla [Kalliopi; his father's father was from Cyprus, hence the name of his café]. His mother's father and Barba Kostas [father of the fishermen, Manolis and Antonis, and a noted player of the goatskin bagpipes] were siblings. Kiriakos is related also to Barba Konstantin the shepherd [not surprisingly, as Barba Konstantin and Barba Kostas were first cousins], and to widow Maria [Ghavalla] who has a grocery shop [probably Kiriakos's mother and widow Maria's mother were first cousins. Widow Maria's maiden name was Kollidha; her mother Kalliopi was the little old lady described in Chapter Three, helping the village secretary's wife, another of her daughters, with threads for loom. I did not realise at the time that Kiriakos's kinship tie with widow Maria also meant that he was affinally related to the village secretary as well, a useful link for a member of the village council].

LETTER 22, ANAFI, SATURDAY 3 SEPTEMBER 1966

... my biggest news is that I have got hold of the village register – it goes back to about 1870 and an older one exists which I'll look at later but I'm doubtful of being able to decipher old-fashioned cursive Greek [I never did get my hands on it]. This register I've got has dates of birth and death, place of birth, and residence (so it has immigrants to Anafi, a few, and Anafiots gone to Athens), and gives the economic status of each head of household: good, middling, poor – I'll find out the criteria later; it also gives occupation. The only thing it doesn't give is dates of marriage, but I can get these from the church register. [I didn't]. There are only two adoptions and one illegitimate child in the whole book and very few children's deaths.

This was because babies were not entered in the register until they had been christened, which tended to be when they were several months old. Babies who died in the first few hours, days or weeks of life (although they were given lay baptism to enable them to be buried in the cemetery) were not entered in the village register. I found this out when I checked my fieldnotes about the exhumation of a baby's bones and found that its birth had not been recorded, see Chapter Six, entry for 21 August.

There were only two remarriages after the death of the first wife (one of these cases is Kiria Margarita Khalari, Nikos the donkeyman's wife). So now I have some facts to investigate; such things as relative ages of married couples, number in family, immigrants to Anafi. Merkuris the fisherman is an immigrant; I know from conversation that he had one family in Simi (near Rhodes), his wife died, he came here (how? when? why?), married, and has two daughters, one of them has come here for the festival on 8 September. I am exhausted with writing it all out onto cards and puzzling out anomalies (like one mother who appears to have had a child at eighty but died before it was born!). I am about halfway through; already lots of people have fitted into place; I begin to see invisible threads between men in the cafés (brothers-in-law, cousins, uncles and nephews) and start recognizing family likenesses. Best of all I feel really enthusiastic... The register has a not-quite-complete system of cross references (family of the wife, and which families daughters marry into) which I am copying and adding to. I've only been swimming once this week, with being so busy. It rained on Thursday night... I ran out on the terrace in the moonlight and danced around in my green oilskin hat.

By the way, I have nearly run out of those pills that help with painful period cramps. Could Mum send me another packet? I was almost doubled up in church last Sunday and had to go outside and sit on a wall until I felt better.

FIELDNOTES, ANAFI, SATURDAY 5 NOVEMBER 1966

Both the Antoniadhis's and Adhriana's cafés were closed. I went to see Margarita Dhamigu (wife of Yiannis the café proprietor); there were strings of sausages rolled around lines hung from the wall and buildings to span the courtyard. Her sister Kalliopi was baking bread in the Dhamigos's courtyard oven, *furno*. There are three sisters altogether, the third is in Athens. Their maiden surname is Vlakhu: Margarita (Dhamigu), Kalliopi (Arvanitu) [wife of Manolis who owned an olive press] and Dhimitra (Allafuzu) live in three consecutive houses down the hillslope; first Dhimitra's, next Kalliopi's, and Margarita's lowest down. One of the rooms in Margarita's house is a flour mill. Margarita's house is her mother's, as she is the eldest and named after her mother's mother; Kalliopi and Dhimitra were said by Margarita to have a

Figure 7   Sisters with adjoining dowry houses baking together

'grandfather's house'. [The Vlakhu sisters' mother, Zabella, was the sister of Iakovos Russos *aspros* (Fair Iakovos), Margarita Vafiadhu's father; Margarita Vafiadhu and Margarita Dhamigu, both née Russu, were thus first cousins, and named after the same grandmother.]

Margarita told me that her neighbour Ariadhni's daughter Margarita (who was awarded a prize at school as the best girl student; the prizes were funded by the Migrants' Association) is her god-daughter. The name is for Ariadhni's husband's mother, not for Margarita Dhamigu. Margarita herself only has one child, a son (Nikolaos), but he is married and there is a namesake grand-son for Yiannis (I saw the son and his wife and baby during the summer). [This close association between the two women neighbours was still strong twenty years later. I called on Margarita in 1988 to find her and Ariadhni reading religious tracts together].

In the late afternoon, I went to see Margarita [Khalari]; she says her husband Nikos is working on building a house down at the harbour, and also gets a day wage from working on other people's fields. Rembelia [grocer's wife] came in and I asked her about her dowry – only a house she said, no fields or money; only her *muni* (cunt) said Margarita, touching my dress in approximately the right place. Later Rembelia told me that she and Yiannis got married during the Occupation; if so she would have been only thirteen years old when the Italian garrison left in 1943; the first child listed in the village register was born in 1948. Her father is Mattheos Nikolis, nicknamed 'the cat', *o ghatis*; her mother is Margarita née Kollidha, who had (at least) ten children over the twenty years between 1929 and 1949, according to the register. Rembelia's mother's mother's house was given to her at the time of her marriage directly by this grandmother 'because of the name' (so presumably this grandmother was called Rembelia). Her husband, Patiniotis the grocer, works his widowed mother's grain fields half-shares; the mother lives out at Rukuna with an unmarried son who is lame. Rembelia has four children, three sons (Mikhalis after Patiniotis's father, Mattheos after hers, Evangelos after one of Patiniotis's cousins who is childless, whose heir they hope he will be) and a daughter, Flora. [As with Markakis's daughter, Flora, I was told that Flora was 'the same name' as Margarita, Rembelia's mother's name. I wonder whether this identification is to do with Margarita being the word for daisy and Flora being a flower? But the Greek for 'flower' is *luludhi*. Could the association of names date back to the time of the Venetian occupation of the Cyclades?].

Rembelia said she was one of 10 children (the village register shows there were five male, five female children) [the point is presumably that her parents could not afford much in the way of a dowry]. In comparison, Margarita said she had a dowry of fields, a bought house, furniture, clothes (20–50 thousand drachmas' worth in all she says, but none of it in cash) also cheese (60 okadhes per year rent from the four mountains she has). [In March 1967 I saw this cheese rent being paid to her, see Chapter Three].

FIELDNOTES, ANAFI, MONDAY 7 NOVEMBER 1966

After watching olive-picking I went to Manolis and Pananos Arvanitis's olive-press. Manolis said he had inherited it from his mother (Maria, née Khalari). It had been her grandfather's, he said; I forgot to ask which: FF or MF? Then it passed to one of that man's sons, Mattheos [not Maria's father, he was Manolis according to the village register] but Maria got the press in exchange for her dowry garden, an orchard with fig trees near the Monastery. Presumably she exchanged the garden with her uncle (or her father did, I rather lost track at this point). Manolis said that he got the olive press (rather than his sister) because he had his mother's father's name. That seems to have been the crucial factor, that the press should go with the name. The house next door to the press was sold, but has now come into the hands of a relative, in Athens. It had been the mother's grandfather's too.

FIELDNOTES, ANAFI, SATURDAY 12 NOVEMBER 1966

Interview with Antonis Arvanitis, the village secretary. His nickname is the student, *fititis*, meaning someone attending high school or even university. This was ironic, he said, because his father sent him to Athens, but not for further education! I asked about dowry. He said here it is never money. The essential is a house, with clothes, furniture, household linen; then fields, usually grain, for bread, some garden land, vineyard – a little of everything. The fields which a man inherits from his father usually go to his sons ('so that the same name will be heard' and not that of the son-in-law, *ghambros*), and the fields of a mother's dowry go to her daughters. The family estate is shared unevenly, with more going to the daughters, because the sons will get from their brides. A father may give a field to his son on condition (he used the verb *epivarevo*, to place a burden on someone) that the son gives him food, etc. when he is old. When the parents are too old to look after themselves they go to a daughter but the other children will give financial help. The reason is that it is all right for a daughter to look after aged and incontinent parents but that it wouldn't do for a daughter-in-law, *nifi*, to have to clean up a father-in-law.

In the Antoniadhis café this morning, Maria told me that they give yearly rent (for the café) to Papakhristos, at 200 drachmas per month; it is actually Papakhristos's wife's building. Adhriana also rents from him at 120 per month. The second room of the Antoniadhis's café used to be a grocery. Both these cafés were Mrs Papakhristu's dowry (her maiden name was Ghavalla, but I don't know which branch). The Dhamigos café is rented from Mattheos

Allafuzos [probably Eleftheria's brother, which would explain how she was able to rent it to 'strangers', non-Anafiot Greeks, in the summer of 1988]. The Vafiadhis' café is rented from a Mikhalis Kollidhas [Margarita's mother's brother, once president of the Anafiot Migrants' Association. I later found at that both the police station and the post office were buildings rented from migrant Anafiot families and were women's dowry houses.]

LETTER 36, ANAFI, SATURDAY 26 NOVEMBER 1966

I've asked 11 women systematic questions about their houses, dowries and fields; I should feel good but I feel rather low about it. It was so hard to get even five minutes question-and-answer done, that I despair of anything more complex. I am thinking actually of presenting the fieldwork for an MA rather than a PhD as I just don't think it's going to be good enough.

Did I ever tell you what happened when the painful period pills arrived? Because the customs slip mentioned medicines, Nikos had to call me in to the Post Office and ask me what they were. I explained and showed him what it said on the packet and I thought that he was embarrassed because he felt I was embarrassed. However, after what happened later, I'm not so sure... A woman came to see and asked if she could have some of the pills I'd been sent 'to bring on the period.' I tried to explain what they were, but she obviously didn't believe me, and I realised that she thought they were to procure an abortion. If I'm right, does Nikos think I'm trying to get rid of a baby? And how did the woman find out, maybe Nikos's wife told her? This is all too sensitive for me to ask about directly.

FIELDNOTES, ANAFI, THURSDAY 5 JANUARY 1967

Irini Ghavalla, elder sister of eleven year old Urania [nieces of Nikos Ludharos the postman], came to see me in the afternoon; she took me to the village secretary's house (Antonis Arvanitis, *fititis*, the student). His wife (Marulia) was sorting seeds in a sieve, Spiridhula (the daughter) was doing the washing, the son was doing homework. I asked my questions very successfully. I saw her weaving-loom in the back room; she said she had learnt to use a loom when the Communist exiles were on the island (she would have been in her mid-teens when they first arrived). This particular loom had been made by Yioryia's husband (Tzortzis Khalaris, nicknamed broadbean, *kukias*, he is a carpenter and makes coffins for funerals), and Manolis Takhidhromos. Three other women in the village have looms. I asked her to make me a rug sometime.

Marulia told me that her father bought a dowry house for her and she has already given it to her eldest daughter Kalliopi (named after Marulia's mother) when she married, but it is shut up now as Kalliopi and husband moved to Athens. Widow Maria, the eldest, has their mother's house, an L-shaped building, with the short side, which had its own door, used as her grocery-store; the house where Marulia is living now used to be her mother's father's. Marulia has grain fields at Modhi; her brother rents lands from her for grazing and she gets 40 okas of cheese as rent. She also has 'two or three' olive trees near the chapel of Ayios Yiannis Eleïmonos, whose feast day is 30 November [I could find no mention of this saint in my Greek calendar. November 30 is the feast day of Ayios Andhreas, Saint Andrew.] Her husband (Antonis, the village secretary) has grain fields and olives lands at Dhrepanos, also a little vineyard and some beehives. His brother Makarios, a shepherd, rents land from Antonis for grazing; the annual cheese rent is 20–25 okas of cheese.

Anezini's mother [Kalliopi Arvaniti] came in. She is Marulia's next door neighbour. Until they built their own courtyard oven, Marulia went next door and used hers. [Old Kalliopi was the wife of a white-haired old man, Dhimitris Arvanitis, nicknamed *kotsifas*, the name of a white-winged seabird. The eldest of their six sons, living in Athens, was Makarios Arvanitis, secretary of the Anafiot Migrants' Association. Makarios told me in Athens that it had been his father's brother who had made it possible for him to go to Athens and get an education, and thus to get a white-collar job in a bank: 'otherwise I would still be herding goats on Anafi'. Makarios named his eldest son after this uncle who had no sons, rather than after his father: 'after all, his name has already "come out" many times [i.e. Dhimitris already had namesake grandsons]', in recognition of what his uncle had done for him.]

Later I went to old Kalliopi's house, next door to Marulia's. There were many pairs of large bloomers hanging up outside on the washing line. Her metal four-poster bed had fabric hangings [she said it was the last curtained bed on the island so I took a photo of it]; she described to me how this bed looked for her wedding – all in white, with money, sugared almonds, *kufetes*, etc., thrown on the cover (adorned by the bride and her friends on the Saturday). The new parents-in-law give the wedding feasts together. She said: 'Now I'm an old woman [she was born in 1896] and wet my pants – I have 21 grandchildren and a good husband...'

In answer to my questions she said that she and her husband usually live out at his holding at Vrisi, but they have this house in the village, too, which was given to them by Nikos Ladhikos's mother during the Occupation, in exchange for a piece of garden land at Lakus [this seems feasible; Stella said that she and Nikos Ladhikos had first met when his family came back to Anafi from Athens during the Occupation to escape the privations in Athens; they might well have needed garden land to farm. Nikos's father had a house below the village on 'the Turk's mound', a little hillock where a shepherd boy was said to have been killed 'long ago' by Turkish pirates to prevent him giving the alarm; in another version of the story it was a Turkish Anafiot who had fought on the side of the pirates who was buried there. If Nikos's mother also had a house in the village it would have made sense to exchange it for land.]

Nikos's mother had already shared out her land at Kisiropi among her children; she gets 10–15 okas of cheese from this land. For their other lands, they employ workmen as day-labourers; it is impossible to get someone to take land on a half-shares basis any more.

FIELDNOTES, ANAFI, SATURDAY 7 JANUARY 1967

The St John the Baptist's service was held in the Kimisi church. Then I went on to Urania's house [daughter of Nikolaos Ghavallas 'Angeletaki' and Kalliopi, elder sister of Nikos Ludharos the postman]. Talked to Kalliopi and a neighbour. The house they live in was bought. Her own dowry house (her mother's) is now shut up, and will be given as dowry to daughter Irini (the grandmother's namesake), but Irini would prefer the present house. [Irini (b.1945), also mentioned above in the fieldnotes for 5 January, was then engaged to Yiannis, son of Manolis Khalaris (Birbilis), they married in September 1968. Urania eventually married Dhimitris Khalaris, son of Yiorghos Birbilis. The two sisters thus married men who were first cousins to each other. Another sister, Maria, married Dhimitris Nikolis, youngest son of Mattheos 'the cat' and ran the village bakery in the late 1980s].

Kalliopi said she had been married during the Italian Occupation (24 years ago) [the Italian garrison left the island in 1943; the village register gives the date of birth of their first child as 1945; maybe Kalliopi was confusing her engagement party with the wedding celebrations]. They had been given permission to kill two beasts (one from each family). The Italian commandant had come over and got drunk. She said that on the Saturday night it is the custom for bride and *kumbara* (female wedding sponsor, rather like a matron of honour) to sleep with groom in the new house, with the groom on the sofa – of course. She suggested that this might be a remnant of an old custom by which they were married on the Saturday night. She said bows, crosses and money were pinned to their pillows and money scattered on the bed.

Then I went to my room to get a torch and go on to the Dhamigos house (to 'greet' a Yiannis on his nameday) but he wasn't there. Margarita, his wife, was just entertaining Yiorghos Kollidhas (married to Margarita Leptaki). This Margarita was born at the same time as Margarita [Dhamigu] and was suckled by her [Margarita Dhamigu's] mother because her own mother had no milk (she said the two of them were milk sisters, *omoghalaktes adhelfes*). They said that if babies of the opposite sex have the same milk mother, they shouldn't marry. Then Manolis Arvanitis (her sister's husband) came in after a long talk about turned wombs and not being able to have babies. Then Stella arrived to 'greet' Yiannis Dhamigos. It seems that a wife can celebrate the husband's name day without him being there.

LETTER 48, ANAFI, MONDAY 29 JANUARY 1967

I acquired a great bundle of sheep shearings yesterday from my next door neighbour [Eleftheria] – the woman whose brother [Petros Allafuzos] died in Athens in November and I heard her mourning through the wall. [The following account from the letter is combined with the notes of Eleftheria's answers to my questionnaire.]

I asked some leading questions about the house, and she told me the story of how she came to live in this particular house. Her own father [Iakovos Allafuzos] was a fisherman and his wife's dowry [she was Aghapia Sirigu] was a house up on the kastro rock [it is the house where Manolis the Takhidhromos now has his storehouse]; then a man from the island of Paros came to Anafi to work in the mines (now closed) and while on the cafenion balcony [i.e. a building belonging to the Allafuzos family, now the Dhamigos café, rented from one of Eleftheria's brothers] looked down into the terrace of the house below and saw a lovely girl [the sister of Iakovos Allafuzos and therefore Eleftheria's aunt] there baking bread. He married her, and she left with him to live on Paros, and the house (which would have been her dowry) was sold to her brother, Iakovos the fisherman, who sold his wife's dowry house on the kastro to someone else (the Takhidhromos?).

The house below the Dhamigos café eventually went to Iakovos's elder daughter Kalliopi, but she went to live in Athens, and exchanged it with Eleftheria for her dowry house, a much smaller one, near 'honey' Anna's house; this house had belonged to one of the sisters of their mother, Aghapia. And so Eleftheria took the house as her dowry and thus became my next-door neighbour. She also had dowry lands at Milies; she said her husband Antonis has no fields at all.

FIELDNOTES, ANAFI, FRIDAY 3 FEBRUARY 1967

I managed to get up by 8:30am [after a late night of pre-Lenten evening visiting at Rembelia's, where *maskari*, veiled and masked carnival celebrators, called in too]. Went to see Stella who was cleaning the stove ready for moving into their new house properly. Khristos [Ghavallas, a tall, thin man who reminded me of the Marsh-Wiggle in one of C S Lewis's Narnia stories] was working on their courtyard oven: 'I wish there was a Chinese here to get into it for me – there's a story of a woman putting the Devil into a bottle, well, the schoolteacher's put Khristos [Christ] in the oven now'; (all this in a very lugubrious tone worthy of a stage comedian). I asked Stella about some of the queries resulting from my interviews. Stella herself has a dowry flat in Athens (as does her elder sister Lula whose name in the village register is given as Adhriani), and gets rents from other flats in the building; so does her father.

[When I was given access to the register of members of the Anafiot Migrants Association, I found out that Lula lived in an apartment block in Pangrati; this was presumably a block built on family land, or on land the *proedhros* had bought, providing dowry flats for the daughters, and a regular income for both the parents and the daughters from the rent of other flats in the building.] The new house in the village, and their holiday house at the harbour, were bought jointly with Nikos [from her rents and his salary?]. They have no fields; her father's lands at Ayio Yianni will go to her brother Nikos. They do have seven beehives at Vunia, in Yioryia Khalari's fields, near Ayios Dhimitris.

Nikos (the schoolmaster) was *kumbaros* (wedding sponsor) to Manolis the fisherman and Marulidhi, and to Maria Antoniadhi's sister and her husband (Marulia and Theodoros Dhamigos); he is godfather to Mattheos, son of Antonis the village secretary, and also to Kalliope, the deaf and dumb daughter of Markakis. Stella was *kumbara* to Nikolaos 'gap-tooth' Khalaris and Marulia.

Coming out from my room about 6:45pm I was called to by Mikhalis Ghavallas the proedhros and his wife Maria from the road to have coffee in Kiriakos's... Tzortzis Russos came in and I asked could I go and see his wife (she is pregnant). She was teazing wool and we sat and chatted – she said I was thought to be a whore when I first came to Anafi, being single and unaccompanied, and always sitting with my legs crossed at the knee which twists up the womb. She answered my questions about dowry and property while her son [Iakovos, then about 8 years old] sat up in bed, laughing at me happily. When Tzortzis came in I had *kurabiedhes* (a kind of shortbread) and *tsikudhia* (distilled grape-spirit) and he told me the story of how he had carried the cot for their first child all the way from Eolu [a street in central Athens] to Guva [a distant suburb]. She said she would have the baby on her own; that she would feel shame and embarrassment, *dhropi*, in front of her husband's sister. There are some things (presumably bloody napkins) one can only ask mothers or sisters to deal with but not sisters-in-law; but in any case her husband will be there. [The baby, Petros, was born in April 1967. By 1983 the family had moved house to the hillslope below the village church, and were renting out rooms to tourists].

FIELDNOTES, ANAFI, SATURDAY 4 FEBRUARY 1967

School bell, then another bell after (possibly for catechism class in church?); went to the grocery for oil for cooking and meths for my paraffin lamp; found onions at my door from Merkuris [the fisherman from Simi who worked with Antonis and Manolis Sighallas]. On the path I met Lemonia Nikoli [the youngest of six sisters and three brothers, the children of Russetos Kollidhas, nicknamed *tsunas* (meaning wriggle, or twist and turn, from the time he unexpectedly caught a partridge with his bare hands); their mother was Marulia Ludharu]. She was with her son Panayioti, he was crying and miserable from flu. She said he had been named as result of vow to Virgin during his birth; and also because he was a son after two daughters. In such a case, even though the child was the eldest son, he would not have an automatic right to inherit land from his father which had come to him from his father, after whom the boy should have been named. [In other words, the crucial factor was the name, not birth order.]

I asked her my questions; and her story about how all the sisters got houses was different from her sister's. Athina (another one of her sisters) and Pliti [wife of Antonis the fisherman] came in and listened. Then I went to honey Anna who was washing, with an 'aunt' of her mother's, Anna Peleki … I asked Anna my questions and it went quite well. Athina came in for a while again, then her daughter Maria; I then went back to see Athina, she too gave me a different version of how the sisters got their houses. She seemed embarrassed not to have anything to offer me and gave me two circular bread-sticks, *kuluria*.

FIELDNOTES, ANAFI, SUNDAY 26 FEBRUARY 1967

After the funeral of Barba Tassos [see Chapter 6] I went to see Maria, sister of Athina and Lemonia. From the village register I knew that she had previously been married to Konstantinos, a brother of Yiannis Dhamigos, the café proprietor. They had two sons, one of whom was engaged to Marulidhi Peleki (nicknamed 'Liz Taylor'). After Konstantinos died, Maria re-married, with Anastasios Ghavallas, and had a daughter, Evangelia, born in 1956 when Maria was 41. This daughter was not named, as the rule seems to be, after Maria's mother (whose name was Marulia). As Anastasios's mother's name was Maria, the same as his wife's, they couldn't use that name for any of their daughters, she told me, because it 'wouldn't do', *dhen kani*, for mother and daughter to have the same name. The same rule applies for fathers and sons.

Her husband, Anastasios, told me a long and incomprehensible story about the division of his patrimony between him and his siblings involving him in all the legal expenses. There was something about a man, possibly a lawyer, who became very ill and had to be fed through a tube – God did it to him because of his wickedness over this affair, but I got very confused about who was who. They usually live outside the village on Anastasios' lands at Kontu, near Milies.

His sister Kalliopi is married to Yiannis four-finger Ghavallas, and his brothers are lame Dhimitri, and Urania's father Nikolaos Ghavallas. Maria showed me a photo taken with her godmother, *nonna*, and other joint godchildren. The *nonna* is an old, old woman I once saw in Athens, said to be nearly one hundred years old. She was the sister of Mrs Rinaki's mother, Zabetta (born 1876), so it's possible she could be nearly one hundred. Maria said that co-godchildren should not marry (*dhen kani* again, but is it Canon Law?), 'because the oil (of baptism) comes from the same house'.

Maria and Anastasios gave me four eggs (they said it couldn't be five because that symbolises the five fingers of the hand thrown up to avert the Evil Eye) and a bunch of narcissus and roses. They said usually such questions as I asked were to do with tax assessment and that people would be uneasy about answering them. So how much of what I have been told has been deliberately underestimated?

LETTER 54, ANAFI, FRIDAY 3 MARCH 1967
I have been trying to get the dowry and inheritance system worked out: what it seems to be is this: a girl gets a house and part of her mother's dowry fields as her dowry, and a son may, if the family has enough land, receive some land on his marriage which is called his dowry. So dowry, prika, *means property given by parents to children at the time of their marriage; but it's usually given to daughters. When the parents die, the remainder of their land, which they have kept to support themselves, employing workmen or renting it on half-shares, is shared out between all their children according to their Will, and the daughters thus may get a bit more than the sons, but daughters are those who are responsible for their parents' funeral and memorial services. So the dowry and inheritance system can only be understood by also understanding ideas about death and the fate of the soul, and the naming system (which also ensures that names of the deceased are remembered) by which sons are named for the grandfathers whose land they inherit, and daughters for the grandmother whose fields they take for their dowry. Often, unmarried aunts, or childless people will leave their houses to the daughter of a family who looks after their funeral and memorial services and often the girl has the same name as the aunt or childless wife. After the three years of interment in the cemetery, most bones are taken out for re-burial in little chapels beside their fields.*

I haven't got the naming bit quite right yet because it seems that after the first two children the reverse occurs: the second son is named for his mother's father and obviously he isn't going to get any fields from him, nor is the second daughter, named after the father's mother, going to get dowry lands from her. But naming and dowry and fields and memorial services all seem to be linked together, and I want to work this out more clearly.

[In late March I went to Athens, in part to collect the next instalment of my grant, and in part to celebrate my 25th birthday on 2 April with the Linetons and Susanna, whose birthday also fell in early April. I returned to the island in mid-April.]

LETTER 63, ANAFI, SUNDAY 16 APRIL 1967

I don't seem to have any energy to reply to my huge pile of mail, so I've written postcards and short acknowledgements instead; rather a cheat really for all those expecting glowing descriptions and humorous adventures. I am dogged by a sense of responsibility and a feeling of guilt for putting myself first. I feel a terrible tension when I relax, a compulsion to be doing something else, preferably something I don't really want to do. And whatever I'm doing I feel there's something else I should be doing instead. I think I'm setting myself impossible goals, or rather I can't really see my goals clearly enough to see how to work towards them with the proper balance of energy and relaxation, allowing myself a glow of pride in the small achievements. The impossible goals are the centrifuges of the different muddles I'm in, and they suck me towards them without satisfying me. So I feel I should be busy, without knowing what I should be busy at, and I feel unable to give myself any credit for any of the things I get done. I hardly understand it myself. Part of me is sure that I've got the key to the thesis now, and that what remains to do on Anafi is just amplification of it. The migrant part is yet to come. There's only twenty weeks now to go until my return flight!

FIELDNOTES, ANAFI, SUNDAY 30 APRIL 1967, EASTER SUNDAY

[The Easter celebrations are detailed in Chapter Six. Here I give an account of the party on Easter Sunday evening to mark Vasiliki Rinaki's betrothal to Yiannis Khalaris. The account shows how much I now knew about people's inter-relationships, and the various cross-currents between them.]

There were children in the courtyard of Vasiliki's house, Vasiliki and her father (Rinakis, the Cretan ex-policeman) were greeting guests at the door of the saloni (formal sitting room). Khristina Vuraki [wife of Mikhalis the policeman] and Maria daughter of Nikolaki Birbilis were helping, later Zabetta Ludharu (postman's wife and also Irini Rinaki's niece) and Maria Ghavalla joined them. In the saloni were: Rinakis, his wife Irini, Yiannis, the 'groom', Yiannis's father and mother, his father's brothers Lambros and Manolis Birbilis, Manolis's wife Athina. Lambros's wife was in the kitchen helping. Also in the saloni were Mikhalis Arvanitis (groom's mother's brother), his wife was in the kitchen, the groom's father's sister Marousi and her husband the aghrofilakas, Yiannis Kollidhas. An important guest was the groom's godfather, the aghrofilakas's father Yiorghos Kollidhas, nicknamed *tsunas*, (does this mean a relative can be a godparent, in this case he would be an affinal one?) and his wife. Also there: Iakovia Mari (born Ludharu, so possibly a relative, but possibly also there because of the connection with the police force), Nikos the teacher and Stella, Mikhalis the policeman and Nikos the astinomos, 'Liz Taylor' (Marulidhi Peleki), her younger brother Zakharias, an older brother Antonis, nicknamed 'the sultan', *sultanos*, and his wife Sofia. Also Nikos Ludharos the postman. At the 'tables' later, Rinakina's sisters (the widow Flora 'Sarpakina', and the unmarried Margarita), Nikos Ghavallas (Urania's father), Andhreas Kollidhas and his wife Lemonia. In the back room was Russetos Ghavallas, (I couldn't see his wife Eleni), also Barba Yiannis Kollidhas, the man with the red and watering left eye (brother of Barba Antoni), and Anna, daughter of the young widow.

When most people were seated in the saloni, the aghrofilakas's father (*tsunas*) began to speak. There were hushes all round. He said that as Yiannis's godfather he had been summoned and had to make sure there was consent on both sides. He started by talking to Yiorghakis, Vasiliki's father (whom he called *sinteknos*, co-parent, the reciprocal term of address used between a child's physical and spiritual parents). Someone interrupted that in such a situation the term *kumbaros* (usually used on Anafi only to refer to a wedding-sponsor) is preferred to *sintekhnos*). Tsunas wanted Vasiliki's father to confirm that there was consent on both sides (presumably Yiannis could speak for himself, but Vasiliki needed someone to speak for her) and Rinakis then asked Yiannis and Vasiliki if there was any sort of barrier standing between them (he said *allos* i.e. another man; presumably Yiannis wouldn't have been there if there was another woman in his life). He then called for an ikon, which was propped up against a flower vase. Yiannis took a ring-box out of his pocket and the rings were moved in the sign of the cross in front of the ikon while Tsunas recited *Khristos anesti ek nekron, thanato thanaton patissas* [words from the Easter anthem: 'Christ has risen from the dead, trampling down death with death'], which at the command of Kiria Mari, who stood up critically to watch, he said three times. No-one seemed annoyed at her bossiness, possibly because she was a priest's daughter? He then put the ring on the fourth finger of Yiannis's left hand, then Vasiliki's ring was put on.

Vasiliki touched the ground in front of him, kissed his hand and then embraced him, then Yiannis embraced and tried unsuccessfully to touch the ground by his godfather's feet but was prevented, but did manage to kiss his hand; then Vasiliki did the same to Yiorghakis and her own father. Yiannis then went over to Rinakis and next to his own father (not touching the floor,

I think, but things were fairly confused and I couldn't see everything), then across to the two mothers.

Then mincemeat-like sweets were handed round, and banana liqueur mixed with *tsikudhia*. Various men stood up and wished the newly engaged couple *ora kali*, a good hour, and *kala stefana*, good garlands (wedding crowns). There was a pause, and Vasiliki brought on the honey and almond sweet accompanied by Maria, daughter of Nikolaki holding a glass of water for the forks, and Maria Ghavalla with a tea cloth. Again a long pause while the *furno* [courtyard oven] was opened and the table prepared; then Rinakis came in and called us to eat. There seemed to be a rough table plan, with Nikos Ludharos, Mikhalis, Nikos the astinomos, on the sofa, Nikos the teacher, Stella, Proedhrina, me and Bella along the same side. Kiria Mari was on the corner, then Patiniotis (his wife Rembelia was helping in the kitchen), Niko Ghavallas, Andhreas Kollidhas, Zakharias Pelekis with Marulidhi his sister, Christina Vuraki, or Anezini Khalari (at different times), Vasiliki, Yiannis, and his godfather and wife at the other end of the table from Kiria Mari. On the other table, Barba Yiannis, the aghrofilakas, Russetos, Manolis Birbilis, Lambros, Antonia and Sofia Pelekis, with Yiorghakis Khalaris at the door end.

I noticed the groom's parents were not much in evidence while V's parents were serving the meal. As the meal ended, V began to sing complimentary songs to the *parea* (assembled company). [My guess now is that these were probably *mantinadhes*, a particular form of rhyming couplet.] The singing was taken up round the table. From time to time other people sang verses, Marulidhi, Bella and Spiridula, the godfather, Mikhalis the policeman and Rinakis himself.

People went out into the parlour to dance; the astinomos called for a *vrasti*, soft cheese (could he demand such a thing in someone else's house because he was a fellow policeman? or a high status guest?), and Lemonia went to get it. People said 'cut it' and he made some sort of obscene reply. There was also a practical joke on Andhreas. They put a pointed-footed ashtray under his chair covering and when he sat down people thumped his shoulder very hard and pulled and twisted him, but he didn't seem to feel a thing underneath him. Someone explained to me that this was because he was a shepherd and was used to sitting on spikey thorn bushes. I wonder.

Vasiliki was very lively, toasting people, but Yiannis, although he sang too, wasn't as forthcoming. Maria Nikolaki appeared to come into the room in tears at one point. She had been acting as their chaperone, I was told. Why was she crying?

I left first, after midnight. The agrofilakas and village secretary brought their musical instruments, *laüto* and *klarino*, lute and clarinet, I think. About

4am I heard the sound of the clarinet and mandolin coming down the street, conducting people home.

In the first publication which resulted from my thesis I tried to condense its main argument into a few pages, linking women's acquisition of dowry at marriage and men's inheritance of property at a later stage in the domestic cycle to the system of naming and to ritual obligations to carry out the cycle of ceremonies which ensured the fate of the soul. I would now write it very differently, but readers might be interested to see not only how all the fieldwork experience and its working out in the thesis was summarised but also how it was presented to a wider academic audience. I wrote in a distanced, objective style, occasionally including the reader in the line of argument by using phrases such as 'let us suppose'. The word 'I' occurred only in the notes and acknowledgements. The first paragraph, imagining a traveller arriving on the island and looking around, uses the 'generic male' ('he would pass... his eye would be caught...'), a form of words which was taken for granted in the mid-seventies. I began the article by describing the Anafiot landscape: barrel-vaulted houses, narrow hill-terraces, a cemetery in which carefully tended plots contrasted with 'open graves, empty coffins and decaying shrouds'; hills and mountains dotted by whitewashed chapels and bone-depositories.

My argument was that to understand these features of the physical landscape they have to be seen as 'the physical expression of rights and obligations which [Anafiots] consider to be the most important and profound aspect of the relationship between the generations'. To illustrate the pattern of naming, and its exceptions, I drew a family tree using authentic Anafiot names and surnames in combinations which did not actually occur. I then used the diagram's central couple and their children to show how houses and fields went to daughters and sons because of the name. I discussed the way in which marriage and inheritance of a share of the family estate was affected by factors of choice and chance such as: migration, elopement, vows to saints at times of crisis, the selection of childless people as godparents, illness and disability, a parent's early death, being an only child, and so on.

After discussing comparative material on naming, dowry, the domestic cycle and the division of the family estate from studies carried out in other parts of Greece, I tried to point out that my own work had linked together aspects of economic, kinship and ritual life which elsewhere had been presented separately. In summing up towards the end of the article, I wrote: 'There is thus a clear connection on [Anafi] between the distribution of the family estate over time (as dowries to daughters at marriage and as lands to sons after the father's death) and the obligation to the souls of dead parents. These rights and duties are further emphasised by ideas about succession to property which are expressed in the system of naming. The connection between property and names seems to contain an explicit notion of replacement and continuity which applies both to families and to the community as a whole in that parents are replaced by their children's children and [Anafiot] men and women succeed to land and houses on the island.'

CHAPTER FIVE

'In a bubble car to see another Anafiot'

Visits to Athens, Santorini, and Mani

∗

When I describe my fieldwork in Greece, I say it lasted for sixteen months, but I wasn't on Anafi for that length of time continuously. Trips to Athens were necessary every three months to collect my Studentship grant, and for other requirements: to have films developed, to buy type-writer ribbons, to stock up on medicines, stationery, and food-stuffs such as tea-bags and instant coffee. In going back over my fieldnotes, I notice that I rarely wrote anything in my note-book about what happened outside Anafi unless it was directly concerned with Anafiot matters, such as contacts with migrant Anafiots in Athens. I can see now that the fieldwork experience, and my developing understanding of Greece, were both informed by what happened outside Anafi as much as by what happened there.

In this chapter, I have collected together excerpts about my travels outside the island, to Santorini, to Athens, to the village in Mani where Mick Lineton was carrying out his research, and to Turkey.

Santorini in June 1966

LETTER 10, ANAFI, SATURDAY 11 JUNE 1966

[This trip from Anafi was primarily to visit a bank and to buy supplies which could not be obtained on the island.] It struck me as very odd that there aren't many more inter-island journeys by small boat. I was commissioned to get a crate of tomatoes, 40 bottles of beer, 15 loaves of bread (better flour on Santorini, they said, and rather a shortage here) and fruit. One of the policemen accompanied me and took the opportunity to get some clothes for his baby daughter and to get photographed for his file at the police station. If I'm a failure as an anthropologist, I could make a fortune as a trader. [The irony of this last

remark was lost on me at the time; I had paid for the caïque trip myself, and did not charge any commission on the items I brought back for people.]

The journey takes about three hours. I got up at 1am and walked down to the harbour in the moonlight. Complete stillness, no wind, no sound except that of the tiny waves on the pebbles and against the quayside, footsteps on sand, oars in the water, a sack thrown down on the deck.

I bought three jars of jam for myself to have with my breakfast-time piece of bread (one of my neighbours gives me bread and is going to teach me to make it), and some fruit which I mostly gave away to women who have been kind to me and to the village president. I also bought Super Tampax and sanitary towels (in addition to the supplies I brought with me) to last me at least until next year, if not until the next decade! The chemist's eyes nearly popped out of his head with amazement, and then disbelief, that I was going to live for a year on Anafi. The people on Santorini said Anafi was a barren and unfriendly place, while 'here the people are full of hospitality...' On Anafi they say Santorini may have refrigerators and electric light, but the people are unfriendly and grasping, while 'here on Anafi...'

We used the sail with the American flour-bag patch on the return journey, there was quite a strong wind, and waves, and I thoroughly enjoyed it. I am a good sailor, by Greek standards an amazingly good one, as most women are sick or terrified on the steamers. The sun was westering by mid-afternoon, shining from behind us onto Anafi, which had a golden glow and marvellous purple shadows. When I got back into the village, there was a party of German tourists, six in all, from a small yacht we had seen down at the harbour. Their leader was a German-Greek from Munich called Ghaitanidhis, who has written several books about Greece. He said he has been doing a study on the island of Amorgos (due north of Anafi, and south-east of Naxos) of three villages and their economy.

Athens in July 1966
LETTER 13, ANAFI, FRIDAY 1 JULY 1966

[Visitors to Greece in the sixties were allowed to stay for up to three months, after which a visa was required. This trip to Athens was timed so that I collect the next instalment of my grant cheque and apply for a visa, but also to meet up with the Lineton family.] Very early on Wednesday morning at about 2 am, I shall go down to the harbour and wait for the 'Elli'. There will be many Anafiot men going off to Athens to work 'on the buildings' as most of the grain harvest is over.

Next time Dad goes to London, could you look at, and price, stainless steel clasp knives with various attachments? The one I bought myself in London for this trip (two blades, corkscrew, tin-opener, bottle opener, screwdriver, marlin spike, nail scissors) has attracted much envy and admiration. As far as I'm concerned, when I leave, it goes to the boatman Manolis. [It did, but on a later visit he told me he had been 'persuaded' to give it to one of the policemen. I don't know whether or not this was true; possibly he sold it]. Perhaps a few others could be given as 'gifts to informants'. When I get back to England next year I shall send a cargo of plastic pants (having held a dozen soaking babies) and boxes and boxes of sanitary towels and Tampax for my women friends (all they have is linen strips which have to be washed).

LETTER 14, ATHENS, THURSDAY 7 JULY 1966

It is terribly hot and sweaty in Athens and the men more objectionable and bottom pinching than ever. I've had a total of six hours sleep since 6 am on Tuesday. I went to the Social Sciences Centre and had a long talk with Helen Aryiriadhis. She says that there will be a Mediterraneanists' conference in Athens in December with the theme: the relationship between the roles of men and women. I've completed visa extension formalities for staying on beyond the three months allowed, and been to the Statistical Office to collect information about Anafi (they suggested I also try the National Library).

The honeysuckle on the fence round the Tower of the Winds and the Mosque is sending up great sprays of perfume with each gust of wind. I am going to visit the Acropolis very early tomorrow (it's free on Sundays) and some time tomorrow Mick and Nancy, Tom and Ben will arrive.

LETTER 16, ANAFI, THURSDAY 21 JULY 1966

Nancy and I had a heart to heart in Athens. She needed someone to talk to after two rather terrible and depressing months. Their house has a dirt floor, no lavatory, steep stairs to the door up which she has to carry the water jars, and there are interfering little girls who ruin Tom and Ben's toys, and also an invading herd of pigs... Mick drove me down to the Piraeus on Tuesday and they all waved me off.

Mani, via Athens, October 1966

LETTER 27, PULAKIS TAVERNA, ATHENS, FRIDAY 7 OCTOBER 1966

[This autumn visit to the mainland was not only another trip to Athens collect a grant cheque but also an opportunity to go to Mani to visit the Linetons in their fieldwork village, Mina. In addition, I began to collect various pieces of information from Anafiot migrants in the suburbs of the Athens, acting as an informal 'takhidhromos' in taking messages and presents to and fro.] The 'Elli' arrived at 5 am. As I had things to deliver to the Vafiadhis family I went straight there from the boat with some other Anafiots to the suburb of Athens where most of them live.

We went in a sort of covered wheeled van, together with a box of chickens, a rabbit hutch (plus occupants), a trunk, four suitcases, five baskets, several cardboard boxes and a child's bicycle. I sat amid this chaos with a girl who has come to Athens to buy items for her trousseau (the one nicknamed 'Elizabeth Taylor'). She kept crossing herself and I felt inclined to follow suit, fearing often for the balance of the vehicle. We arrived safely, then found Mrs V was on night duty (she's not a nurse, but is privately employed to sit with sick people in case they need anything). She was not due back til 9.30am, so there was a lot of time to fill in. The house is composed of three flats; the top flat is owned by an Anafiot woman, the sister of Kiriakos Antoniadhis, the proprietor of the café opposite Mr V's. Her elder daughter Popi (Kalliopi) married Mrs V's step-brother [Tzortzis Russos], and has the bottom flat (very luxurious with refrigerator, stove, tiled bathroom) while the V's have three rooms built on to the side (really little better than a lean-to shack). I then got the bus into the city (walking to the main road up the dirt tracks). These suburbs have electric power lines criss-crossing the roads while goats and sheep are driven along the dirty paths next to the lorries and the newly built houses.

I had a struggle today to find the right bus station but managed to book a ticket to Mina for Monday, leaving 6.45am, arriving 4.30pm. I am exhausted by being back in a city, there are too many people. I keep thinking: walking along this street there are as many individuals as the total population of Anafi. I took the 'squeeze' of the altar dedication to Apollo from the Monastery to the man at the American School of Archaeology [see Chapter Seven].

I've also been to the Agricultural Bank to see the director who spoke excellent English and knew various people at the Social Science Centre and was really in tune with what I was doing. He also rang up the Agricultural Bank on Santorini and told the manager there to help me whenever I went to see him.

LETTER 28, MINA, FRIDAY 14 OCTOBER 1966

The bus journey down to visit the Linetons on Monday took ten hours, the road getting worse and worse with each town we stopped at. The landscape was like glimpses through windows in paintings of the Madonna and Child; dark flame shaped cypresses, red tiled-roofed stone houses. Then after Sparta, the first Maniot towers. Some are broken off at the top and stick up like shattered fangs, with the houses near them like stumps of teeth. The road is just rocks and soil, and the driver's mate was busy distributing paper-bags to the travel-sick passengers.

At Mina I saw a little fair haired boy standing by the roadsign. Tom and I had composed a story about this moment: he was to be so brown that I thought him a Greek boy, and I was to have hair down to my waist so he wouldn't recognize me. Then I saw Mick in his old denim shirt and jeans, and Ben, now *very like Tom when I first knew him, much more of a little boy and less of a baby, and Nancy in a red striped t-shirt, her hair tied back with a yellow ribbon...*

We drove to Yithion, about an hour and a half's drive from Mina. We shopped and had a swim before lunch at a café on the seafront. They usually go on Fridays when spare seats in the microbus are taken up by a vying mass of journeying peasantry who disorganize and monopolize their day with stops to visit relations in villages en route, and for mysterious 'things', praghmata. This time they only had three extra people. I think they get into the same state as me about the Anafiots, although it's worse for them because the villagers are nearly always carsick and try to spit out of the windows which don't roll down but open on a vertical hinge, so have to be cleaned off after every trip. There is a bus which runs every day but of course Mick doesn't charge and goes at a more convenient time.

We've been comparing 'hardship levels'. Mick and Nancy have the advantage of a car, and can drive to Yithion for supplies , but they have a house with only two rooms for all four of them. The house is surrounded by a crumbling stone wall with a gate made from an old rusty bedframe, with some of its wires broken and twisted.The bedroom has a wooden floor, the kitchen has just stones and dirt, so that the tables and chairs slant and slope and wobble. Their well is outside down a flight of steps, and has a very small opening, peculiarly shaped so there is only one way the bucket will come up. They have no lavatory and have to use a disused pigsty, putting paper in a special box as next door's hens scratch it up and spread it all over the garden. The stables are both flea pits and one night we caught 15 between us as we undressed – no possibility of discreet modesty as Nancy with a shriek wrenched off her dress to capture one attacking her stomach...

The village of Mina itself is like a dwarf New York; a few of the famous Maniot towers rise up from the crumbling roofs and walls, like embryo skyscrapers, the mountains behind them block the rising sun, which sets beyond the road in the gulf between Mani and the most western peninsula of the Peloponnese. All around are olive trees on stony ground with cattle fodder crops sown between them. The sea is two hours away.

One evening we had a supper of boiled eggs and bread and butter with retsina, followed by tinned apricots, while listening to Beethoven's 'Pastoral' and then Mingus, Monk and Bob Dylan on Mick's fieldwork tape-recorder. During a quiet pause we heard a rat scuffling behind the food boxes and set a trap which successfully caught it. Then we had to find a way to kill it, and drowned it in a bucket of water, which I found very upsetting.

We went on a picnic one afternoon, carrying a thermos, some bread and fruit and tins of sardines, and felt very English among the olive groves. Tom and I played noughts and crosses by scratching on a rock (a puzzle for archaeologists

Figure 8   *Picnic in a Maniot olive-grove*

of the future) and Ben climbed into the lower branches of the olives and pretended to be riding donkeys. I met some of the villagers with whom Mick was building up good relationships. One of them, Niko, the village secretary in Mina, described my living on Anafi as a perpetual Lent, Meghali Sarakosti, *that is, the forty-day fast leading up to Easter.*

Mick and Nancy think they will move to the Piraeus after Christmas for Mick to investigate migrants from the village. But they are certainly coming to the conference in Athens which is being run by the Social Sciences Centre in December. I hope the sea isn't too rough for me to leave Anafi then!

PERSONAL DIARY, ATHENS, THURSDAY 27 OCTOBER 1966

Back in Athens, waiting for the boat back to Anafi. In the middle of the afternoon, I made a sudden decision to go Anafiot hunting so I seized writing pad, a biro and Greek-English dictionary, and some photographs which had been developed in Athens while I was in Mani. I set off to see Khristina [the seventeen year old daughter of Yioryia and Tzortzis Khalaris (the carpenter nicknamed broadbean, kukias]. I got the 108 bus and asked for the Olimpia stop. In the kitchen Khristina's elder sister cut up wild greens, khorta, and I asked about dowry, fields and houses. The information seemed so little in comparison with the effort to get it...

Then we went off over the appalling unmade roads in a bubble car to see another Anafiot, a restaurant owner, nicknamed Foksakis *whose daughter, Rita, had holidayed on Anafi in the summer, and caused a stir by wearing a bikini on Klisidhi beach. Sitting there was Yiannis Khalaris, Vasiliki's young man [whose engagement to her the following Easter was recounted at the end of the previous chapter]. They drove me back to the Pulakis taverna dodging between buses like an ant scurrying along between huge stones. It was a terrifying ride, swerving past the lit columns of Olympian Zeus's temple and madly through the Plaka. They drank orangeade at the taverna before they left. I must say I felt pleased with my evening's work and was glad to sit quietly and eat my supper watching the changing lights of the son et lumière show on the Acropolis in contented solitude.*

PERSONAL DIARY, ATHENS, SATURDAY 29 OCTOBER 1966

On my way to Sintagma, to catch the bus to visit the Vafiadhis family and to ask them and the Karamalengkhos family my questions about property, I rang Kalliopi Khalari, a daughter of Yiorgos (one of the Birbilis brothers) and Anezini, a distant cousin of Khristina, and arranged to meet on the steps of the Metropolis church tomorrow. The pretext was to show her photographs I had taken in the summer and to give her copies of ones with herself in them.

I have become familiar with the 108 bus route now and anticipated the stasis strofi *[the name of a particular bus-stop]* before the conductor called it. The diggings and ditches seemed more extensive than last time. It feels rather pioneerish to cross wooden slatted bridges to get to people's houses. As I was approaching the place where the V's live I saw Vivi and Popi, the Karamalengkos sisters. Maridhi ran out and hugged me, and Margarita Vafiadhu welcomed me with a special kind of cake. Rula, the elder daughter, did her mother's hair while she answered my questions about dowry and property. After Mrs V left for the hospital for her all-night job, I went to Popi's flat.

Popi ushered me into the dining room and we sat formally around the table. I made a joking reference to my notebook and said I wasn't a police inspector, an astinomos. Mrs Karamalengkhu answered my questions about family property and dowry, with Popi elaborating and explaining.

PERSONAL DIARY, ATHENS, SUNDAY 30 OCTOBER 1966

Woken early by bells ... I was early to meet Kalliopi, so went up to Sintagma and bought the Observer and returned to meet her in front of the Metropolitan cathedral. As we walked to the tube station at Monastiraki I seemed to tower over her. Have I got taller or is she very short? She kept repeating 'Bravo Margarita', as if not knowing what else to say to fill in the gaps in our conversation. She asked to see the photographs and commented in detail on them until we arrived at Kato Patission. Her younger sister, Zoï [who had acted as my guide to the festival of Ayios Panteleïmonos in July], looks after Kalliopi's boss's children. Zoï seemed very subdued and pale, perhaps homesick or downtrodden. I barely saw her. The boss was in bed, and the glass screens were drawn between his room and the saloni where I was given cake and tea. A minor argument took place in the kitchen. Kalliopi had come to take Zoï to their uncle's, without checking first with Zoï's employer. This was resolved by K leaving with me, and Zoï to follow later. As she got out at Omonia to go on to her uncle's house, I promised to go and see her at her job one morning. From Monastiraki I took a taxi to the Archaeological Museum...

LETTER 31, ATHENS, MONDAY 31 OCTOBER 1966

I went to the Archaeological Museum yesterday and saw the gold grave mask of Agamemnon and the statue of Zeus or Poseidon throwing a thunderbolt. I opt for Poseidon but mainly because the sunlight was shining on the green bronze, making him look like a man-fish. The most exciting thing there was a marble sarcophagus just like one on Anafi – except for the carving on one of the long sides. Last night I went up to see the Acropolis by full moonlight. It was rather cloudy and windy, so only about twenty people were there. The marble was cool – not holding the sun's warmth as it does in high summer – and everything was silvery and still.

I had lunch with Helen Aryiriadhis of the Social Sciences Centre today and she suggested lots of ways of handling a survey I might carry out on Anafi (testing the questions out first on a 20% sample), ways of leading onto new themes – such as self-ranking in the village stratification system – it seems almost definite that Anafi as compared with Mick's village has a wider range of valuation between people's standards of living which might give the basis for calling it a 'class' system. We talked for about three hours, and she told me how Kolonaki Square, which we were looking down on, used to be surrounded by beautiful residential houses so that Likavettos hill could be clearly seen from all around – now large, plain blocks of flats hide it from view. She also described how people used to be almost besieged on their name-days by callers, distributing sweets to them and answering their wishes of khronia polla *(you shouldn't need a translation of that now!).*

Tomorrow I'm seeing Peristiany in the morning ... and then visiting a cellar sweat-shop in Nikodhimu Street where pillow cases and sheets are made. An Anafiot girl [Kalliopi Khalari, mentioned earlier] is working there, and I am to take a letter from her to her parents. I went there this morning; at one side of the cellar is a machine which embroiders leaves and flowers on pillow cases. It has a roll of punctured brown paper, like a player piano roll, to set the pattern. Kalliopi was hemming up the pillow cases on an electric treadle machine, the finished ones falling softly to the ground on the other side of the machine in a great snowflake heap.

Rula Vafiadhu will bring me a basketful of goodies to take to her father and then on Thursday at 11am the 'Limnos' sails for Anafi. Because of the new route and day, I'm not sure quite when it will arrive. The route is Naxos, Paros, Siros, as usual, and then Dhinoussa, Amorgos, and I suppose, Anafi. I'm looking forward to going back, I feel much refreshed and heartened, full of ideas, ready to face everyone and keep things in proportion.

PERSONAL DIARY, ATHENS, WEDNESDAY 2 NOVEMBER 1966

Rang Khristos Vurakis (brother of Mikhalis the policeman) to ask him to bring anything he wants to send to Mikhalis direct to the boat. I collected Kalliopi's letter... the bubble car drew up outside Pulakis's taverna and Khristina, Nikos Sirighos, and a man called Yiannis leapt out like chickens hatching. Another parcel to encumber me now. Uneasy moments drinking together, Khristina repeating messages, Yianni making odd jokes, the younger boy bored and impatient...

On board the 'Limnos'
PERSONAL DIARY, THURSDAY 3 NOVEMBER 1966

Just before the 'Limnos' sailed from Piraeus, I was surprised when Khristos appeared with a pair of trousers for Mikhalis and a barrow with a huge basket in it for him, which I am to keep an eye on. We shouted farewell and the journey began... A nun is sharing my cabin and snores excruciatingly. When I combed my hair, I could see, in the mirror, up her nose and all her fillings.

Athens (and then Mina) in December 1966
LETTER 38, ATHENS, TUESDAY 6 DECEMBER 1966

As we steamed into the Piraeus this morning, all the ships were bright with flags and church bells were ringing – it is St Nicholas's day and he is the patron saint of sailors and seafarers. Mr V looked like Napoleon in his military greatcoat. He had a trunk, a sack of onions, two boxes of hens, three wicker-covered glass bottles of wine, a suitcase, two baskets, and a bunch of flowers (which he made me carry). The sea was perfectly calm all the way but the two women in my cabin were sick so I went on deck until they had both fallen asleep.

The shops are full of tinsel and plastic inflatable Father Xmasses... I sent you a message tape and a postcard today. The card has one of the special issue stamps of Greek embroidery. One of the issue, for letter weight, is an Anafiot embroidery [see book cover]. The Battle of Hastings stamps on your letters to me are a great success with the rival stamp collectors (one is Mikhalis the policeman's son Evangeli, the other Nikos the postman's son Manolis Ludharos).

Yesterday I rang up the president of the Migrant Anafiots Society, Iakovos Ghavallas, who has a seed and fertiliser shop in the Piraeus. He met me at the tube station at Piraeus and we walked through the wet streets and past the Piraeus fruit, meat and fish market on one side, and the bustle and hooting of the steamers at the quay on the other side. His shop was down three steps behind a theatre and the doorway was flanked by trees in tubs. He is the son of one of my favourite old ladies on Anafi, Marusi Gavalla, 'Granny Glasses', and I met him on Anafi in September.

I arranged to meet him again in the evening so as to see the former President of the Committee, Yiannis Ghavallas, (brother of the nice old man Marinos Ghavallas, who always brings me flowers and fruit from his gardens when he comes into the village once a week). When I went back we sat among the bags of fertiliser chatting, then they drove me into Athens to a building in Panepistimiu (University) Street, where the past president has a gentleman's tailors establishment on the first floor overlooking the bustle of the traffic going into Omonia Square. There were various wives and young lawyers assembled and they talked to me for about three hours on the history and present state *of Anafi, and the work of the Committee, which sends money for roadmaking, repairing churches, lightning conductors, etc., etc.*

One interesting thing I learnt is that the monastery has some link with the patriarchate at Constantinople [it was 'cross-founded', stavro-piyiako, meaning that it had a direct link with the Patriarchate, rather than being linked into the ecclesiastical hierarchy through the local bishop]. We sat in this vast room with shelves of suiting material lining the walls, and a copy of Rubens' 'Judgement of Paris' looking down through the gloom. They showed me the list of members of the society which I could copy (a very handy guide to addresses so that I can see if certain families congregate in certain areas and go and see a selected few) and arranged for me to meet them at the office of the society next Wednesday evening. The President of the committee took me off for a meal (with his wife and one of the young lawyers). The lawyer is a nephew of the man who recently died, Petros Allafuzos, whose sister Eleftheria, my neighbour, I went to 'weep' with before I left Anafi. The young man was wearing a black tie and I felt a pang at the mourning signs in Anafi and in Athens for the same man's death. Back to the Taverna in pouring rain...

LETTER 39, ATHENS, FRIDAY 9 DECEMBER 1966

There are oranges on the trees in the Mosque garden opposite the Taverna, but the last few days it has been raining furiously, the roads and gutters running with muddy water, and Athens has become a city of umbrellas. Everyone in Greece is mourning the loss of over 200 people drowned in the steamer 'Iraklion' en route from Crete to Piraeus. Just north of Milos, at the island of Falkonera, the tremendous seas broke through the doors in the bow ... 47 people have been saved – probably those travelling deck class who managed to swim or float free – the 1st and 2nd class passengers will have been trapped in their cabins. I can just imagine the moments of chaos before they went down.

I have been working on the Migrants' Association records: making a list of where the various Athenian Anafiots live to try to work out if certain families live in particular areas of the Athenian suburbs. It seems so, judging by what I've done. Now I have to decide how many of them to see and for what reasons. What do I want to find out from them? Why they left Anafi (schooling for bright children; for work after a series of bad harvests; because relatives starting businesses offered jobs and a share), what they have done with their houses and land on Anafi, etc. Is it possible to do this by writing to them through the Society? Should I send a questionnaire, very simple, and a stamped addressed envelope for their answer? Is this feasible?

There are two Japanese tourists staying at the taverna at the moment – they bow to the Pulakises and clear their own plates away and lark about like two children.

I think the most pretentious sentence in modern fiction is in Durrell's Alexandria Quartet "Truth' said Balthazar to me once, blowing his nose in an old tennis sock, `Truth is what most contradicts itself in time" ... I wish I could write about Athens the way Durrell does for Alexandria. To capture the many moods of the city, the junk market at Monastiraki with old boilers, mangles, spiked German helmets, mincers, brass door knobs and knockers, bedsteads, radio parts, pillars of old magazines, and bound copies of old newspapers. The meat market with its swaying naked light bulbs, the red carcases, sawdust, white aprons; the fruit market with melons, peaches, tomatoes, all colours and smells bombarding eyes and nose. The round blue cushions and the square orange ones of the two most expensive drink and pastry shops in Sintagma Square, with the ragged beatniks and hitchhikers just arrived, slumped in the shade, clinking the ice in their lemonades, while the group who have come down from the American Express Mail Office are obliviously reading their letters and reaching for their glasses without looking, groping for the cold side of the glass while the airmail pages flutter in their hands. The screech of taxi-tyres, their musical horns playing 'Colonel Bogey' and 'Love is a many splendoured thing'; the itinerant nut-sellers and the sponge man bouncing his cargo from table to table, the blind guitar players and the men with their roasting corncobs (chestnuts now) on iron-barred charcoal fires. The streets of button and trimming shops, all crowded with all colours and shapes and patterns; the streets of electrical shops, shoe shops, with creepers of plastic slippers dangling in the doorways, the elegant streets where imported French fabric costs as much as one month's rent for me on Anafi.

PERSONAL DIARY, ATHENS, SATURDAY 10 DECEMBER 1966

After hot milk and bread and honey for breakfast, I began a walk up Athinas Street to find a wick for my winter heater. In one shop the man was so helpful he took me to two others to find one. On my way back I went into the Textile Museum in the old mosque at Monastiraki. There were wonderful flared-backed sleeveless coats with heavy gold embroidery, glittering jackets, heavy jewellery, bedspreads embroidered in cross-stitch, long heavy white canvas dresses with thick bands of colourful close designs round the hems. There was a piece of embroidery from Anafi depicting a wedding procession, the one on the new stamp. The place was marvellously warm and all the inside of the dome was whitewashed, so it was lofty, cool-looking and warm feeling. I then went out to the airport to meet Marie and John [fellow postgraduate students, coming from fieldwork in Spain to the conference] and found them a hotel. I took them to a meal at the Pulakis taverna where Dino, the one-time exile on Anafi joined us over dinner, seeming to be delighted to see me and offered us green-leaved oranges from a paper bag.

LETTER 40, ATHENS, MONDAY 12 DECEMBER 1966
End of the first day of the conference at the Athens Hilton – vast, marble, sculptures, fountains, free refreshments. Very very posh indeed. And some interesting papers. But no time to write as yet in detail – I met Marie and John at the airport on Saturday and we talked until about 2am. They came to the Taverna Pulakis with me for a meal and were delighted with the place and its atmosphere; they said it was so different in emotional tone from Ronda. Then on Sunday I went to lunch with Thetis and then up to the Acropolis in the chilly, fresh, sunny afternoon. I could see right down to the Piraeus where the water was gleaming like metal.

PERSONAL DIARY, ATHENS, MONDAY 12 DECEMBER 1966
First the chairs were put in rows for a speech from a Minister in French and Greek; after coffee, all was rearranged – a table with silver jugs and sparkling goblets for the participants, and chairs around the sides for observers. Peristiany read an impressive paper summing up the polarities of male and female in Cyprus...

When one of these 'observers' asked a question after a paper, we were told that only paper-givers could make comments or ask questions. Then, that evening, arriving at a conference reception held in the Hotel Grand Bretagne, Mick was refused entry because he was not wearing a white shirt; Nancy and I were told we could go in, but wouldn't do so without Mick. The three of us went to Apotsos, a bar just off Sintagma Square.

We each downed several glasses of brandy and I burst into tears which dripped down onto my plate. Then we walked back to the taverna and ate, getting more and more furious about our inability to participate in the conference discussion and to attend the Reception... and so, what with our pre-reception ouzos, we were all very drunk ... about 3am we were alternating between tears and anger, returning to our rejections and reinflaming our fury.

PERSONAL DIARY, ATHENS, TUESDAY 13 DECEMBER 1966
I think I was still drunk when I got up this morning and went to the conference. Pitt-Rivers read his paper on the similarities between strangers' and women's roles, straddling his legs across a chair ... Harry Levy [husband of Ernestine Friedl] capped it by moving from the spectators' chairs to the table, reciting the plot of Euripides' Alcestis, and returning again in a storm of applause.
From the conference I went on to the Anafiot Migrants' Association office in Makriyianni. After the bus journey I found a few people there all intent on a party, planned without informing me. I had to force myself to keep my temper

and to insist on asking the questions I wanted to. Doggedly we went through the surnames of members of the Association, which I had copied from the membership register at Yiannis Ghavallas's menswear shop on 8 December to see which ones had vanished from Anafi – my respondent here was the editor of the newspaper 'Old Athens', Palia Athina. Then I asked Marinos's brother, Yiannis, about the work of the committee, sinedhrio, and the plans for a ten-room tourist hotel on Anafi. A trolley of lush cakes and brandy was wheeled in from the tiny kitchen. The hubbub was incredible and all my energy was bent on finishing the cake and escaping. I knew it would have been good policy to join them all for dinner but I just couldn't bear it...

PERSONAL DIARY, ATHENS, THURSDAY 15 DECEMBER 1966

Breakfast in the café next door to the Taverna Pulakis, and late for the first paper... Almost a mass exit before the paper in French to get coffee; the café in the Hilton is like the chapel at Coventry Cathedral, circular, with a tent-like roof, and a chandelier below it, a hushed and reverent moneyed atmosphere and even canned organ music.

I went with Mick, Nancy and the children for lunch to Barba Stavros's Taverna in Plaka. The walls have strange pale paintings of trees growing into people, people growing into trees, walking false teeth, elephants with feathered tails, other animals with flowers growing out of them. A planking roof over the outside tables had spaces cut for trees; Tom and Ben played with the gravel.

LETTER 41, ATHENS, SATURDAY 17 DECEMBER 1966

The conference finished today with papers by Russell Bernard on the Kalimnian sponge fishermen's wives and one by Andromedas on the position of women in Mani (in which he mentioned the sexual segregation of donkeys). Tolosana had the conference in fits of laughter over a fertility orgy which he described very soberly: 'The women as they detrousered the man cried "Hurray for trousers", and he as he grabbed at their legs, "Hurray for petticoats".'

It's Monday now, yesterday we went on an excursion to Mycenae, Epidavros, and Nafplion. All the serious professors became jolly, even silly, and Gellner decided to stop off at Nafplion and stay the night at a hotel in the middle of the lake – in an old castle-fortress. So my last view of him was getting into a small boat with an old battered rucsac setting off for his island castle in the dark. [Ernest Gellner acted as External Examiner for my doctoral thesis five years later.]

There were beautiful anemones in the grass among the ruins at Epidavros, and everyone stood in the middle of the theatre dropping pennies, rustling paper and whispering messages to the other professors at the top of the amphitheatre. There was a Frenchman and his Greek wife there and I had to speak to them in

Greek as every time I tried to say things in French it came out mangled: 'Je ne sais pou einai...' The boat to Anafi goes on Thursday so I'll try and write again before I leave...

PERSONAL DIARY, ATHENS, THURSDAY 22 DECEMBER 1966

Nancy and I went to the Post Office to send our Christmas mail, rounding together on a man who was following us and pinching our bottoms. The post office was like a refugee camp with silent lines of people waiting in front of tiny windows in temporary partitions. Nancy joined the parcel queue and I the letter one. We were made to peel the sellotape off some of the parcels as only string is allowed. They were setting up stalls all along Eolu Street, with tinsel, clockwork pigs, combs, kitchenware, vases, jumpers and the roadway was marked with numbers in white paint for future stalls.

I went to say goodbye at the Social Sciences Centre ... and dripped rain onto Peristiany's suit from my oilskin's sleeve when I shook hands. The government had just fallen and he was in a panic to get all his projects to the new minister; 'I'm a professional beggar' he said, 'and I've lost my self-respect.'

LETTER 42, ATHENS, THURSDAY 22 DECEMBER 1966

Well, as usual, a delay in boats, so one more day in Athens while it rains and rains and we all suffer streaming colds. We've been going Christmas and provision shopping and I looked after Tom and Ben last night and took them to the milk shop for tea while Nancy and Mick went out shopping for their presents. After I read the Smiley Lion for Ben and Winnie-the-Pooh for Tom, they went to bed and I recorded Beethoven's Pastoral, Getz, Mingus and Dylan from Mick and Nancy's tapes.

LETTER 42 CONTINUED, ARGOS, SATURDAY 24 DECEMBER 1966

...here I am on my way down to Mina again with the Lineton family. I was ready to go yesterday, said goodbye, and then heard that boats had been cancelled because of the weather (it had been raining all morning). I rang up the harbour master at Piraeus who said that the boat for Anafi wouldn't be sailing and would probably not leave until next week. So what to do? Go to Santorini, if there was a boat the next day and try and get a caïque over to Anafi? wait in Athens until there was a boat? I went slowly upstairs again and told Nancy. 'If you'll be lonely' said Tom 'I'll stay with you.' So I burst into tears!

Nancy suggested another alternative which was to spend Christmas with them and to return to Athens to get a boat in time for New Year. We drove down from Athens to Argos yesterday afternoon and evening in a thunderstorm, the sky was purple and the sea was like a bruise. This morning the sun is shining and the Argive girls' band is beating drums and blowing trumpets round the square. All the shops are full of Christmas trees and coloured lights. I am disappointed about the boat because I did want to see the celebrations on Anafi, but I suppose that as a consequence of the 'Iraklion' disaster they are being very cautious.

LETTER 43, ATHENS, WEDNESDAY 28 DECEMBER 1966

God (and the harbour master at the Piraeus) willing, I sail tomorrow for Anafi and the New Year celebrations. I arrived back in Athens this afternoon after one of the loveliest Christmasses and one of the most surprising!

The whole of Christmas Eve resounded with the tune of the carol, Ta Kalenda, which the military bands in each town and village of the Peloponnese were playing. I wrote to you from Argos where we had spent the night and woke to the fresh cold morning and the sound of trumpets. Each orchard had a stall hung with plastic bags full of oranges outside its gates. We stopped in Yithion to shop and got meat for Christmas (and heard its town band) and drove to Mina in the sunset, getting to the village about 7pm. Mick and Nancy had bought two paraffin stoves which worked wonderfully well, so we were warm throughout all our preparations. Mick decorated a little silver tree, Nancy wrapped the children's presents and made up their stockings with balloons tied to the tops. While we were busy we played a selection of records which John Pulakis had given to Mick; lots of old, normally unobtainable favourites, and juke-box-only issues...

I woke up to hear Tom exclaiming 'I got a clockwork pig!' and the pink plastic pig juddering across the floor, its curly tail spinning. Ben was overcome with his balloon. We had just got back from church and given the children their presents when we heard village children's voices, and up the stairs, accompanied by them, came – Susanna! She had arrived in Greece the day before and went to find us at the Pulakis Taverna only to learn that we had just left. She got on a train to Kalamata overnight and caught taxis down to Mina. So we had Christmas lunch all together and then she and I travelled back on the bus today. She will wait for a trunk to arrive and to get a Research Assistant (she's on an American grant and can afford one), then go out to Santorini to choose which village to start off in. I think she has been given a good idea how tough fieldwork can be from the Mina situation and also of the practical difficulties she hadn't foreseen – like warmth and water...

Santorini, February 1967

LETTER 49, ANAFI, THURSDAY 2 FEBRUARY 1967

[The next trip, arranged at short notice, was six weeks after my return from Christmas in Mani, when I went over to Santorini to help Susanna get established in her fieldwork village.] Tomorrow I'm going to Santorini by caïque.

Susanna rang me up from Athens; her Research Assistant can't return with her on this second visit, and she has to arrange the renting of a house (she chose a village and found a house on her first visit), as well as buying things and settling in. As I have to go there anyway sometime to see the Manager of the Agricultural Bank, I may as well combine altruism with self interest.

LETTER 50, SANTORINI, THURSDAY 9 FEBRUARY 1967

I left Anafi on the large caïque at 10pm last night. I went down to the harbour on donkeyback with Nikos Khalaris. Rembelia, the grocer's wife, walked beside us with a storm lantern which threw our enormous shadows onto the rocks and down the slopes, and the lights of the village on the ridge above us were mixed up with the stars. We waited in the shed with old fishing nets, driftwood and possibly a door from the wreck of the 'Iraklion' which had been washed up on the beach. At about 9pm we saw a small red light, heard the sound of a motor, and then as the boat turned towards us, saw the green light on its right side. Shouts across the water: a dinghy was launched, Rembelia and I climbed aboard, and she arranged for the unloading of various sacks of animal fodder, sugar, and flour.

Finally, when the unloading was over, I was wished good journey, kalo taksidhi, *and off we went into the starry night, the sea calm and breaking in little phosphorescent wavelets along the side of the boat. I sat in the bridge for a while, then went below, wrapped myself in a blanket and slept fitfully and draughtily for several hours. I woke at 2:30am and looked out to see the lights of the main town, Fira, like a straggly Z: the top stroke made by the street lights of the town on the rim of the crater, the downstroke made by lights on the winding path to the harbour whose lights were strung out along the quay. Everything was quiet; just the sound of water, and a little rain. The captain advised me to sleep until dawn, but as I was resettling myself, a man called out: I had asked by phone from Anafi for a donkeyman to wait for me, and he came.*

I rode up to Fira in the falling rain, on a huge horse, with two small dogs following behind. Finally we reached a lighted courtyard and Susanna's greetings. She has a rented room in Fira and will be moving out to her village, Kypseli [a pseudonym], on Sunday. There were many people who remembered me from my one-day visit with the Anafi caïque last June when I came over to the bank, and from a visit of a week in September, so we were often called into shops to be offered coffee. All these coffees were brought to us by the same man from a nearby café, who turned out to be from Susanna's chosen fieldwork village and his wife is the schoolteacher there.

I don't feel that a ten days' absence from Anafi is a bad idea, it has been six weeks since New Year and I have been 'anthropologizing' solidly. My hair is very long now – I had it washed today, at Santorini's only hairdresser. There's hot water but no plumbing and the basin runs out into a bucket which has to be emptied between each rinse.

We went out by bus to a village which was celebrating a patron saint's day (Ayios Kharalambos) and people were busy wiping small pieces of cypress twig against his ikon and relic box. As it is a Friday, and good Orthodox Christians abstain from meat and fish (and because the Bishop was there) instead of a feast afterwards, there was a distribution of bread and olives. I know that Anafi has an Ayios Kharalambos in the village so it will be interesting to ask what happened there, when I get back. It has been raining almost continually since I arrived: the crater of the volcano is smoking as the rain hits the hot sulphurous lava: one feels rather near the edge of doom looking across at it. Anafi, in the other direction, looks as insubstantial as stage scenery – dark purples, pinks, golds. I can't help feeling some envy of Susanna with a research assistant and willing friends to help her, compared with my own beginnings.

LETTER 51, KYPSELI, SANTORINI, WEDNESDAY 15 FEBRUARY 1967

I am now settled in with Susanna in Kypseli, 25 minutes walk from Fira and on the side of Santorini looking towards Anafi, which sometimes disappears in the mist like stage scenery and reappears magically, the village just visible on a pimply mountain peak, like icing on a fairy sponge-bun.

We came out for a look-round on Saturday afternoon. We lost the path and reached the lower village down the hillside by a track of tumbling stones like a stream-bed: black volcanic lumps, maroon and blood-red, and orange pebbles, and white, hollowed-out caves. So much black stone and gravel made the paths look dirty. There were wide terraces on the sloping hillsides, the grey earth like huge folds in an old elephant's skin. Kypseli is on a slope, but divided into an upper and lower village between which there seemed to be some rivalry. Each part has its own shop and telephone and track into Fira. The lower village has a dirty gravelly square.

On Sunday afternoon we set off with three laden mules and one which was unburdened and galloped behind or in front, rolling in the dust, jumping over fences, grazing at lush verges; Susanna and I followed the caravan in laughter and apprehension. It was worse at first than I could have thought, people were idling, looking for a focus of interest. Women and children crowded the doorway, the owner of the village shop and brother of S's absentee landlord seemed to be taking control. S was a little worried over this as she doesn't want to be in with any particular power group. Anyway, all the drawers and cupboards were full of things and locked; eventually we won an empty wardrobe and another table. It was very much easier for me to ask for things, to get information, to ask questions for someone else than it is for myself.

The house is just above the school and on the path to the shop. She has four rooms, one with its own external door is to be her office-study. All her books (three cratefuls) and tapes are in there but as it has no window pane and the weather is freezing cold, we are living in the room beside it. The house is on a slope, so the kitchen window is at ground level and some of the snotty-nosed children who came to gawp at us went round to spy at us from there.

I seem to be a successful interpreter, and many things are coming up which compare and contrast with Anafi. Here, being a more agricultural island, there are few sheep and goats, bread is brought daily from the baker's in Fira, there is no spinning or weaving, all the wool is bought ready. There used to be large landowners here whose power was broken by a spontaneous cooperative movement which now runs a wine-press, a tomato juice factory, etc., etc.

I went to the Agricultural Bank. The Manager said they have almost no information about Anafi; the cooperative there has been in operation since 1957, and he only has figures for the sale of fertiliser. But what about the barley? I asked. He said that they had never sold it to the Bank – so perhaps I was told this on Anafi just to shut me up. Or else the Bank Manager doesn't know.

I also found out that the Monastery of Patmos owns land on Anafi (as well as on Santorini). [At this time I didn't know that there had been several monasteries on Anafi: one dedicated to Panayia Kalamiotissa, on the peak of Mount Kalamos, had been founded by the Patriarch of Constantinople (as I had been told in Athens by the Migrants' Association), another (dedicated to the Lifegiving Spring, Zoödhokos Piyi, an epithet of the Panayia) at the foot of the mountain, and another at the chapel of Ayios Antonios]. But I realise that these are background details, really secondary to the main work I am doing. It's when I'm unsure of the main work that I retreat to the historical details and try to pretend that they are important, just as important as how the villagers live today (but it doesn't really affect them who owns the lands they rent or who founded the monastery).

Monday and today (Wednesday) we have been setting the house in order and receiving gifts of eggs and cheese brought by highly curious women. Susanna put only her most modest dresses on view in the wardrobe and hid her mini-skirts and gold stockings. I lined the kitchen shelves and scrubbed out an evil-smelling food safe, but after an energetic morning the freezing cold drove us back beside the heater to eat omelettes and our own supply of macaroons! Yesterday, after the visit to the Agricultural Bank, we went to the police station for Susanna's permit and a licence for her motorized bicycle. We had forgotten to bring photographs so have to go back tomorrow; I also collected the prints of the film I took at the conference outing, in Mina over Christmas, and on Anafi at New Year.

One of S's tapes is of the 'Gymnopedies' by Satie, a contemporary of Debussy, [which still reminds me of Santorini]... We went to see a hilariously funny, Greek sub-titled and badly cut version of Calamity Jane in Fira. This is only the second time I've been to the pictures in Greece – the first was in December when I saw Who's Afraid of Virginia Woolf? in Athens.

Athens, April, 1967

The visit to Athens in April was timed not only to coincide with the last instalment of my grant cheque, but also to celebrate my 25th birthday on 2 April and Susanna's 26th birthday the previous day. The occasion of my quarter-century justified one of the few international phone-calls I made while in Greece. The Linetons were just about to move from Mani to Athens for Mick to make a study of the Maniot migrants in Piraeus to complement his work in the Maniot village of Mina. My great friend from undergraduate days, Rosalind Horner, was flying to Greece for a holiday after finishing her Master's thesis, and before going to Burundi to start her own doctoral fieldwork. Her arrival time also coincided with my visit to Athens. The plan was for her to visit me on Anafi at the end of her holiday, just before the Greek Orthodox Easter on 30 April. Chapter Eight, which gives an account of Easter on the island, and also of the reception and effects of the Colonels' coup there, also includes a description of her visit.

LETTER 59, ATHENS, TUESDAY 4 APRIL 1967

I'm writing this in the ruins of the agora, on a late sunny Tuesday afternoon; Tom and Ben are rushing about on the hillside picking wild flowers (which I'll enclose) while Mick and R are looking at flats. Susanna's birthday, 1 April, was cloudy. In the evening she lit her cake with 26 candles ... Sunday, my 25th birthday, was lovely and warm and we lay on the balcony and listened to different tape-recordings and read the Sunday papers and then had lunch at the restaurant on Likavettos, overlooking the city, and looking across to the Acropolis. It's getting cold now, I'll try and write again later. I went to see Mr V on Thursday afternoon and took him a tin of 36 eggs from his chickens on Anafi which one of the neighbours collected, and he sends you his compliments.

LETTER 60, ATHENS, THURSDAY 6 APRIL 1967

Lovely to get your letter this morning – it upheld me through a tremendous crisis: I walked around the Acropolis and its lovely cool museum with my mind in a tremble, vibrating with unhappiness and guilt and sadness and exhaustion. I made an unpremeditated remark last night which suddenly fired an already awkward situation into one which set each one of us against the other. These currents had been there all the time so I feel now that my remarks didn't really *cause them so much as reveal them – and now, later on in the day, the air has cleared. Although there is a strain between the four of us, it involves the embarrassment of starting our friendship again.*

While I was walking I was preoccupied but also noticed that a huge concourse of students had gathered in the Zappion Park beside the parliament building. It might have been the beginning of a demonstration as there were policemen at all the tables of the park café. [The students were probably demonstrating in support of 21 students at the University of Thessalonika whom their university senate had subjected to disciplinary action because of participation in 'illegal activities'. As the report in The Times states on the following day, 'the Athens police announced tonight [i.e. the evening of Thursday 6 April] that for reasons of public order all outdoor demonstrations and marches were banned. The National Students' Union, however, announced a rally at Athens University tomorrow night [Friday 7 April] to protest against the Kanellopulos Government and to demand immediate action' (The Times, Friday 7 April 1967).]

LETTER 61, ATHENS, SUNDAY 9 APRIL 1967

We are sprawled out on the Pulakis's terrace in our bathing costumes, listening to tapes, reading the Sunday papers and eating bananas. 'We' consist of Susanna, Rosalind and I, with Ben and Mick darting across the scene. I met Ros at the airport on Friday morning. Her plane was delayed for three hours so I walked up and down until the dark night became soft dawn and then suddenly she had arrived. We had coffee and croissants in Sintagma Square, Ros commenting all the time on the sunshine, and the smell of sandalwood. We went to the beach after leaving her rucsac at the taverna, and we got sunburnt; there was a slightly chilly wind and we didn't realise how unused our bodies were to the full sun. Yesterday she went to the museum while I rushed about shopping. I go back to Anafi tomorrow.

Rosalind stayed on in Athens for a few days, and then went travelling around Greece, ending up in Crete, from where she took a ferry to Santorini and then the weekly steamer to Anafi. Shortly after her arrival on the island, there was a coup d'état in Athens on 21 April by which a military junta seized power (see Chapter Eight). After she left, I expected to continue my fieldwork until mid-July, then meet my parents in Athens. They were intending to drive to Greece and wanted me to travel home with them. I hoped to make the journey back with the Linetons, particularly as we had to be back in Canterbury in time for a de-briefing meeting with our supervisor on 2 September. Then my plans changed; Susanna came over from Santorini and we decided that the only thing that would get either of us through the next months of fieldwork was the thought of a treat in the offing, and we decided to go together for a short holiday in Turkey. As Susanna said: 'my favourite of all emotions is anticipation'. And in the event, it became too difficult to coordinate a return with Mick and Nancy in the Volkswagen microbus, so I travelled back to Britain by air on my own.

Turkey June 1967

NOTECARD FROM ISTANBUL, TUESDAY 27 JUNE 1967

Turkey seems to me like Greece with camels. We are taking things very gently – staying in Istanbul until the weekend to visit a friend of Susanna's who owns an island, called Spoon Island I think, in the Bosphorus. I can speak a few words of Turkish, which is the most incredible sounding language; 'scurabundi chiribiribim' it sounds like to me. Walking in the streets we are bumped and pinched and stared at and followed; last night it got rather frightening and in the end we walked up the drive of the Hilton to escape. We were still followed and pestered until I swung round and hit one man with a sideways sweep of the arm, and Susanna clonked him on the head with her bag. The city actually looks and feels like Liverpool with its red buses, the ferries, scurrying people. Today is sticky hot and all the lovely trees cast still, cool shadows.

We went into the Blue Mosque this afternoon at prayer time – it was lofty, light, cool, deeply peaceful. I thought: this is the first religious ritual I've ever attended which I don't understand and have no emotional response to. We washed our feet outside – there were cool soft carpets inside for our rather swollen bare feet.

We met a woman last night who commented (in Greek) that she was surprised that we could speak 'Romaïka', meaning Greek as the language of the Eastern Roman Empire. I felt we had stepped back to the time when the Greeks regarded themselves as the heirs of the Roman Empire.

Athens, July 1967

Susanna and I travelled slowly down the Aegean coast of Turkey, finally stopping in Bodrum where June Starr, a friend of Susanna's, was carrying out research. Susanna stayed on there, while I took a caïque from Bodrum to Kos, and then a steamer back to Athens, where I met up with my parents who arrived in Athens by car on 13 July. They stayed less than a week, leaving on 18 July, taking with them some of the luggage I had stored at the Taverna Pulakis.

LETTER 73, ATHENS, MONDAY 24 JULY 1967

I'm wondering how your journey has been? It was good that you came to Greece when you did as it has got much much hotter since then. The day after you left Mick rang, and I went round to see them and have since spent an afternoon in the park with Nancy and the children, and all last Sunday at Vuliagmeni beach. We took wine and buried it in the sand at the water's edge, just the thing to go with chicken and cucumber sandwiches!

Andromedas, who is an authority on Mani (he was at the Mediterraneanists' conference in December), has arranged an informal conference. Informal, because since the coup, meetings of more than five people are illegal. We are to meet with Peristiany, Ernestine Friedl, and another anthropologist working in Athens. We had the first talk today about revising the training of anthropologists, and the way that human geographers seem to be able to talk government language and get things supported which are really third rate sociology whereas anthropologists don't seem to be able to get their voices heard by government. The monumental Social Atlas of Greece isn't in any of the Greek Information Offices so the Centre is sending free copies as these offices have no budget for them.

I'm writing on my knee in Sintagma, very shakily, drinking an ice-cream soda and going to buy some material for a dress. My old green one was drying on the line and blew away off the Pulakis balcony and over the Tower of the Winds! I went and asked all the neighbouring shops to rescue it if they saw it waft by, but it hasn't been seen; Eolus, god of the winds, must have kept it for himself.

I've been to an Anafiot café in the suburbs and found that what I'd planned to do here in Athens in these next weeks would be well nigh impossible in the time I've got left; it's a real man's society, no room for me and my questions. More anon from Anafi...

CHAPTER SIX

'Crossing myself from right to left'

Saints' day festivals and other rituals

✳

Some of the events recounted below are celebrations of saints' days, taking place in the main village church or in chapels dedicated to those particular saints, in the village, or in various parts of the island. Attending saints' day celebrations, particularly in these outlying chapels, gave me both a sense of the religious geography of the village and the island and of the way in which the islanders' year was patterned by the strict, or lax, observance of feasting and fasting. Most important for the development of my ideas about the underlying structural principles of Anafiot social life was the cycle of rituals which took place after death: the funeral, followed by a series of memorial services, and culminating in exhumation and the placing of bones in a family vault.

The main village church was dedicated to Ayios Nikolaos, patron saint of sailors and seafarers, whose festival is on 6 December; next to it was a small chapel, possibly an earlier main church, with the same dedication. There were seven other churches or chapels in the village. Just outside the village was an unfinished chapel, eventually to be dedicated to Ayios Spiridhinos (Saint Spiridon, 12 December), built in memory of the proedhros's son, Spiros, who had been killed in Cyprus in 1952, probably while on military service.

Further afield I knew of eleven other chapels by name, some of which I had visited in my first week on the island in company with Thetis, the ikon expert from the Byzantine Museum, and others which I was to visit when their saints' days were celebrated. Dominating the religious lives and ritual calendar of the islanders, and of the migrants too, was the celebration on 8 September of the festival of the Birth of the Virgin at the Lower Monastery church, where the miraculous ikon of Panayia Kalamiotissa, the patron saint of Anafi, was housed. It was built on the site of an ancient temple dedicated to Apollo and Artemis.

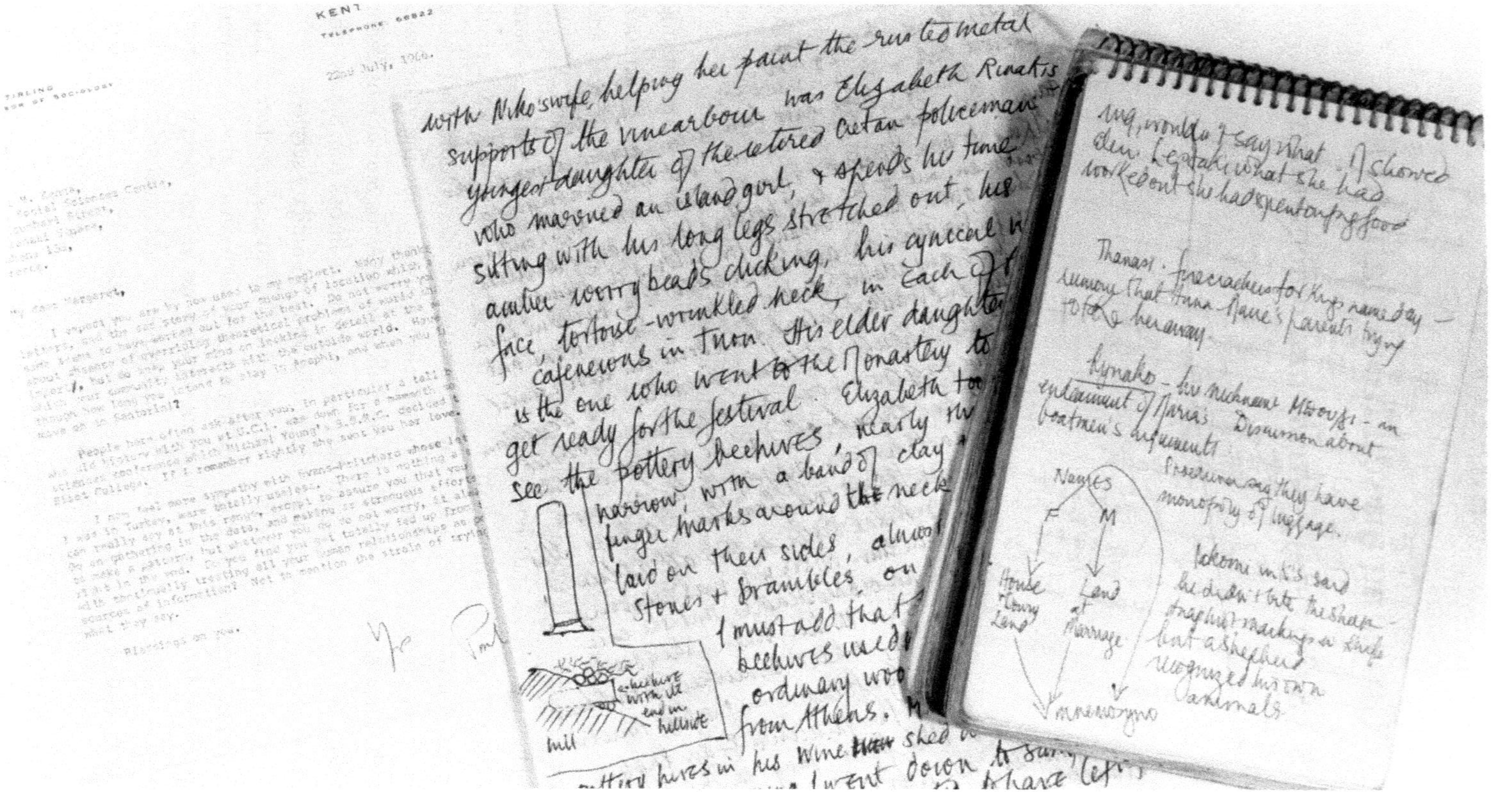

Scrapbook i) From my files: notebook, letter to parents, letter from supervisor

Returning from Ayios Panteleimon, July 1966

Anna and Zoï, daughters of Yiannis Kolliahas, agrofilákas, on terrace outside my room.

With Ben Lineton, Mani, October 1966

With parents, University of Kent, about to leave for Greece, April 1966

Taverna Pulakis, Athens. 25th birthday, April 1967

With village girls and Danish tourist. Kalliopi, Fleuri, Theoni, Yannoula, Urania (in sunglasses)

ii)   Photographs taken in Canterbury, on Anafi, in Mani and in Athens

unloading the steamer, July 1966

An exhumation, August 1966

New Year's Day 1967: women with ikons to "first foot" their houses. n.b. "Liz Taylor"

Bringing sheep and goats to caique, April 1967

Abbot and Flora "short sleeves" at chapel of Ayios Andreas, Nov '66

Kalliopi Arvaniti and the last curtained bed in the village; note ikons and wedding garlands on wall.

Young shepherds celebrating, Ayios Antonios Day, 17 Jan '67

iii) *Imports and exports: unloading the steamer and Easter livestock sales*

Discussion in a café: Vinzenzos, proedros, Manolis Takhidromos

Margarita and Kostas Khalaris harvesting, 1967

Kiria Polidhorou

Urania and Pananos Arvanitis ploughing, November 1966

Nikos Postman (in mourning for father), Zabella with Apostollos, Manolis Efthimia, Irini

iv)   Work and leisure: indoor and outdoor scenes

Other rituals I attended during my fieldwork were what anthropologists call *rites de passage*, transition rituals, in which a change of status takes place: nameless infant to named member of a family; single persons to married couple, and unrelated persons to relatives by marriage; dead person to sin-laden corpse to expiated soul. No weddings took place on the island during my fieldwork, and I had to wait until the summer of 1987 to attend one, the double wedding of two sisters. Between May 1966 and August 1967 I attended a number of christenings, two funerals, an exhumation, and a number of memorial services. I gradually came to realise that these services, called *mnimosina*, were related to property inheritance, and thus to naming.

FIELDNOTES, ANAFI, WEDNESDAY 27 JULY 1966, AYIOS PANTELEIMONOS

I left the village on donkey-back at 4.50am with Zoï Khalari and her brother Vinzenzos [two of the children of Yiorghakis 'Birbilis' Khalaris and Anezini]. The route was down from the square, steeply down past Kisiropi (where Zoï said her family gardens are) to Vayia, past the chapel of Ayia Paraskevi (who cures eyes), and the double chapel of Ayia Varvara and Ayios Nikolaos, a picturesque, double vaulted chapel. We were the only people who came from the village that morning. Everyone else came yesterday and had stayed the night [a practice called *enkimisi*, literally 'sleeping-in', translated as 'incubation' by some experts].

As we arrived, I saw the Abbot in the doorway of a house below another chapel. I found out later that this was the house of Kiria Polidhoru, a devout old widow; the chapel housed the bones of her husband. A basket of *artos*, brown bread with seeds on top, was brought into the chapel and blessed at end of service. Stella did most of the singing, and her husband Nikos the schoolteacher read a sort of 'lesson' during the consecration. The Abbot seemed to be composing a list of names, possibly people who were asking to be helped by the saint. At first there were only four of us in the chapel, by the end there were about 20 women and six men and lots of children. One woman knelt down for the consecration. I was kept busy crossing myself from right to left. [I didn't realise at the time, but this list was made up of the names of the dead whose relatives wanted them to be remembered in the Liturgy; the Abbot was given a small sum of money for each name.]

Afterwards, the basket of artos was brought outside, also a tray of sweet cakes, a box of loukoumia, a bottle of ouzo (given out by Russetos), banana liqueur (by Katina), small plums. All wished each other a phrase I couldn't understand which sounded like *theos se khorestu* [o *Theos sinkhores' tu*, may God forgive him]. Lots of photos demanded of me and taken.

We saw the boat 'Elli', the weekly steamer, far below and far out from the shore. A harbour-inlet called Prassa, on this coast of the island, can be

Figure 9   Women and girls at Ayios Panteleïmon

reached from the chapel of Ayios Panteleïmonos. After the service we went to the house of Kiria Polidhoru. She offers hospitality to visitors the day before and the day of the feast: ouzo, loukoumi, coffee, paksimadhi, small plums, for the sake of her dead husband. The Abbot, Nikos, Stella, Khristina, Vivi, Rita and I sat inside. Older Marulidhi and Russetos's wife helped serve. Those sitting outside got coffee, paksimadhi and water. Most people there agreed that this was a 'small affair'; in past years, there has been music and dancing afterwards. Has this lapsed because of labour migration? [This was my first experience of the distribution of food and drink 'for the soul', connected with the memorial service, *mnimosino*, customarily carried out three months after a death. This saint's day was chosen because there would be a large number of people whose prayers would assist the soul of the dead man. The photos taken on this occasion were developed on a later visit to Athens and then provided an opportunity for me to visit migrants in the city and suburbs.]

Kiria Polidhoru's children are in Athens, she told me. She will come into the village in the winter, she has a house near the police station, above Patiniotis' grocery. I left her house at 11am, arriving in the village an hour later.

LETTER 17, ANAFI, TUESDAY 2 AUGUST 1966

After the saint's day at Ayios Panteleïmonos, I had a day of unexplained malaise, feeling generally off-colour, no appetite. This is told not to worry you but because it was popularly attributed to the Evil Eye, to Mati. Someone with more 'power' (they also used the word elektrismos) than me had admired me without either spitting, or calling on the Virgin to avert the implied envy which was making me ill.

LETTER 18, ANAFI, MONDAY 8 AUGUST 1966

I went to a christening yesterday afternoon. The baby was the village barber's daughter; the godfather was one of the rich summer visitors who has a wind-driven generator on his house, his name is Papakhristos and his wife is from an Anafi family. Swearing, promising, spitting, censing, immersing, is all done three times. We had almonds and honey and banana liqueur afterwards, and the godfather gave money to the child's parents and close family and to the priest. His handful crackled, so I expect it was at least a 50 drachma note.

They were sweeping out and decorating the church of the Assumption ready for the festival next Monday, August 15. It's a privately owned church with a Russian ikon, one I saw with Thetis in May. I went to help, but wasn't allowed to (but I think good marks were chalked up in my favour for offering). [I realised later that it may have been because the other women didn't want to ask me if I was menstruating, as this would have put me in a state of ritual impurity for tasks such as dusting ikons.]

Letter 19, Anafi, Monday 15 August 1966, Kimisis Tis Theotoku

I'm afraid I've been ill the last two days, a combination of food poisoning and stomach chill – the worst diarrhoea I've ever had, migranous headaches, the shivers, then hot sweats and terrible weakness. I greedily ate half a watermelon, imported by the Takhidromos, in one sitting and I don't think I'll ever be able to face watermelon again. I couldn't make it to vespers, esperino, *at the church dedicated to the Dormition of the Virgin last night, but with my bag full of toilet paper in case I had to take to the hills or a nearby house, I crept up there this morning after the first bell went at 6:30am, and sat through most of the two and a half hour service. I'm glad I went; everyone was in best clothes; it seemed one of the few occasions when whole families came together to church, although of course men and women were on different sides of the church.*

I was told that the chapel was built by a man who was the unexpected child of a couple who kept having miscarriages and stillbirths, in fulfilment of their vow to the Virgin, and it is used only this one day every year. An albino boy was taken up for communion at the end of the service with many other children [I was asked later to take a photo of this boy; he died before my next visit, in 1973, and I found that my photo had been placed on his grave.]

After the service there was a procession including the cross, monstrance, a candle-lamp and two ikons round the hillside to the North, counter-clockwise, and into the church in the square 'from the back way' and then back down the village street. I didn't get to see what happened in the main church.

Fieldnotes, Anafi, Friday 19 August 1966

Margarita Dhamighu told me that the ikon of Panayia Kalamiotissa was found on a reed, *kalamos*. It moved three times from the church where it had been taken to where it wanted to be, that is where it had been found, on the peak of Mount Kalamos. Margarita says wounds appeared on the hands of the ikon during the war (which war? presumably World War II?). Someone else told me the scratches appeared on the Virgin's hands after the 1956 Santorini earthquake; people were killed on the next island, but nobody on Anafi was hurt, thanks to Panayia Kalamiotissa.

Fieldnotes, Anafi, Sunday 21 August 1966

The church was packed by the end of the service, about 40 men and women. A little to the left of the centre was a table with four candles, draped in purple cloth, and on it, two round discs, covered in sugar with silver crosses worked into the 'icing'. One of these was for the Abbot's mother, Kalliopi Arvaniti, who died a year ago, the other for a man who died three years ago.

At one point in the service all the men were given candles and the church was ablaze, the top chandeliers were lit. Afterwards, there was a distribution outside the church of artos, cognac, honey with cinnamon, and instead of the usual 'your health' when taking the cognac, one says 'may God forgive him (her)', *O Theos sinkhores' tu (tis)*.

I went to the Abbot's house for cognac and coffee in memory of his dead mother, and was then taken to the graveyard for the exhumation of the man who had been commemorated. The three women and others were chanting what I assume were *miroloyia*, laments, shrieking 'my father' and putting words into the dead man's mouth: 'daughter', 'niece'... After the priest said words over the grave, it was broken open, the women shrieked and held each other back, children pushed forwards to look, some of them seemed genuinely frightened. As the bones of the corpse came up, Granny Glasses (Marusi Ghavalla) poured wine over it, incense was burnt. It was covered with a sheet, taken into the church, one candle put at feet and two at head, and later the priest read prayers, holding a candle and burning incense.

Meanwhile, a child's grave was opened. I later found out this was Mikhalis Arvanitis's first child, who was born prematurely at 8 months, and lived only 17 days. [Neither the birth nor the death was recorded in the family entry in the village register]. The grandmother (which? Mikhalis Arvanitis's mother? or Zabella's?), dressed in brown, wept quietly. The bones were put in a pillowcase with a sprig of basil. The bones were going to be placed in a family vault out in the fields.

That evening, because I was feeling so unwell, Vasiliki Rinaki and Zabetta Ludharu came and gave me *venduzes* (literally 'leeches', here 'cupping'). They commented that I must indeed 'have cold' as the jars gripped tightly and my skin went very red.

LETTER 21, ANAFI, TUESDAY 30 AUGUST 1966

Nikos the donkeyman and Margarita's baby was christened on Sunday afternoon and we feasted afterwards on honey-cakes. Which reminds me about spitting. At a christening when the godparents are promising to abjure the devil, to hold fast to Belief, they spit three times on the floor and rub it away with the sole of their shoe (I haven't got the exact meaning of this yet.) People also spit when they admire a baby or an animal so as not to bewitch it. I had a touch of heat exhaustion that evening (anything inexplicable is attributed to the evil eye) and people said I was bewitched. The postman's wife and the Takhidhromos can diagnose this; Kiria Zabetta by dropping oil in water (if it disperses one is 'eyed', if it stays in a drop one isn't), the Takhidhromos by saying certain prayers in three breaths, using one's baptismal name and then asking one to stand up.

LETTER 22, ANAFI, SATURDAY 3 SEPTEMBER 1966

I am off to the Monastery on Monday morning, returning Thursday, hence I must post this today so it can go on Wednesday's boat, by which even more people will arrive for the Festival. Last Wednesday 78 people came, plus an English couple called Steve and Margie wondering why the island they had been told was the most isolated of the Cyclades was suddenly so popular! Steve had long hair and Margie was wearing shorts; Anafiots made honest mistakes about their respective sexes, and I had to keep insisting that they weren't my friends from Mani. It was marvellous to speak English with them. And of course they goggled to hear Bert Jansch and the Beatles on my tape-recorder.

FIELDNOTES, ANAFI, TUESDAY 6 SEPTEMBER 1966

I hired one of Nikos's donkeys for the journey and Margarita came too. We passed Marinos Ghavallas's house where his son Nikolaos and wife from Mani and three children (youngest named after Marinos) are staying. We were called over and given loukoumi and grapes and coffee. Margarita came to the Monastery to revere the ikon, *na proskinisi. Proskinisis* is translated in my dictionary as 'veneration' but here it seems to mean a particular physical form of revering something; she knelt three times in front of the ikon of the Virgin crossing herself in between each kneeling, then made the sign of cross with a cup of incense in front of each ikon on the ikon-screen. She crossed herself passing each church on the journey and on first catching sight of the monastery. Nikos stayed to collect fuel; thorn bushes for their kitchen hearth and for their courtyard oven. Presumably anyone can take it from Monastery land?

When I arrived at the Monastery, Rembelia the grocer's wife and Yioryia Khalari, Khristina's mother, and the Abbot's unmarried sister, wearing black in mourning for their mother, were making bread: *prosforo* (the Host?) and *artos* for the church services, and ordinary bread for the evening meal on the Eve of the feast. There were three loaves for the liturgy, two had five separate stamps with letters on them in a cross shape, ICXC for Jesus Christ, and ICXC NIKA: Jesus Christ conquers, and one which was more elaborate: it had five squares making up a cross shape. Three squares had ICXC NIKA in them in a vertical row, with one square to the right with nine triangles in it and one square to left with alpha and omega in it. There were five small artos loaves (for a special reason but the women didn't know what it was, presumably someone had vowed them in thanksgiving for some favour from the Panayia) and large ones on another table with the stamp in the middle but concealed with seed. The bread is made from grain from the monastery fields. The meal served to the pilgrims on the Eve of the Feast, *paramoni*, will be meat (eight slaughtered calves and kids), *makaronia* [pasta], wine, cheese, provided by the monastery [I found out later that the pasta was provided by the Takhidhromos, Manolis Arvanitis, as a result of a vow to Panayia Kalamiotissa on behalf of his wife]. I was told that only 'clean' women can touch this holy bread (i.e. they should not be menstruating) to do so would be a sin, *amartia*. [The women were too discreet to tell me that 'clean' also meant not recently having had sexual intercourse.]

Yiannis Ghavallas, the man with four-fingers on one of his hands after a shot-gun accident, and the Abbot were cleaning out the the sanctuary, *ieron*, and taking out the ikons for cleaning; the women and girls don't go in, just reach in and around. The water which washes things from the church mustn't be dropped on the ground, one must wash one's hands over the basin and not shake the water off, as I did, in all directions. The rags and pieces of cotton-wool which have cleaned the ikons are powerful amulets.

Kiria Polidhoru is here from Vayia being looked after by a woman called Eleni; also here are Rembelia, Vasiliki and Zabetta Rinaki, Merkuris's daughter, Yianni four-finger and his daughter Maria, the family of the Takhidhromos, and the Tzakalis family. The monks' cells are being swept out for the pilgrims to sleep in, and as helpers, we are able to give ourselves first pick.

I was told that a woman with a period cannot *proskinisi* the ikon, she can just make the sign of the cross; *dhen kani*, 'it won't do, it wouldn't be appropriate', to do more; but it was not described as 'a sin', like making the holy bread if menstruating. A wreath of plastic flowers, red, white, orange and pink, and white tulle, to decorate the ikon, was sewn by Vasiliki. Again, this shouldn't be done by an unclean woman. Vasiliki told me she was helping because she owed it to the Virgin who effected a cure when she was in hospital with a hurt back.

The women who have been cleaning and are already here, gave their names to the Abbot to write down to mention in prayers, plus money for this favour. [This was a misunderstanding on my part, the names given were not their own but of those they want mentioned in prayer of intercession.] And in the evening there was a service of intercession, *paraklisis*. Hymns were sung by candle-light, there was a small censing and the Abbot read out the names. When he read out the gospel extract about the meeeting of the Virgin Mary and Elizabeth the mother of John the Baptist, several women and girls knelt round his feet, Kiria Polidhoru holding a candle for him to read by. I noticed that the ikons are censed just as if they were members of the congregation. Ilias Tzakalis is running a café in the *kella* of Apollo's temple (presumably on behalf of his sister-in-law Adhriana?), Kiriakos has a make-shift café by the refectory (do they rent the venues from the Monastery?).

FIELDNOTES, ANAFI, WEDNESDAY 7 SEPTEMBER 1966

Up at 5am to go to the Upper Monastery on Mount Kalamos; up the hillside among the prickly bushes. The track is good and built up with stones. Ruined houses but no sign of a Venetian citadel (the Gibitroli). The old monastery church is cracked by the Santorini tremor of 1956 and full of powdery thick dust. Zabetta Rinaki brought candles and incense, and lit a fire in the middle of the floor over which she crouched, sprinkling incense. A cave was pointed out to me near the summit where a holy hermit is said to have lived.

From up there we saw the steamer arrive at the harbour of Ayios Nikolaos; there is a clear view from the Upper Monastery all along the south coast of the island. The village at a distance of about five miles looked like icing sugar on top of a bun. There were cisterns of rain-water at the Upper Monastery, but no buckets to reach it with. On our return, the first arrivals from the village and the steamer were going into the church and then to find rooms. A few like Rembelia and the teacher and Stella had rooms with keys. The Takhidhromos brought boxes of sweets and biscuits to sell.

The slaughtered animals were being cleaned, the innards washed and cooked up for lunch, the hides hung out to dry. Yianni four-finger appeared to be the expert at chopping up the carcases. [He also acted as butcher in 1973.]

About 5:30pm the bell rang for the *esperino*. Long candles were tied to candle-holders, white ones from weddings and some new ones. Kiria Polidhoru was looking after the candles. The ikons and the congregation were censed, the censer is decorated with bells. Tzakalis brought in a round loaf, took it to the left door of the ikon screen; later all the *artos* was piled on a table with a three branched candlestick. The bread was censed and kissed by the Abbot, then taken into the sanctuary and cut up, put in cloth-lined basket and distributed. At the end of the service the Abbot wished everyone *khronia polla*.

The women changed out of their good clothes and began cooking *makaronia*, the meat was put in wooden troughs. There were three sittings; at the first one and at the top table were the two priests and women I recognised as the godmothers at Kiria Margarita's baby's christening. [They must have been important women from the Anafiot migrant community in Athens. My guess is that they were on the organising committee of Saint Simeon, the Anafiot chapel in Anafiotika]. Yianni four-finger and Rembelia's father, Mattheos Nikolis 'the cat', served the *makaronia* and the meat. Two old women washed up.

Afterwards many people stayed up all night drinking in the two cafés. The young people went and danced to a battery record player outside the monastery walls. There was a service during the second sitting, probably another *paraklisis*. Lambros the barber, some old women, and several old men 'incubated' in the church.

FIELDNOTES, ANAFI, THURSDAY 8 SEPTEMBER 1966, YENESIS TIS THEOTOKU

The liturgy to celebrate the Birth of the Virgin, *Yenesis tis Theotoku*, began at 6:30am. Most people came before the second bell, at which point the candelabra were lit. There were about eighty people in church. After the service, all the ikons and the altar instruments were taken three times anti-clockwise round the church, Yiannis four-finger and his son Vinzenzos carried the ikon of Panayia Kalamiotissa in the procession. [They carried it together again in 1973.] Prayers were said outside, then people went inside for communion and to get holy oil for the ill and to perform *proskinesis* in front of the ikon. Almost immediately people began leaving. A Santorini fishing caïque, with Antonis's dinghy tied on, and later Vinzenzos' boat, were ferrying at 10 drachmas a time. Everyone wished each other *khronia polla ke tu khronu*, many years, and may we all be here again next year.

Steve and Margie, the English tourists previously mentioned, came to the Monastery with the main body of visitors on the Eve of the Feast, and slept outside the Monastery walls. The reaction of both islanders and migrants to their long hair and 'hippy' clothes, was continuous questioning of me about their sex: were they both male, because of the trousers, or both female, because of the long hair? It seemed that they constituted a threat to Greek? or Anafiot? ideas of male and female.

I had assumed that everyone came to the Monastery 'for the Panayia', but the village secretary's sister's son (a migrant) said he was really 'only there for partridge shooting'. Several people had come over from Santorini, I was told, but not the Bishop.

LETTER 32, ANAFI, THURSDAY 10 NOVEMBER 1966

On Tuesday 8 November it was the Feast of the Taxiarchs (Archangels) and the nameday for all Michaels. So I had a jolly time in the evening going first to the policeman's house and then to the Village President to wish them khronia polla*. Their poor wives had to serve all the wellwishers with candied fruits, sweet cakes and banana liqueur or ouzo, and the Michael in question had to sit and be toasted and wished to reach 100. Now approaching are the name days for Maria (Nov 21) Catherine (25) Andrew (30) and Nicholas (Dec 6) so I should be well sweeted and liqueured.*

FIELDNOTES, ANAFI, FRIDAY 2 DECEMBER 1966

Woken by a bell tolling. Three slow strokes, then many. Through the party wall, I could hear Eleftheria weeping next door. I found out that her brother

Petros Allafuzos, whom I'd met in the summer, had died in Athens. I went in to 'cry' with her and she told me that she had heard the news last night and also wept, i.e. mourned, then. She has only been out of black for her father for a few months and ought to wear it again now for two years. She and her husband went out to the fields as usual today. Zabetta Ludharu, Nikos postman's wife, said that Eleftheria's husband's relations had been with her to mourn. [In other words, people related by marriage are part of the circle of those affected by a death.]

A very still day. Cold in the evening. Vasiliki was sitting in the Ludharus' kitchen when I paid a visit, telling a dream of a boat sailing in the street which she says foretold Petros Allafuzos's death. Zabetta Ludharu used some dough from the last time she made bread (*prozimi*), mixed it with flour and water and then made the sign of the cross in it, and covered it to keep warm. She said that sometimes 'the coat of an angry man' put over the dough will help it to rise quicker. She will make bread tomorrow. The Abbot was at the proedhros's house. The proedhros was eating fish but Maria, his wife, said she was fasting (there is a sort of mini-Lent leading up to Christmas).

FIELDNOTES, ANAFI, FRIDAY 30 DECEMBER 1966

In the evening, in the Dhamighos café, the agrofilakas brought in a blue painted wooden box about one foot square, addressed to the monastery of Michael the Archangel at Simi [an island in the eastern Aegean]. The islanders say such a box would probably contain oil, incense, candles, money for *mnimosina*. It will be thrown back into the sea to be taken on by the current. There is a monk at Simi who goes round the beaches to find such offerings. This has happened at least once before and they wrote on the side of the box that it had been washed up on Anafi and an acknowledgement was sent from the Monastery on Simi. It was argued that with the wind from south, *siroko*, the box wouldn't go in the right direction; response: the saint would look after it. No one would open it as it was protected by Saint Michael. Simi is a very important place of pilgrimage. The Takhidhromos's daughter was baptised at Simi (because her parents had made a vow?) and Nikos Ludharos went on pilgrimage there.

FIELDNOTES, ANAFI, SUNDAY 1 JANUARY 1967

About 40 to 50 men and countless women and children in church. Everyone seemed to be wearing new or best clothes. The Doxology was said after the service; some people were already outside. Many women took household ikons (which they had put in the church last night) home with them to 'first foot'. The Ludharos family's ikon had been put overnight in the Kimisi church. I went to eat *lukumadhes* with them (batter balls dipped in honey and cinnamon and sesame) and to cut the *vasilopitta* (St Basil's Day cake) which had lemon and orange grated into it. The first slice cut was for Christ, the second for the Virgin, the third for the *spiti* (house, i.e. family), then each person chooses a slice; whichever slice has the one coin baked into the cake gets good luck for the year.

FIELDNOTES, ANAFI, THURSDAY 5 JANUARY 1967

Today is called the festival of light, *ta fota*. I went to church when the second bell rang; there were about eight old men and 14 women. Lots of children all holding plastic mugs and cups. At the end of the service the Abbot 'baptised' the cross, with the sprig of basil tied to it in a copper samovar-like thing on a small table in the centre of the church [a portable font; in other parts of Greece, this service takes place by the sea, into which the cross is thrown, and young men dive in to retrieve it]. Then everyone in the church came to him to be sprinkled with the water which was shaken off the basil, to kiss the cross and the priest's hand. As the service ended, all the children and adults rushed forward to take the *ayiasmo* from the container, dunking their tumblers and jugs in the water.

A few minutes later (after a cigarette and a conversation about Greece's low educational standard) the Abbot, together with Ariadhni's son, and Manolis Ludharos, Nikos the postman's son, went round the houses to bless them with the holy water. He went first to the Post Office, then to Kiria Polidhoru's, then Rembelia's, then down past Margarita Khalari's to Kiriakos's café, then back to the Astinomia (police station) where he had coffee, then Vinzenzos's... Everyone slipped money into the holy water container.

FIELDNOTES, ANAFI, FRIDAY 6 JANUARY 1967

I was told that this celebration is called *olo fota*, all lights, in comparison with yesterday's which is called just 'lights'. I'm not sure what the difference is. There were about 35 men, 40–45 women in church. Water in the font was blessed with three crosses of the Abbot's hand.The altar cross and a sprig of basil were immersed three times, each time proceded by a cross-shaped movement. Last year's *ayiasmo* was poured in from a bottle, and new water taken out to refill it at the end. Very sick people are given this as communion and one can only drink it fasting as it is like communion. The *ayiasmo* has to be sprinkled in buildings the same day it is blessed to be effective. Vasiliki could not go to her family's properties (I presume she was menstruating), hence her father (Rinakis), her sister Elizabeth, and her mother went with *ayiasmo* to various holdings. Adhriana sent some to her sister, Marinos Ghavallas' wife, by a workman. More water can be added to the ayiasmo and takes on its qualities.

Merkuris came up to the village with fish about 2:30pm and Manolis brought the Simi box back; it had been washed up again and burst open.

FIELDNOTES, ANAFI, SATURDAY 7 JANUARY 1967, AYIOS YIANNIS PRODROMOS
The St John the Baptist's service was held in the Kimisi church. Yiannis Dhamighos the café proprietor and Nikos the astinomos were chanters. About 30 men, 40 women (fewer than yesterday). When the line of men and women went to put offerings behind the left side door, one woman gestured upwards and Pananos stood on a chair and lit the lamps above the ikons. People wished each other *khronia polla* and greeted them for their brothers, fiancés, fathers, called John.

I was asked to take more photographs. After lunch Anna the aghrofilakas's daughter and Efthimia, Nikos postman's daughter, came to my room and sang Christmas songs for me to tape. Then I went back with Irini to the aghrofilakas's house to wish him *khronia polla* on his name day. His wife, the youngest child of Birbilissa, wanted me to photograph them. She said she had been 'stolen' (that is, she eloped, and her parents could therefore refuse to give her a dowry. Was this a way of avoiding my questions about dowry and property?). Her sister is married to 'Foksakis' who runs a restaurant in Athens, he is Petros Ludharos, father of Rita who wore the bikini. I went on to greet Patiniotis, another Yiannis; other callers included the proedhros and his wife, Vasiliki, her father Rinakis, and Pliti, Rembelia's sister.

Yiannis Dhamighos said he knows how to cure the evil eye, but he says a sufferer can't find out who did it to them. In other words, you know if you've been 'eyed' but there are no procedures for identifying the 'Eyer', although people have their suspicions. When his son was born, he went and said spells against the evil eye over him immediately (they only have the one child).

This story was told à propos the Simi box: a man from Crete was in danger at sea near Anafi and called out: St Anthony save me and I will give you whatever you need. Then he saw that the chapel on Anafi needed a door (another version says that the saint gave him the dimensions in a dream) so he made a door when he got back to Crete, threw it in the water with a northerly wind, and it was washed up just below St Anthony's.

PERSONAL DIARY, ANAFI, MONDAY 16 & TUESDAY 17 JANUARY 1967
Yiannis Sirighos and I, together with Nikos Khalaris, whose donkey I had hired to take me to the chapel of Ayios Antonios, left the village at 10am on the Eve of the Feast, passing Khristina Kollida gathering wild greens, khorta, and Eleftheria shepherding. It was so cold and windy on that north-east coast path, that I got off the donkey, as my legs were numb with cold, and ran along between the

stones and low prickly bushes, waving my arms, jumping and singing, my cheeks burning and my blood bubbling. Near Ayios Antonios we met Eleni Leptaki and her son gathering khorta on their way back from sweeping out the chapel and I went back with them to their land-holding. We walked by the side of the fields in the soft soil near the sparse low green shoots on the shelf-like terraces. Holdings in the area belong to Barba Konstantin and to his brother Yiannis Sighallas, also Yiannis Sirighos himself; he said it was ex-Monastery land, probably from the time when Ayios Antonios was a monastery, redistributed by law to those men classified as landless, aktimonon; *if so, his name should be in the register.*

Late afternoon, at the chapel of Ayios Antonios: Nikos the schoolteacher was roasting two small birds, tsikla, *over a fire in the angle of the path wall and the chapel wall. He said St Anthony had helped him more than any other saint, hence his devotion to him. Also there were Stella, Anna Sirighu, daughter of the young widow (Yianni Sirighos's niece), Tzortzis 'broadbean' (husband of Yioryia, and father of Khristina) and his son Aryirios. Later, Kalliopi arrived, the wife of Barba Konstantin the shepherd, whose daughter was killed on Mount Vigla. The craggy rocks above were very spiky, the chapel's rounded vaults like an old pebble, the whiteness contrasting with the blue foam-flecked sea behind it and the outlines of Amorgos and Astipalia in the distance. Difficult to imagine that it was here that I experienced a solar eclipse last May, when I visited the chapel with Thetis during my first week on the island.*

Mikhalis and Nikos the two policemen were in hunting gear, the Abbot had a slightly fluffy three-quarter jacket over his cassock, like a worn teddy-bear. Yiannis Sirighos had brought yellow satin curtains for the door of the ikon-screen. Eleni had swept out the chapel and put narcissi on the candle stands. I had a candle and some incense which Adhriana had given me to bring for the saint. After the service, we shared a feast of cold stuffed vine leaves, fried fish, and underdone hardboiled eggs. My own bottle of wine was drunk but not praised [it had been made by Thanasis Vafiadhis]. Then another service took place, one of intercession I think, both for the living and the dead, for Stella called out the name of her dead brother. When we went out in separate groups to pee, the wind blew with an aftertaste of snow round our bared bottoms. While we settled down to sleep in the chapel, the Abbot told legends about Saint Anthony. The floor was very hard and I got bad hay-fever from the sacks of donkey fodder some people were sleeping on.

A very early rising and all the uncomfortableness of no washing and no food. I felt so faint and empty during the beginning of the service that I pretended to cough and went out into the freezing air where dawn had come. A group of about fifteen people arrived from the village. The wind was very strong and cold, the sea immediately below was churned and foaming; there were pink clouds. All during the service more groups arrived from the village, reproved by the Abbot for talking in church. Then there was a distribution of sweets and drinks. Yiannis Sirighos gave out lukumia, Aryirios had banana liqueur, his father more loukoumi; the Abbot was grumbling away "God forgive him' and another loukoumi' and he shouted at Aryirios and others for talking. Another communal meal, inside the church, with a wearied jollity and a rather forced and belligerent drunkenness. Then people dispersed.

Once again I returned to Eleni's house with Yianni to wait for Nikos and the donkeys. While there I read aloud from the beginning of St John's Gospel. When I reached the phrase 'and the light shineth in darkness' (skotia) Yianni asked 'where exactly is "Skotia" (i.e. Scotland)?' The Light of God shining only in Scotland. How the Calvinists would approve.

On the way back to the village we passed a field-cottage where they were dancing inside. I saw Nikos the astinomos in his shirtsleeves dancing, leaping up and slapping the sides of his legs. The wind seemed to take all my clothes off and pared away the skin until I felt colder than a skeleton from the Ice Age. We passed a group of young men lying singing among the scrub with their empty plastic wine bottles.

Back in the village, frozen from the waist down, I heard the tsabuna *(goatskin bag-pipes) and drum; those who had stayed in the village went out to greet returning pilgrims and brought them back with songs and more wine. I was told that Antonios Ghavallas meraklis had got so drunk he fell over the wall by the police station, a drop of about ten feet, but was unharmed. I got into bed with two hot waterbottles to warm up. Name-day visits were being paid; Margarita and Nikos the donkeyman were calling on Pliti (whose husband, Antonis the fisherman, wasn't there). They said that they had to return visits made on Nikos's name day (6 December).*

Personal Diary, Anafi, Tuesday 17 January 1967

At about 10:30 pm Rembelia and her sister Pliti (Antonis the fisherman's wife) came for me to take me to a name-day party. I felt hemmed in by hospitality (or is it not knowing the right formulae and ways of escaping when I want?) having been pushed from the men's to the women's end of the room furthest from the door. I was really bothered by the drunken horse-play and laughter. I physically loathed it and felt that I had no real sympathy or understanding for the people there. Perhaps on an intellectual level I could see what this sort of party, and loss of constraint, means to the islanders, but as a person I hated it. And now I feel rather ashamed.

Fieldnotes, Anafi, Saturday 25 February 1967

Shopped at Patiniotis' grocery; the news there is that Barba Tassos (Ariadhni Nikolis's mother's brother, Anastasios Ghavallas) is ill and cannot recognise anybody. Later, I went to see Marulidhi, Manolis the fisherman's wife, and she told me that Barba Tassos had died. I hadn't heard the bell. Women visitors agreed that it was sad Barba Tassos had no child to be with him at death, and no one to really mourn for him. They said tomorrow after church people would go to the house to see him in the coffin and then take him to the church, then to the cemetery. After the burial, further visits to the home. No-one seemed upset about his death, everyone agreed he'd had his life and then went on to discuss his money and will.

Fieldnotes, Anafi, Sunday 26 February 1967

A beautiful sunny day, but with occasional chilly wind. Second bell at 8:45am; about 20 men in church, 30 women. Apostoli, younger son of Niko postman, and another baby had communion. The communion spoon dropped on the floor and the Abbot wiped up the drips with his hand, then Lambros mopped up with a cloth; no special sense that the Blood of Christ had to be treated in a reverent manner. Neither Ariadhni (niece, and closest relative of Barba Tassos) nor Yiorghos (her husband) was there.

I asked Efthimia what would happen; she said the funeral would be in the afternoon. I went into Kiriakos's café which was very full, some people sitting outside. Maria said 'Broadbean' had made the coffin. Yiorghos Nikolis came and sat outside, he seemed to be shuttling backwards and forwards between his house and Barba Tassos's. Kiria Polidhoru passed with two candles and a bunch of grasses (?) to see the corpse. Maria said Tassos had his own tomb (*tafos*, but I thought she meant vault rather than grave) ready, built three years ago by Dhamighos (Yiannis, I presume).

I went up again to the Kiriakos cafenion at about 3pm, there were a lot of men sitting on the low walls outside, talking and enjoying the sunshine. Barba Tassos had been taken care of by his sister's daughter Ariadhni Nikolis, and her husband Yiorghos was sitting among the men saying he still hadn't had the official permission for the funeral, and was waiting for the police to come back from lunch. As everything was ready, he went off to look for them. His little daughter went by to get something from the grocer's for the *kolliva* [a mixture of boiled wheat, pomegranate seeds and dried grapes]. It seems that the burial must take place within twenty-four hours of the death [presumably in places without morgues and refrigeration].

At about 3:30pm, the Abbot and a group of small boys holding lanterns and other church ornaments went down the village street to Barba Tassos's room. All the men followed, taking their caps off as they approached the doorway, some went inside and others stood outside with women and children. I heard the jingling of the censer, then the Abbot came out, followed by two women with purple-draped candles and a man with a coffin lid which

Figure 10   The funeral of Barba Tassos

had been leaning up against the wall outside with initials in white ribbon either side of a cross. After the lid came the coffin with Barba Tassos's corpse in full view. His hands were tied together with black material, and his trousers laid on top of his legs. The jacket had been put on him. He held an ikon and there were purple stocks inside the coffin, on top of the white cloth lining it. There was a pillow, too, which was buried with him. A great crowd followed, the cafenions were shut.

There was a nasty moment outside the church when the coffin got stuck in the gateway. Once inside the church, it was then put on two chairs, and white candles, purple-draped, placed at head and foot. Mattheos 'the cat' (a distant relative of Barba Tassos but quite how I'm not sure) was holding a tray with lots of long candles, these were given out to the men in church [later I learnt that candles are given to non-related men; relatives are assumed to be praying for the dead person in any case]. Yiannis Dhamighos and the astinomos were chanters. Lots of chanting, then the Abbot walked around the coffin censing the body, then turned and censed the congregation. At the end, people kissed the church cross which had been laid on the body, and the corpse's forehead (or the pillow he was lying on). Yiorghos Nikolis, Vinzenzos, Patiniotis, and someone else I couldn't see were coffin bearers. The procession moved out of the village towards the graveyard. Many women commented how quick the service had been (only twenty minutes) and that the reason was because he had no children to mourn him, no godchildren, no close relations. Ariadhni had been the only one crying; she, Lemonia (married to Yiorghos Nikolis' brother), and another old widow (probably Ariadhni's mother, Irini Ghavalla, and therefore Tassos's sister?) were by the coffin.

Lots of women had brought oil with them to the cemetery to light the oil lamps on relatives' graves. We stood by the white-domed sepulchre that had been prepared three years ago, an old lady (Yiorghos Nikolis's mother) took the jacket and trousers off the body, a man climbed inside the sepulchre and after a censing and a few prayers, the coffin was put in, and the lid fixed on afterwards. The Abbot was asked by various women to cense graves, which he did after censing the vault of his own parents. I saw one woman kissing the photograph on the cross on the grave of her mother and whisper into the headstone. Meanwhile the new grave was closed and the top-stone fastened down with a mixture of soil and water. Outside the graveyard Yiannis Sirighos was giving out loukoumi, Mattheos Nikolis was handing out small change, and someone else had a flask of menta liqueur and one small glass. Yiannula Nikoli, daughter of Kostas and Katina, who was carrying my jacket while I took photographs, said that before I went home I should go into an animal pen, *mandra*, to wipe my shoes in the manure and shake out my clothes so that

I wouldn't bring death into the house. Men I told this to said it was women's stories, and Rembelia said it was rubbish, *kolokithia*.

We walked away from the cemetery, everyone dispersed but a few went into Barba Tassos's room where Ariadhni and a few old women were sitting. They were wished 'may you live to remember him' and 'God forgive him'. Kalliopi, the old lady with the curtained bed, commented that he must have had a good soul as he had died with so little trouble and it was such a beautiful day for the funeral (with the implication that appearances had been very much to the contrary). There were no tears. Ariadhni was asked if the kolliva was ready. When the Abbot had gone by, she took a basket, and with an escort of children, some holding candles, went to the church for it to be blessed. It will be shared out tomorrow morning; more will be made in nine days, forty days, three months, one year and at three years when he is exhumed and reburied. Rembelia said that the minimum amount of kolliva was nine wheat seeds 'for the soul', necessary to absolve the sins.

The talk turned to Sunday's Carnival which marks the beginning of Lent, when, Patiniotis assured me, anything could be said. For example, he said, you could say that men had beards on their chins but women had beards under their arms and between their legs, and no-one would take offence (or was he saying this to see if I would be shocked?). It was a 'free day', *eleftheri mera*, a day of freedom from ordinary constraints.

FIELDNOTES, ANAFI, SUNDAY 26 FEBRUARY 1967

Urania, Flora, deaf Kalliopi, and Anna came to my room wearing lovely old island clothes, heavy damasks and silk, with their faces hidden by views or masks. On other nights I have heard running feet and giggles in the street outside. There is a lot of activity when there is a full moon.

LETTER 54, ANAFI, SUNDAY 5 MARCH 1967

Windy but sunny now, it rained suddenly mid-morning after church. It is a week after the death of Barba Tassos and his nine day's kolliva was blessed in church and shared out after the service. The boiled wheat and pomegranate seed mixture was decorated with sugar and silver baubles and a candle was stuck into the middle of it. The table was flanked by the purple-draped candle-sticks.

Yesterday in the late afternoon I went out to the cemetery to take some photos for the proedhros. He wants to send them to the Nomarch on Naxos to show the unkempt condition of the graveyard, to get some money to tidy it up. I was taking the photos when I saw Yianni the whitewasher hurrying across the hillside toward me and I thought 'Oh dear, he's come to tell me it's unlucky or disrespectful or something', particularly as I had just jumped down from on top of one of the family vaults from which I wanted to get a better angle. He told me he was coming, as on every Saturday, to light the oil-lamps at the head of the graves, so he is a kind of sexton. So I learnt something from my trip out there. Did I tell you that in Greece, St Michael is the Angel of Death? On his feast day he writes down the names of all those he is going to smite down in the coming year with his sword.

LETTER 56, ANAFI, TUESDAY 21 MARCH 1967

The Proedhros' wife said that as she was observing the Lenten fast I was to come every night to take a share of the milk brought in every day by their workman Nikolaos from Ayio Yianni, so I am feasting on crème caramels and enjoying hot milk with my diminishing supply of cornflakes.

On Sunday afternoon a week ago, the last day of the Apokreas carnival, men were sitting about outside the cafenions waiting for something to happen; small girls were wandering up and down dressed up in long skirts made of curtains or old dresses, and with lipstick smeared on their cheeks and mouths. Suddenly there was a shriek and two men came running out of the grocer's house. One was wearing a long pink dress with white bloomers underneath and his hairy legs in plastic slippers, a rubber mask on his face, kerchief on his head, and carrying a chamber pot with some rice-pudding in it. The other (Patiniotis the grocer) was wearing a tall hat, a mask of sunglasses and an old stocking, a pajama jacket, and a sort of apron over old trousers. Under this apron he had tied a string above his knees, looped round a painted stick, which, when he flexed his knees outwards, stood up and erected like a penis. He kept flicking up the apron and flexing his knees at giggling girls and women who pretended to be horrified, and chasing them with the pot of rizogalo. Followed by children and various villagers, they made a tour of the whole village, going into different houses and chasing people. They ended up in the square while an evening service was going on in the church. There was a great deal of chasing about and finally Patiniotis threw the pot up into the air and as it shattered he capered out of the square.

In the evening I was asked to a party at Manolis the fisherman's, I took my tape recorder and played the tapes with Barba Kosta's bagpipes, and recorded some Lenten songs. We had roast goat and lots of wine, men were sitting on the sofa chatting, children were sent to different houses to invite people, and women were cutting up cabbage for salad and heating up plates of potatoes, meat and sausage, and preparing tit-bits of sardines and cheese. Vasiliki brought her record-player, pik-ap, and women began to dance, with little girls and one nimble footed boy. Eventually some of the men got kefi, got in the mood, the spirit; and there was some tremendous clod-hopping dancing in their heavy working boots. One of them danced as if he had terrible corns or his knees were going to give way. One of the women kept trying to dance and her baby daughter screamed in hysterics every time she was put down. The hostess disappeared from time to time to reappear with fresh plates of fried sausage and flagons of wine. I danced quite a lot too and found it was a very enjoyable evening, especially as I was able to work out who was there and why (wife's brother and his wife, neighbours, wedding-sponsor and wife and daughter, cousin, etc.).

The deaf girl, Kalliopi, was encouraged to put on a mask and make fun of one of the young men. He had either been jilted or been refused, because she made garlanding and ring-wearing gestures. He was a bit embarrassed, but not very, and everyone laughed. Children fell asleep on the floor and over the side of the sofa and people got jollier and jollier and clinked glasses and shouted healths to each other. A crowd of young lads filled the doorway with wide eyes and open mouths, and called out 'It's quiet' whenever there was a delay in putting on a record. The party finished about 2am, and at 6am I was awakened by the ending of another party at the aghrofilakas's house as they rolled down the street to the sound of the clarinet.

The Monday was terribly warm and sunny and a few people went down to the beach for the traditional outing on Clean Monday, but a stiff breeze prevented any small boats going out to the islets. It was the first day of the Lenten fast and no meat should be eaten but that evening, I saw people eating up their roasts and frying sausages.

LETTER 63, ANAFI, SUNDAY 16 APRIL 1967

Today was again sunny and gloriously warm, after two fiercely windy days with dust blowing through the cracks in the window panes and the sea frothing around the islets and into the harbour. This morning the 40-day kolliva was distributed for Barba Tassos. The table in the church was flanked by white candles draped in purple, the mound of kolliva was covered in sugar and decorated with sugared almonds, silver balls, a cross and initials. The dead man's niece came and stood by it at the end of the service, then everyone surged outside for the chocolates, and the liqueur, with handerkerchiefs and scarves to fill with kolliva. During the service men are given candles to hold, these in some way help the soul, lighten or purge it, or act as a symbol of prayer, but even the Abbot wasn't very sure. These things may not have an explicit meaning, or be understood in the detail of their significance by the islanders and yet they are essential – but I suppose Irish peasants don't fully understand the Mass, or Bowdon villagers the constraints and unwritten rules underlying the subtleties of social stratification there. I'm trying to work out a way of justifying my interpretation I suppose, and it's rather frustrating to find that no-one here has very much idea what the ritual side is all about, except that it is intrinsic.

Fieldnotes, Anafi, Thursday 20 April 1967

Stella said that the feast on the Friday after Easter, the zoödhokos piyi, meaning the life-giving spring, a festival connected with the Panayia, is celebrated at the Monastery as this is the festival it is really dedicated to. Only since the earthquake [i.e. since 1956] has the festival of the Birth of the Virgin been celebrated in the church at the foot of Mt Kalamos. [This does not seem to be correct, as historical sources record that the Upper Monastery was struck by lightning in the 1890s and that as a consequence, the ikon of Panayia Kalamiotissa was brought down to the Lower Monastery. I was told by village women that the lightning bolt to the Upper Monastery was a direct punishment from the Panayia on the day of the festival; the Abbot at the time was killed by it for blaspheming, and other wrong doers were also killed. Scott O'Connor reports the same story.] So it is the top church which is really the original Kalamiotissa one and monastery, and not the one at the bottom.

Letter 66, Anafi, Saturday 6 May 1967

I got back last night from a two-day trip to the monastery for the feast of the Life-giving Spring, a feast of the Virgin. The Abbot didn't know its significance, but the schoolmaster looked it up and it has something to do with a church near Constantinople where the Emperor Justinian was cured, and which later, on the fall of the City to the Turks in 1453, had a spring where the half-fried fish one of the monks had been cooking, swam around! I went with the teacher and his wife Stella, on Thursday morning; it was misty and windy but good for walking, then it cleared but always with a slight breeze, very pleasant. When we reached the Proedhros's garden at Ayio Yianni we stopped for a picnic under the shady pine trees with the scent of lemon flowers all around.

At the monastery the Abbot had been attending to his bees and was putting away his white outfit, with his long plait straggling down his back. Soon Mikhalis the policeman and his wife and son arrived and later the astinomos. Mikhalis had a bad headache and I was the only one with any aspirins, so he had to thank me, and we established a minimum conversation level again, so the incident about the tape-recorder seems to be healing over.

Nikos and Mikhalis bought two baby kids from the Monastery flock and had them killed for us to eat. Afterwards I learnt that the Abbot should have done this as we were pilgrims. We were allotted camp beds to sleep on. The two shepherds who live out by the monastery with their wives and children came in for the evening service: on our arrival I went to explore the temple ruins and was called over to sit in the chicken run while one of the women, peeling broad beans, brought me a cheese cake and wished me Happy Easter. The prickly pear is beginning to sprout little bright green bristly buds, and red whiskery fruits, and the mountains are dotted with gorse. Next morning after the Liturgy, there were greetings between the pilgrims, those who had overnighted, and those who had come that morning, about twenty people, and then most of them set off to their fields or to the village. We ate up the rest of the meat and then set off again, this time it was hot and sunny and the path seemed to be all uphill. We stopped again at Ayio Yianni, ate, and everyone fell asleep under the trees. So 'in the cool of the evening' we went the rest of the way, getting back to the village about dusk. It was a marvellous break and I also heard gossip that Vasiliki's 'uncles' (her father's brothers or husband-to-be's father's brothers?) don't approve of her and that's why they weren't at the engagement party.

LETTER 69, ANAFI, SUNDAY 28 MAY 1967
Do you remember the blue crate with wax and incense and money that was found in the sea and thrown back again after village contributions? Well, a letter came to tell us that it arrived at the monastery at Simi and they said a Liturgy for all the names, so you and I have been recommended to St Michael along with the Anafiots, so that should ensure our safe meeting in Athens in eight weeks time.

JUNE 1967 REPORT TO SUPERVISOR
The most exciting ideas I'm investigating are those which link the naming system, inheritance and dowry, and the funeral and memorial rites. I know that I have mentioned these things individually in previous letters, now I am sure there is a connecting network between them; understanding each aspect involves an examination of the other two, and the whole construct links past, present and future relationships and ties them to property.

LETTER 72, ANAFI, SUNDAY 18 JUNE 1967
On Friday I spent the morning watching the preparation of kolliva for the evening service on the Eve of Soul Saturday. This service is for the souls of all the recent dead; instead of the memorial services which are linked to the death date of a particular individual, Soul Saturday unites the whole village in a commemoration of their dead. I saw the whole process of cleaning and boiling the wheat, censing it and drying it in the sun, and mixing it with sesame, pomegranate and dried grapes.

At the service the separate plates of kolliva made by each household had been tipped into one basket and each plate's candle put in too (there were about 30) so that when they were lit the whole corner of the church glowed. The Abbot read out the list of names of those commemorated, as he did next morning during the Liturgy, before the kolliva was shared out.

There were about 20 men and 40 women in church this morning, which someone said is good for harvest time. There were bunches of herbs below one of the ikons and these were taken at the end of the service to be hung in fig trees for a good crop. As today is the equivalent of Whit Sunday there was a special reading after the service and we all had to kneel down three times. The village secretary and the president of the cooperative studiously avoided me after church. I went and had a good cry behind the windmill in the square after yet another rebuff this morning. I feel very at the end of my tether and in need of a holiday – anyway, off to Athens on Tuesday, and possibly off to Istanbul on Thursday.

CHAPTER SEVEN

'An island-centred view of Greek history'

From Argonauts to exiles

When I was carrying out fieldwork, I tried very hard to do what I thought an anthropologist should do and study what was going on, to capture the essence of the social system at the time I was there, as well as to find out what were the long-term underlying structural principles which persisted. I attempted to explain what I was doing, and to convince the Anafiots, islanders and migrants alike, that I was not an archaeologist or a folklorist, but interested only in the way people were living on the island at that particular time. However, just as 'cheerfulness was always breaking in' for Boswell's friend Oliver Edwards when he tried to become a philosopher, so the past, and the history of Anafi, kept impinging on what I was doing, and prevented me from staying totally in the present. During my postgraduate training, I had been made aware that for anthropologists working in the Mediterranean area, history was an essential aspect of their work; but I was unsure what history, or whose history, was essential for my work on Anafi.

I became conscious that, for the islanders, trying to turn my attention away from the present and the recent past to the more distant past was a strategy to keep me away from sensitive contemporary issues. My questions about the division of a family's estate, for example, were too close to the kinds of question asked by officals to determine tax liability; my questions about decision-making on the village council required explanations in terms of political rivalry and personal antagonism which were difficult to reveal to an outsider whose silence could not be assured.

The history of Anafi to which I was encouraged to turn, however, was an uncontentious past; mythical Anafi revealed to Jason and the Argonauts by Apollo; classical Anafi with its own coinage and a flourishing cult centre located at the temple of Apollo and Artemis; Venetian Anafi with its noble overlord, pirates, and picturesque peasantry; patriotic Anafi, sending a boatload of men to fight in the War of Independence; post-Independence Anafi, sending its young men to help build King Otto's palace.

There was an area of recent history which continued to impinge on the present, which I was aware was too sensitive to probe: the time in the 1930s when Anafi was used as a place of political exile. I had direct contact with people (particularly my landlord), who had experienced exile; I knew islanders who claimed to have helped members of the exiles' commune, and others who said that they were profoundly antagonistic to the 'godless Communists'. If I was interested at all in the exiles, my focus of interest was the effect of the exiles on the islanders, rather than the experience of the exiles themselves (to which I only turned twenty-five years later). Not only did Anafiots have first hand evidence as witnesses of the consequences of political dissent, they also realized just what those at the centre thought about them and the place where they lived through the use of their island as a place of punishment and exile. For anyone in Athens, Anafi was indeed 'far from God'. I was too naive to understand why Anafiots would not freely answer questions about those times. If I had thought about my own experience, as a six year old Australian 'alien' in Berkeley, California, in the McCarthy Era, hearing my parents talking of the Loyalty Oath, I might have understood a little better.

I can see now that I resisted, without understanding them, attempts to divert my inquiries by urging me to talk to old people about the old days and old ways. I countered by saying that I wasn't a folklorist, and I now feel I missed important opportunities by not exploring what people thought I ought to be told about the past. I suspect, from some experience of such interviews, that I would have collected a fascinating mix of heritage, generalisation and personal experience.

My attempts to find out more about Anafi, both through my own visits to libraries in Athens, and through my father's occasional trips to the British Museum Reading Room, resulted in a mass of diverse materials which I tried to put together in a short historical section in the introductory chapter of my thesis. One examiner criticised this section in the thesis, saying that it offered 'an island-centred view of Greek history'. My response today would be: what else would you expect?

The sources I drew on for this historical account ranged from travellers' tales and maps ('Isolarii', island guides) of the Aegean Islands under Venetian and Turkish rule to nineteenth-century archaeologists' descriptions of the ancient sites and the accounts of travellers interested not only in the sites at Kastelli, the ancient harbour at Katalimatsa, and the Monastery but also in the lives of the islanders. Some of their comments about local conditions helped me to find out more about the island and its economy: for example, a reference to mulberry trees and the raising of silkworms which I mentioned casually resulted in a gift to me of mulberry vinegar and the recollection of a grandmother's vivid description of placing silkworm larvae in her bodice to keep them warm. Once alerted to the now defunct silk-industry on the island, I found on my trips to Athens embroidered silk scarves and towels from Anafi in the Benaki Museum and in the Museum of Folk Art, and later I investigated the collections of Greek embroidery at the Ashmolean Museum in Oxford and at the Fitzwilliam Museum in Cambridge. Reference in another source to the growing of cotton on both Santorini and Anafi led me to ask about this and the suggestion was rejected by islanders as unlikely, but the consequent discussion took me to Patiniotis the grocer, to ask about the tobacco his father was said to have grown, bringing in migrant workers to harvest it (which meant that pre-war islanders had access to an untaxed source of cigarette tobacco). A number of sources mentioned that the island had been plagued by partridges which continually threatened the crops but villagers said that nowadays wild birds were not such a problem. However, with children going to school instead of being able to act as bird-scarers, maybe the plague would return? Local men, as well as visiting migrants, enjoyed going out hunting for birds and rabbits: it seemed that it was the introduction of firearms which had reduced the numbers of partridges.

A nineteenth century Danish account of Anafi in the summer of 1850 mentioned that monks at the Lower Monastery welcomed travellers by offering them cucumbers dipped in honey. I was assured that this refreshment was still extant, using Anafiot honey and the local ridged cucumbers, known as *katsunia*, rather like gerkins. The account concluded with a description of the monks standing in a line and firing rifles in farewell. Why would monks have had such weapons? To shoot wild birds and rabbits, just like other farmers trying to protect their crops and get a 'snack', *meze*, to vary their diet.

Another nineteenth century account I consulted was Bent's *Life among the Insular Greeks* (1885). James Theodore Bent, an English clergyman, visited the Cyclades in the winter of 1880–81. He gives a lively picture of life on Anafi in January 1881, although some of the detail must be based on what he was told rather than what he actually witnessed for himself. 'Their windmills grind their corn, their fields produce a sufficiency of grain, their looms make all their materials for their clothes, their hill slopes produce excellent grapes'. The only export he mentions is *paksimadhi*, a twice-baked bread rather like rusk. He, like other authors, mentions the stories about the red-legged partridges and confirms that when riding to the village from a landing-place on the north side of the island, they stirred up 'coveys of partridges and lots of wild pigeons... at every turn'.

The only island surname Bent mentions is Khalaris, being that of a man Bent calls the 'demarch' and also of 'a deaf, shrivelled-up old man of ninety, who had assisted [the German archaeologist] Ross to dig in 1836, and was prepared to tell us of all the antiquities in the place. [He] insisted on our first visiting his house, which consists of one room, and is furnished with a bed, sofa, chair, table, and endless archaeological trophies scattered around. With pride he pointed out the various objects he had collected – the torso of a statue let in over his door, an inscription let into his well before the house...' On a visit in 1988, when I referred to the possibility that there might be such items in local homes, I was shown a marble tombstone kept in a donkeyshed and told of marble blocks built into the walls of houses which had been heavily whitewashed over to prevent detection and possible interference. A portion of a classical pillar could be seen forming part of a village bell-tower, a long inscription had been recorded on the lintel of a small chapel, and a carved stone provided one of the steps of the main village church. The island's past was built into its present in a perfectly ordinary taken-for-granted manner.

Bent also gives a detailed description of a woman's festival dress which he was told was authentic, but by then (1881) outmoded: 'one of the old Anaphiote costumes ... consisted of a violet silk brocade skirt, green velvet bodice, gold embroidered stomacher, and a short pink satin jacket, edged around the cuffs and down the front with pink fur. The headdress somewhat resembled the *pina* of Siphnos, but here it is called `the circle' (*o kiklos*); it consists of a tall wedge of cotton inside, over which Oriental handerchiefs are gracefully arranged, so that the ends hang down over the shoulders' (Bent 1885, 91).

This description came to mind during the time I was carrying out further research on both the island and the migrants from Anafi; in the autumn of 1987 I was shown the costume which had been designed by a teacher of Greek traditional folkdance for the Anafiot Migrants Association Dance Troupe. For the young women dancers the costume consisted of a green flock-velvet skirt trimmed with white lace, a white blouse and a black velvet waistcoat or bolero jacket. For the male dancers (some of whose parts were danced by young women; the young men were more interested in joining the Association's football team) the costume was a white shirt with coloured neckerchief, dark trousers, and a fringed sash around the waist. Young women with long hair who were dancing the male parts wore woollen caps and tucked their hair up inside.

I am cautious in presenting Bent's description as more 'authentic' than the costume designed a century later. For one thing, elderly island women at the time of my fieldwork (some of whom were old enough to have been babies at the time of Bent's visit) mentioned that their own grandmothers had worn *vrakakia* ('Turkish trousers') and, when bitten by fleas, pulled the trousers up over their heads, disappeared inside, and hunted down the culprits (all this mimed with hearty laughter). If the 'traditional' Anafiot everyday costume for women was of this kind, it is certainly possible that the festival costume consisted of a skirt rather than baggy 'harem' trousers, but there is also a chance that what Bent was shown was a costume brought to Anafi from the mainland.

When it came to twentieth-century accounts of visits to the island, such as O'Connor's *Isles of the Aegean* (1929), Birtles' *Exiles in the Aegean* (1938), and Kininmonth's *Children of Thetis* (1949), many details were recent enough to link up with the memories and experiences of people I knew. In some cases they confirmed and embellished them (as in O'Connor's recounting of the blasphemous pilgrim to Panayia Kalamiotissa's chapel), and in others gave a fascinatingly different account. When I looked at the descriptions of Anafi given in guide-books I doubted that the writers had ever visited the island: one described it as circular, others drew heavily on the historical sources I had been consulting, whose style I recognized.

Anafi and the Greek state

I felt that these anecdotal responses to 'real history' were not appropriate in a scholarly work like a doctoral thesis, and that I needed to find solid and documented facts. Sketching in the mythical and ancient history of Anafi, and its centuries under Venetian and Ottoman rule, every sentence seemed to be qualified by 'possibly' or 'perhaps'. I seemed to be on much surer ground the nearer I came to the present. Systematic information about Anafi appeared after the War of Independence in 1821, and the incorporation of the Cyclades into the state in 1832, after which census data and other kinds of information were asked for by the government, and had to be collected at local and regional levels, impinging not only on the time and energy of local bureaucrats but also on the lives of members of these administrative units. For example, every local community of the Greek state had to keep a register of male children, entering boys at their date of birth so that at eighteen years of age they could be called up for military service. For most Anafiot young men this was their first experience of a wider world and marked their transition to manhood. The local community secretary also had to keep records of, and sometimes compile annual returns on, a whole range of topics including agricultural production. Although I was given access to the village register during my fieldwork, it was twenty years before I was able to take full notes from the annual agricultural statistical returns. Later experience of how the raw data were collected and recorded cause me now to view some of the official statistics with some doubt as to their accuracy. Back then I felt relieved to be able to tabulate population statistics and information about land use so as to back up the rest of my material.

What is certain is that from the mid-nineteenth century onwards Anafiots were migrating from the island and settling in Athens. The area immediately below the Acropolis is known as Anafiotika, and it is here that the first migrants are said to have settled, building ramshackle houses for themselves overnight to evade building restrictions (which were in force so as to allow archaeological excavations) and to take advantage of a law which said that extant dwellings could not be pulled down. Oral tradition gives the names of the first two men to build houses in Anafiotika as Yiorghos Dhamighos, a carpenter, and Markos Sighallas, a mason. And there is some solid evidence for the Anafiot presence in Athens at this time, in the form of a plaque in the chapel of Ayios Simeonos (at the Acropolis end of Mnisikleus Street), giving the date 1847 as the time at which Anafiots placed 'an ikon of Panayia Kalamiotissa' in the chapel. Anafiot migrants from the city and suburbs who are unable to go to the island still come to this chapel to celebrate the festival of their patron saint in early September.

What of the migration of island women? There does not seem to have been a practice, as there was among other Cycladic islanders, of sending girls and young women from Anafiot families to work as domestic servants in Athens, often for no wages but in return for their food and board and a contribution from their employers towards their dowry when they left to get married. It is possible that Zoï Khalari, whom I visited with her sister Kalliopi in October 1966, was in this category, but I think she is much more likely to have been employed in an *au pair* capacity. Some Anafiot girls and young women went to the city to live with and work for relatives, sometimes with godparents, with the hope of an eventual dowry contribution (or even being made heir to property) as a return for their labour. Often the receiving family saw their obligation simply as one of giving a little city polish to a country bumpkin. Exploitation, as well as misunderstanding, was common. In the sixties I knew of only a few cases of young women going to Athens as domestics or nannies; a much more common pattern then was for a young woman to go and housekeep for migrant brothers, or to get a factory job while living under the care and protection of migrant relatives.

Twentieth-century Anafi

An early edition of the Naval Intelligence Handbook summarises conditions on Anafi in the early years of the twentieth century: 'Owing to its isolation and the simplicity of its life, the island is self-supporting to an unusual degree and there are few exports... the islanders' isolation (due to the nature of their coasts) and perhaps the conditions of land tenure (cf. Ios) discourage great activity and the island is not as closely populated nor as productive as it might be' (1919, II, 174). The reference to Ios reads: 'what good land it possesses is mostly in the hands of larger owners and it is not energetically or intensively worked ... lack of personal ownership discourages industry' (1919, II, 136). The large land-owners on Anafi at the time this was written probably included the Monastery of Panayia Kalamiotissa (a foundation which was directly linked to the Patriarch of Constantinople) and the Greek Orthodox Church (unworked Church lands on Anafi were distributed to 'landless' men in 1956; the register was shown to me in early 1967). The later edition of the Handbook adds: 'the islanders have little interest in the sea and do not engage in fishing and trade... There is little trade with other islands or the mainland... and although the inhabitants sometimes migrate to work on the mainland of Greece, Anafi is one of the most primitive and self-contained of the islands' (1945, III, 486). I do not know the Handbook's sources for these assertions; they were certainly of great importance in moulding my own assumptions about economic life on Anafi.

The earliest reference to Anafiot migration to Athens in the twentieth century comes from an account of a visit in the 1920s but the author, Vincent Scott O'Connor, seems (like Bent) to be reporting what he was told rather than what he knows for himself: 'The island population of seven hundred souls is concentrated in the one town; there are more Anaphiotes in Athens than in Anaphi... Over there they live in a quarter of their own under the Acropolis, known as Makri Yianni, and every lad who leaves his island makes for it as another home. They make good masons and builders' (1929, 221–2).

When I began to investigate the island migrants in Athens during my first fieldwork I found that the registered office of the Anafiot Migrants Association was in Makriyianni, an area below the Acropolis, bordering the Plaka and also touching Anafiotika, the area on the lower slopes of the Acropolis, just above the Plaka, where the Anafiots had first settled. The office is still located there; but with a large increase in the Association's membership, they created a cultural centre, *politistiko kendro*, in a sizeable semi-basement room where large gatherings can take place. This centre lies a block or two from Leoforos Vuliagmenis, in the suburbs of Iliupoli and Ayios Dhimitrios, probably best known to travellers who arrive at Athens' Western Airport as the dual carriageway lined with multi-storied shops glittering with light-fittings and chandeliers.

O'Connor's chapter on his visit to Anafi ends with an account of the murder of his host, the proedhros Nikolaos Ghavallas, in November (presumably 1928) 'by a young man of 25; a degenerate; for the sole purpose of robbing him' (1929, 223). Nikolaos and his wife Maria, according to O'Connor, had lived in Egypt for twenty years and kept a bar and coffee-shop in Cairo.

Not only did this contradict the picture of Anafi as a tiny place cut off from the rest of the world, where the inhabitants had little knowledge of anywhere beyond their restricted environs and the occasional journey to Athens, it immediately made me think of the proedros in 1966, Mikhalis Ghavallas, whose family nickname, *khiliadhatos*, I was told then, derived from the fact that his father had made 'thousands' running a café in Egypt. Mikhalis's father was also named Nikolaos, and I wondered why this dramatic story about him had never been mentioned to me. Stella (Mikhalis's daughter) told me later that the man who entertained O'Connor was not her grandfather but his cousin. The young man was a relative who wanted money to finance a court case and, when refused, shot the *proedhros* and tried to hide the body. O'Connor arranged for a marble plaque to be erected in Nikolaos Ghavallas's memory, and this can still be seen, set into the wall of a building on the right of the path up from the harbour near the village school.

Exiles on Anafi

At the time of O'Connor's visit to Anafi in the late twenties there were Communist exiles on the island; these must have been exiled under the regime of Pangalos. He mentions meeting 'the leader of the Communists imprisoned on the island... (who) had been editing a Communist newspaper in Athens... the house in which he lived with a dozen others of the same conviction was next to ours [i.e. the house of Nikolaos Ghavallas, the proedhros, with whom O'Connor was staying]... a very slight change in externals and he might have passed for an undergraduate at Oxford' (1929, 216–17).

O'Connor mentions only the political exiles, but other kinds of people who had offended the law and were classed as 'public nuisances' or even 'public dangers' were also deported to the islands. Sometimes exile was additional to a jail sentence, sometimes an alternative. While the political exiles formed communes and pooled their resources so that they could rent houses, eat in communal dining-rooms, study in the evenings, and produce their own newspapers, the common-law exiles lived much less well. They included animal thieves, bouzouki-players, hashish smokers, drug addicts and drug-dealers. Exile was devised as a punishment for them and a form of protection for society: contact with friends and family who might have brought money, food and clothes to them in prison could only be by post, and the addicts were supposedly kept away from sources of supply in isolation hospital-like conditions. While a few who had been in prison together, or were friends, might join forces to rent a room and arrange for meals to be cooked for them, most slept in stables and outhouses. The addicts who were sent money by their families for rent and food used it to try to bribe locals to get hold of drugs for them. Some turned to drinking methylated spirits. Most of

Figure 11   Two political exiles in the 1930s

the villagers would have nothing to do with them, and, not surprisingly, they were accused of theft and damage which otherwise could not be accounted for. Letters in the Migrants' Association correspondence book show that requests to the Minister of the Interior to remove the exiles, reduce their number, or increase the number of police went unanswered, despite a veiled promise of votes.

It was a clever strategy of the authorities to send those whose offences were political to the same places of exile as these common-law deportees so as to produce an association of the two in the consciousness of the general public. Those in authority hoped that all good citizens would come to realise that political deviancy was as anti-social as drug-addiction or as characteristic of 'low-lifers' as the blues-like music of the bouzouki and baglama, instruments so closely associated with the underworld that simple possession was good grounds for arrest.

A later non-Greek visitor to Anafi was the young Australian Communist journalist, Herbert (Bert) Birtles. Accompanying him was his wife Dora whose knowledge of French proved invaluable. The visit was made early in 1936, when there was a small 'collective' of exiles in the village, the remnant of a larger group most of whom had gone on hunger strike for amnesty in late 1935. The main aim of going to Anafi was for Birtles to collect accounts of the hunger-strike, and to write about the exiles themselves. He hardly mentions the local people, although there is a brief vignette of a conversation between one of the exiles and an old peasant, and an account of the various attitudes of the police, justice of the peace and village secretary to the Birtles' visit.

Later in the year when Bert and Dora had visited the exiles' commune, hundreds more political exiles were sent to Anafi (and to other islands) following the seizure of power by Metaxas on 4 August 1936. I have written elsewhere about the social organisation of the political exiles on Anafi. Here I will simply point out that the effect of successive waves of exiles on the islanders was multi-faceted. Some people, of course, made money out of them: migrants and locals rented them houses, fields, olive trees, garden land, mules, donkeys, sheep and goats. Grocers imported bulk quantities of goods for them and sold on credit. New ideas and techniques were introduced: a flat-bed loom being used by an island woman in the sixties had been built by male exiles and used by the women exiles; the exiles' doctor, Perikles Zikas, attended sick villagers; his attestation as to causes of their deaths, as well as to those of exiles, appears in the Death Register. Some villagers became familiar with new left-wing political ideas which changed their orientation completely; others reacted against Communism and had nothing to do with the exiles.

A few exiles struck up friendships with locals; a very few eventually married women from island families. My landlord, Thanasis Vafiadhis, told me how he saw Margarita Russu from a distance and immediately fell in love with her. She was visiting her father (Iakovos *aspros*) to get his signature for permission for a tonsillectomy which she was about to undergo in Athens. Kiria Adhriana, who ran one of the village cafés, was said to have been married to a man who had been exiled on the island. Another young woman from an island family (the daughter of Granny Marusi Gavalla) married the senior policeman who was drafted in to oversee the exiles.

Occupied Anafi

The island was occupied by an Italian garrison from May 1941 until September 1943. The first to arrive were naval officers, but they were replaced by soldiers and later by 'caribiniere' (police). Islanders in the sixties remembered the men of the garrison as likely to commandeer livestock arbitrarily for their own consumption, but described them as basically good lads, *kala pedhia*. Conditions on the mainland, particularly in the cities, worsened in the autumn and winter of 1941 and early 1942. Poor harvests in 1941 (partly as a result of the absence of able-bodied men in the army), distribution difficulties, commandeering by the occupying forces, and a blockade of Piraeus by the British, all combined to produce famine (Mazower 1993, Chapter 3). Some people say that Anafiot migrants began to return from Athens, and to cultivate holdings which they had earlier abandoned or reclaimed them from tenants, and, according to some, the island took on a new lease of life with this increase in population. If this is the case, how did the migrants get back to the island from Athens? Surely it was difficult to find steamers or caïques to transport them as diesel fuel was hard to obtain? Maybe only a few of the wealthier migrants were able to leave the city. Or were my informants transposing the events of the Civil War back several years? At this point, or a few years later, urban-based ideas and ways of thinking and behaving were introduced to the island in a more powerful and persuasive form than previously, because migrants stayed for long periods of time rather than for a summer visit. I was told that many island customs and celebrations were revivified by returned migrants' involvement and at their instigation. Marriages took place between the sons and daughters of island and migrant families. Stella Ghavalla, younger daughter of the man who was proedhros at the time of my fieldwork, had first met the man who was to become her husband, Nikos Ladhikos (later the village schoolteacher), when his family came to the island during the Occupation.

Members of the exile commune on Anafi began to experience shortage of food and illnesses linked to malnutrition. Shortage of imported food is understandable because of mainland conditions and the Piraeus blockade. The exiles were also not receiving their state allowances, *epidhoma*, and had no cash in hand; receipt of letters and parcels had also been forbidden. In addition, the exiles were told by the Italian garrison that they would soon be transferred to the mainland and would therefore have to give up their land renting arrangements and dispose of their stock-pile of provisions. They made all the necessary arrangements and then were not transferred to the mainland after all. They could not renegotiate their land leases nor buy any more provisions as their government allowances had been stopped. Eventually they were reduced to eating wild greens, *khorta*, and snails, and several members of the commune died of illnesses brought on by their weakened conditions (one Death Register entry as to cause of death reads 'toxic gastritis'). The descriptions of the exiles' attempts to gather food for themselves and their sick companions make hard reading. How much the situation resulted from deliberate strategy and how much from the unfortunate coincidence of circumstances is unclear. No sources mention that returned migrants taking back their land to cultivate for themselves may have been a factor which exacerbated conditions but I think it may have played a part.

If these were the conditions for the exiles, what was the state of affairs for the islanders? Certainly, some regular exports were halted because of shortages on other islands and the mainland; diesel for boat engines was in short supply so fishing was mainly done by hook and line or from row-boats and sail-boats. My guess is that paraffin for lamps and heaters was also being conserved, but beeswax candles could be used for lighting, and also oil-lamps. Fuel was always a problem, but brushwood, still being used in the sixties alongside bottled gas, could be brought in for kitchen and oven fires from hillslopes and mountainsides; imported coal for the village forges (primarily engaged in making and repairing plough-shares and cistern covers) could be replaced by charcoal. Villagers kept hens and rabbits, and there were thousands of sheep and goats as a source of milk and cheese in season, and of meat. Resident islanders and returned migrants were probably able to provide themselves with a reasonable and seasonally variable diet under such conditions. But without extraordinary communal goodwill, it was not possible to feed another two hundred people on existing resources and so the exiles gradually starved.

There were instances of individual kindnesses, by both villagers and the Italian garrison, in giving food to those with whom particular ties had been formed, and also of extraordinary rigidity on the part of the exiles' commune to the exigencies of the situation (two men who were out collecting wild greens were expelled from the commune for taking and eating vegetables from an islander's garden plot). However, it was not only exiles who suffered: there are two Death Register entries in March 1942 for island men (one a 73 year old, the other aged 27) which give the cause of death as 'privations and hunger' in the first case, and 'privations' in the second. The only other death in which 'starvation' is given as a cause occurred late in 1944 (a 29 year old woman).

All this raises the general question of the degree to which Anafi could ever have had a self-sufficient economy, even in the days when the cult of Apollo was bringing wealthy pilgrims to the island (in other words, bringing in resources with which imports could be obtained). Information about the causes of the famine in 1941–2 in Greece makes it clear that although some regions produced a great deal in the way of subsistence crops, many other parts of Greece did not produce basic subsistence needs and so imports were vitally necessary. Islands with particular specialisations exported for cash and imported other necessities and luxuries. Data from other countries suggest that many so-called 'subsistence' or 'self-sufficient' economies are anything but this; there is an ideology of self-sufficiency (as on Anafi: 'enough for bread and oil') and migrants' remittances and imports are concealed or underplayed. The differing effects of the Famine Winter on other islands are discussed by Mazower; here I can only speculate that Anafi, however impoverished it appeared to the exiles, probably produced enough over all to allow its inhabitants a basic staple diet. However, as we have seen, access to land was not equal, so it is likely that during the Famine Winter some islanders had enough and to spare and others just about got by.

Two factors helped the exiles. An appeal (in March 1942) to a new Italian colonel in charge of the Cyclades who visited Anafi, had an effect. He allowed the most seriously ill to be transferred to mainland hospitals, and negotiated for the exiles' allowance to be sent along with letters and parcels. As soon as the commune had cash in hand again, they were able to buy supplies, including meat. This implies that most villagers had enough to eat at this time. The exiles also sent over to Santorini for some supplies. Leasing arrangements were also re-established and all the Monastery fields were taken over (Tzamalukas 1975, 100). A windmill in the square was brought into use with multi-coloured bed-sheet fabric as sails so that the exiles could grind their own grain. Telegrams from the exiles, supported by confirmation of their plight from the *proedros* and village priest, also had results. A boat flying a Red Cross flag arrived in March 1942 with supplies both for the islanders and for the exiles.

By the end of the year all the exiles had left the island for hospital, other islands, and for prison camps. Many of them were killed, some died of illnesses and bad treatment; some escaped and joined the Resistance, a few survived, although some of these were re-imprisoned during the Civil War.

The German Occupation of Greece ended in the autumn of 1944 (Athens was liberated on 12 October that year); some of the migrants left Anafi and returned to Athens, only to find themselves soon caught up in the Civil War; others remained on Anafi until after the Civil War ended. Their experiences during these years convinced many migrants of the importance of retaining a house and some land on the island. Even the most prosperous urbanite in the sixties remembered the massive inflation and deprivation suffered in the city, and the lifeline provided by having a rural source of subsistence. While migrant Anafiots might sell some of their land – and they found it increasingly difficult to rent it or find half-shares tenants – they always retained a few hill terraces and olive trees on the island as a hedge against dramatic changes in their political or economic circumstances.

Post-war migration

Along with migrants returning to Athens went islanders looking for work in the massive post-war reconstruction which was under way. From this period onwards islanders, particularly men, regularly engaged in various types of migrant labour in Athens, some of which led them to leaving the island permanently. The type of migration usually depended on their stage in the domestic cycle: young unmarried men tended to go away for several years, returning to visit their parents at Easter or for the festival of Panayia Kalamiotissa; if they married in the city they rarely returned. Married men with wives and children on the island, who worked on their own, or on parents' lands, and as agricultural labourers for most of the year, went to Athens for three to four months' summer seasonal labour after the grain had been harvested and before olive-picking began. Some of these families remained permanently on the island, but often the lack of provision of secondary education there was the deciding factor in a move to Athens.

After I had carried out some more research (in 1973) to fill out the material I had already collected about island migrants to Athens and the life of the migrant community there, I began to reconsider my previous views about migration from the island. During my first fieldwork, I had seen migration as a continuous process which had been taking place for over one hundred years and was slowly but surely draining away the most active members of the community; a process which would eventually result in depopulation, or the kind of village which my friend Mick Lineton had seen in Mani containing only 'a few old women podding lupins'. In the seventies, taking a less island-based perspective, and seeing migration from the Athenian end, I interpreted migration from the 1950s onwards as different in character from pre-war migration. Before the war, migration was a slow and steady process which seemed to me to have acted as a built-in economic safety valve, removing the surplus population and enabling the island community to keep going as a result of the money which migrants sent back, and because of the houses and land which they left behind. The land could be rented, or worked on a 'half-shares' system, the houses were available for daughters' dowries. After the war,

1836	1844	1848	1850	1870	1879	1889	1896	1907	1928
620	870	895	982	700	687	658	643	579	550

1929	1940	1951	1961	1971	1981	1991	2001	2011
700	785*	532*	471*	353*	292*	261*	—	271*

* census figure

Figure 12   Population figures for Anafi, 1836–2011

the rate of migration increased dramatically and threatened the very existence of the island community.

In trying to collect figures for the population of Anafi I came up against problems which were partly historical and partly cultural. The figures I put together from travellers' accounts and national censuses are collected in the table above. I was told by the village secretary in 1966 that the increase in the size of the population in 1940 was due to islanders who had migrated to Athens returning to Anafi during the Occupation and Civil War but the date is much too early for such a explanation: the Occupation of Greece by German and Italian troops dates from May 1941, the Civil War from 1944. The reason for the apparent increase in population is obvious when the number is broken down into male and female components: the large number of males makes clear what one might suspect: the increase is due to the large number of (mainly male) political exiles, around 185 of them.

My fieldwork in the sixties might have become, in its turn, a historical record of a now vanished community. However, within a decade of my departure, the population stabilised and began slowly to increase. Islanders were no longer leaving, either for work in Athens, or to give their children access to secondary education, and migrants were returning to the island. The 'push' and 'pull' factors affecting migration had altered. An electricity generating station had been built at the harbour in 1974, providing power and light for the village, the harbour, and for migrants' holiday houses at Klisidhi Beach. Within another decade, a deep-water jetty was constructed which enabled car-ferries to disembark passengers and supplies direct onto the quayside. A secondary school department was established in the village school. In Athens, inflation and changes in building regulations encouraged migrants to look for investment opportunities elsewhere. They soon became involved in the tourism development of the island, and formed an island-based association to preserve and revive old customs. Government ministries now offered incentives for those with occupations in rural areas, with special subsidies for farmers and for shepherds in peripheral areas, and EEC grants were available.

Anafi is now offered (by tour operators on Santorini) as 'a truly unspoilt island' to visit, and listed in guide-books for travellers who are prepared to make an extra effort to go somewhere off the beaten track. Whether or not tourism should be the islanders' main source of livelihood is hotly debated. The very qualities which attracted the first tourists are now threatened. The beaches on the south coast are spoilt by litter, sewage disposal contaminates sea-bathing, amplified music from bars and discos has driven migrant holiday-makers away. Back-packing tourists are moving on to the new 'unspoilt places', particularly in Turkey. Returned migrants now dominate the village council and some stress that a more viable economic base than summer seasonal tourism must be found. Whatever happens, I doubt that the island will ever suffer the threat of depopulation again.

CHAPTER EIGHT

'Letters might be censored'

The Colonels' coup and Easter 1967

✳

After a year's research, I was writing fieldnotes very differently from when I first arrived on Anafi. I could now identify almost all the islanders, and trace relationships between them, thanks to record cards based on the village register. Fieldnotes were not only long and detailed, taking hours to type, but also interspersed with the personal observations and comments I had previously reserved for letters to my parents. Excerpts here describe ten days in April 1967 leading up to the celebration of the Greek Orthodox Easter on 30 April, a period during which the 'Colonels' coup' took place, on 21 April. For some of the time I had the company of my friend Rosalind Horner, whom I had met in Athens during my 25th birthday visit there. She was about to begin doctoral fieldwork in Burundi, and this was our last meeting for several years.

FIELDNOTES, ANAFI, FRIDAY 21 APRIL 1967

The merchant caïque, quite a large, rather ugly ship, arrived with Patiniotis's provisions from Naxos and two of the sailors came up to the village. Nikos the postman was listening to the radio in the post-office, and Nikos the astinomos said that there was a government crisis and the banks had been closed.

Rembelia and Katina Nikoli went with donkeys down to the merchant ship and brought up bottled gas, flour, a bundle of brooms and other things; the shop was full of sacks. Rembelia was obviously distracted, and later I heard from the Proedhrina she had been crying about her children in Athens. It was difficult to tell if there were lots of people around the grocery shop because of the new provisions, because they wanted to take a look at Rosalind, or because they were stocking up at a time of crisis. Some women were buying *khinos*? some kind of Lenten soup stock made of sesame.

About three in the afternoon we went to see Stella. On passing the Kiriakos café I asked what news? Nikos postman, Merkuris, Vinzenzos and Lambros the barber were all there listening to the radio; Kiriakos seemed to be explaining what had happened and mentioned that Papandreou and his son had been arrested. They also said there was a curfew and that all buses, boats, etc., had been stopped. When I asked what had happened Kiriakos said there had been a take-over by the army. It seemed that no-one was making any comments on the situation or expressing any personal opinions, in fact we learnt later that comment was forbidden.

We left Kiriakos' cafenion and passed Yiannis Dhamighos outside his café. When I asked what was happening he said 'disturbances in Athens'. As we passed the school on the way to Stella's house, widow Maria called out that there was trouble in Athens and that there had been a movement of the Left in the night which had been counteracted by a take-over by the army and the King. She looked very grim, said all communications had been stopped but did not mention her son in Athens. Note that she was the one to initiate the conversation whereas in every other case we had to ask, except for the policeman telling me in the morning.

Stella was in the kitchen with Yioryia Khalari who was knitting. Stella said that she had realised something was wrong when she found that only one radio station was broadcasting, and it was all folk music, *laïki musiki*. She said that a military dictatorship was in force. There had been some Left-wing rising in the night which had been quelled by the army and the King, who curtailed all movements and had imposed a ten-day period of strict rule. She said that a dictatorship was preferable to a Communist take-over.

We went out to sit on the porch at the front of Stella's house and saw that someone was baking; smoke was rising from a courtyard oven nearby. The merchant caïque couldn't leave because all movements were stopped, but another caïque had left earlier before the ban was known. The mother of 'Liz Taylor' peered through the gate and moaned about the worries of the situation; Stella seemed to be ignoring her.

The merchant caïque men were in the post office trying to get a call through to Naxos, and the astinomos was backing up their attempts to leave. He did this by insisting that the harbour was too unprotected for such a large ship. No-one spoke openly about the situation.

We changed into jeans and went up to look at the castro, passing the donkeys outside the grocery being unloaded by the donkeymen Nikos Khalaris and Kostis Nikolis. When we descended, Eleni Leptaki took me to task for the trousers: it wasn't nice, but Sarpakina said I was sensible not to wear a skirt which could get blown up in the wind.

As we passed Athina's house, she and headache Margarita and Lemonia her sisters were conversing, Athina had a hen under her arm. Margarita said that there was now a dictatorship, but Athina was saying it would blow over. We came past the church (we had heard the esperino bell go just after four from Stella's) and changed to go into the cafenion. On the path we saw the Abbot talking quietly to Mikhalis the policeman. We went first into the Dhamighos café. Yianni four-finger was sitting with Nikos Ghavallas, son of Antonis *meraklis*, and I mentioned we had seen him ploughing yesterday. Talking about cheese, he said that his fields nearby were inherited from his father. Then Lambros Birbilis came in and said he had wondered if the cafés might be shut. Dhamighos said 'you are not meant to make any comments, sit down and shut up. They have got Papandreou and his son for opening their mouths too wide'. Then he commented that Rinakis had underestimated the possible scale of the fuss last night, and laughed that he had been proved wrong. He turned the radio on, possibly to make conversation difficult to hear and then did a little dance between the café tables. I asked him why and he said because his party, ERE (Centre Union), had come out on top and squashed the Communists. Markakis had come in by this time and was sitting with Lambros. The Santorinian meat merchant was also with Yianni four-finger, and he and Nikos (Antonis' son) moved out of the café together and were talking outside and followed us into Kiriakos's café which was very full.

FIELDNOTES, ANAFI, SATURDAY 22 APRIL 1967
We heard the first bell about 6am for a service commemorating the Raising of Lazarus, but neither of us felt like getting up. Apparently the schoolchildren all took communion at this service, or so I was told in the grocery later. Someone there commented that I hadn't gone to church (interesting that my absence was noted). We made porridge because the weather turned cold and the sea was rough.

After five in the afternoon we went up to the Post Office but Nikos was out 'on a message'. We leaned over the wall and talked to Marulidhi [Manolis the fisherman's wife, whose house was near the post office] who was clearing up after the house had been whitewashed (I saw Yianni whitewash in there a few days ago; presumably these preparations were in honour of Easter?). I asked what was happening and she said she didn't understand but that it had something to do with the Communists and that people might be being shot in Athens if they went out of doors.

Then Nikos came back and I mailed my letters and asked if I could phone Susanna and he said come back at 6pm. When I did, all his family were in the post office. Susanna said that people in Kypseli were saying that it was forbidden to talk about the situation but were in fact expressing opinions, for example that P's election campaign was to have started on Sunday and the King feared that P would get enough support to boot him out of his job [i.e. abolish the monarchy]. Hence he arrested Papandreou and his son, and the previous Prime Minister, to make it look not such a move against the Left. Papandreou was proposing various electoral reforms to take power away from the Centre Union and give more to the smaller parties thus getting more assurance for his position. On my return from the post office to the house I had a long talk with Ros about my fieldwork problems.

Ros thought it important to find out more about the political affiliations of the island families and their tie-up with their cafenion patronage. She also suggested that wealth differences on Anafi might be connected with the island's ties with Athens: rents from the city combined with self-sufficiency here. It might be that the need for cash forces some people to leave some of their holdings in order to work the holdings of Athenian-living islanders in return for wages and this leads to the purchase of things like flour which they might have grown. I remember the comment that it was almost impossible to get workmen now to work on the half-shares system. Hence it might be worth looking at the flour-mill records to see the names of those with large quantities of grain, and asking the grocery and the mills who bought flour from them. I must ask the village secretary for the poll and land tax records as a way of assessing incomes, and I should also ask him how he arrives at his classification of Rich, Medium and Poor.

The section of the study in Athens should aim to complete this picture rather than to be an insufficient study of migrant life. It is the Athenian end of the Anafiot economy and social organisation which is important. Ros said I should look at the correlation of status and economic ranking – do similar economically classed families have similar or different statuses? She suggested it might be Stella's money and the schoolmaster's status which accounted for their influence. Granny Marusi says she owns half Anafi, yet lives in a rather shabby house; the cash with which the workmen on her family lands are paid presumably comes from Athens, and why does her son, or daughters, go to this expense? I should concentrate on process rather than structure. [Rosalind was a postgraduate at the University of Manchester; with hindsight, her advice to me, and her own interests and concerns, seem to reflect the dominant themes of the Manchester School in the mid-1960s.]

FIELDNOTES, ANAFI, SUNDAY 23 APRIL 1967

First bell went about 6am and the second at quarter to eight, church was over by quarter to nine. On the way to church noticed Rembelia by the grocery store-house, she said flu [as a reason for not going to church] but things were coming up from the harbour. There were 39 men, including Manolis the fisherman, the doctor, and other non-regulars. When Iakovos *mavros* came in, several men moved aside to give him a stall, and the Proedhrina moved out of her stall for another old man. Seven people took communion: four men and three women.

There was an incident when the Abbot threw the olive branches (which were to act as palms) through the sanctuary gates and Lambros Birbilis' son had to pick them up from outside the altar screen and carry them back in, Niko the postman helping. People clustered around the screen to take the olive twigs. The post office motor was working, unusual for a Sunday, and Mikhalis was in the police station...

After breakfast we went for a walk as far as Ayios Andhreas [see Letter 64, below]; a fierce wind, frothing the sea and rippling the barley, coming from the south-west, shifting round to west in the afternoon. There were goats grazing on the slopes. On our way back we passed Barba Konstantin talking to another man and to Pananos' son. He said he made cheese down at the Vafiadhis' hut every afternoon [a cottage just off the harbour path]. As we came back into the village, people commented that our visit to the church [i.e. Ayios Andhreas] would be to our good [in other words, it was assumed we would get a religious benefit from it].

We met Stella who said her mother [the Proedhrina] wanted to see us to give us fresh milk from Ayio Yianni. We went into Kiriakos' for a vanilla, and when I asked what was happening Kiriakos said it was forbidden to say, but I should, like them, listen to Radio Cairo. We went on to see the Proedhrina, passing the store-shed filling up with sacks, Rembelia supervising.

Maria the Proedhros's wife was not forthcoming about the situation in Athens, but when I told her about Margarita and Nikos over-charging for our donkeyride to Kastelli and for cheesecakes [see Letter 64 below], she said they were like 'money-loving Judas'. I remember her saying one evening last week, that Margarita Dhamighu was not an evil gossiper and conversed about food and clothes, and never slandered, and that it was a shame they lived so far apart because she would enjoy her company. We left gifted with fish and beetroot, and the milk.

We sat on the balcony writing letters and Eleftheria shouted from next door that I was to send her greetings to my parents. Yianni four-finger came for the dinghy-fare owed after Ros's arrival, he was quite apologetic about it. I assumed the boatmen were doing a share-out just before Easter. Then we had lunch and lay on the balcony, Eleftheria was baking and called out to ask if I would like some *fakies* and *fava* [lentil-based dishes]. She later sent these across, together with a loaf, by her son Yiannis [blown to bits by dynamite while fishing in 1986].

We went up later to the Kiriakos' café for an ouzo. Rinakis was in the doorway when we arrived, but went out. There was the atmosphere of a close intimate discussion, which returned when I announced to Kiriakos that we had heard the Voice of America news:

K: Oh you heard the news, did you? Bad news.
Me: Yes, we learnt what is happening.
K: You asked me to tell you, but I couldn't, and now you do know.
Me: And can I tell you? Perhaps as I'm a foreigner the law doesn't touch me?
K, and others: Yes, foreigners are not affected.
(intense interest during this part of the exchange)
Me: We heard that Kanellopulos has been released but the other two are still
     …
K: Yes, still held inside. Bad news.

At this point we became aware that Anastasios Kollidhas was outside the door dithering. He walked in; a silence fell very obviously, and he looked very unsure whether to stay but K brought him a chair and he sat down. K immediately said in a sort of neutral continuing way, '… yes it's difficult to say…' and I said 'well I don't understand anything that's going on.' People returned to muttered small-group conversations.

I became aware that they were discussing a regulation prohibiting firearms. Mikhalis the policeman stalked in and put up a notice, and in reply to a question from Kiriakos said very sharply 'not the day after next, tomorrow it has to be'. Apparently the notice said that all firearms had to be given in at the police station. The discussion moved, prompted by the Abbot, to a comparison of Greek and English seasons and weather, following my remark that we had been for a walk and gathered wild flowers. As we were leaving I asked what they thought about me coming into the café. Vinzenzos and K answered together, saying that Athenian Anafiot women came into the cafés in the summer, that foreign girls did too, so it was all right for us. When I asked about Anafiot women, Barba Yiorgos said that they were too busy at home.

All the afternoon the church bell kept going for women to go and help clean the church, and while we were in K's café, the bell went and someone said 'there goes the bell for the esperino and the Abbot is still in the cafenion.'

LETTER 64, ANAFI, SUNDAY 23 APRIL 1967

Just one year today since we arrived in Greece. This morning after church Ros and I went for a windy walk inland and picked poppies, periwinkles, petunias, small purple and red snapdragons, white and yellow daisies, dandelions, and the tiny flowers off the prickly bushes that look like green chicken-wire. The hill terraces of barley and wheat are green, and mixed with so many flowers that the distant hillsides looked like Impressionist paintings, spots of colour, brilliant and moving among the rippling ears of grain. There was brilliant rust and yellow lichen on the rocks, the sea opaque and capped with lines of foam; fluffy goats in camouflaging coats of white and black, biscuit colour, grey, moving across the slopes with their bells tinkling. Last night the wind smelt warm and of lemon flowers and sandalwood.

Yesterday we ate the tinned chicken I bought for the Christmas I wasn't able to spend here so today we've had a wonderful soup of the jelly and stock, with truffle paté and Ryvita. A most delicious meal, with tastes I haven't enjoyed for such a long time.

I was telling Ros about the bits of Anafi's history that nobody seems to be interested in: the time of the Venetian occupation in the C14. Do you remember anything about it from the photocopies Dad sent me? The Dukes of Naxos, who seem to have gone in for assassinating one another, gave islands to their followers and I suppose the one at the end of the list got Anafi! Someone called William Crispo [Guglielmo or Guillelmo in some of the photocopied sources] built the fortifications just above the present village, and visible from Santorini. They're the ruins still referred to as to kastro, the castle. William also built a second fortress, which some authors refer to as Gibitroli, but it's not clear where it was. Some people here say it's near Ayios Antonios on the north-east coast, but Ros and I haven't got time to go and see if it's there.

Well, William of Anafi became Regent when one of the Dukes died, leaving a baby son, and then was Regent again when the child died aged seven (I wonder why?!). Eventually William became Duke but just for his lifetime, because his only legitimate child was a daughter, Florence. Florence was left to look after Anafi. Ros and I have decided that this would make a wonderful historical novel. What had happened to Florence on Anafi after her father went off to Naxos? We've devised the plot which would bring a weary soldier who had fought on the walls of Constantinople to Anafi to fall in love with her. We've also tried to bring in a volcanic eruption on Santorini (there was one sometime in the fifteenth century which we think will do).

Our scenario had to be scrapped when we discovered that the historical sources indicate that Florence Crispo was married in 1469, aged six, to Luigi Barbaro (who presumably became the active overlord of Anafi). Two daughters, Daniele and Zaccaria, were later born of this marriage, and Florence died in 1528, aged 65. Anafi then passed to the Venetian family of Pisani.

On Thursday last we went by donkey to see the ruins of the ancient city at Kastelli, about an hour and a half away from the present village. There were marble walls, house foundations, steps down into a deep cave, its walls covered with the initials of shepherd boys as far back as 1820, headless statues, ground level openings into what must have been tombs. I bravely crawled into one and found a black beetle, some seeds blown in by the wind, warm still dust and two niches in the rock face. All very mysterious. We continued down the hillside to the chapel at the foot of the mountain where a marble sarcophagus is built into the wall, and then down to the Proedhros's garden where his daughter Stella and his workman's wife, jolly Kalliopi, made us coffee. The workman had gone off to his own holding to cut hay, so Kalliopi was struggling to milk the goats. The only sour note to the day is that Nikos the donkeyman vastly overcharged me (at least in Anafiot terms) for the two donkeys for the outing, and his wife Margarita baked me a batch of cheese-cakes for Ros's visit and over-charged for them as well (again, by Anafiot standards). I was too nervous to complain to their faces, but mentioned the cost to a couple of people to get a check on whether I was right to think I was being over-charged. Maybe, as this is the time of year when running bills at the groceries have to be settled, they were in financial difficulties and needed the extra money.

Having Ros here has been wonderful, not only having her company, but the stimulation of an outsider asking me questions. She has been suggesting lines of inquiry, commenting, re-thinking the material. I am inspired to new labours!

I suppose you heard about Friday's coup; we weren't able to send any reassuring telegrams as Athens was kept incommunicado; other places couldn't put calls through to the capital nor through it to the outside world. The first we knew was a dark hint from the policeman as I passed the door of the police-station, and then on the Cretan-American Air Force programme the announcement that people out on the streets were liable to be shot... We found it very funny, and frustrating, to hear these announcement about curfew and other prohibitions from Crete without them telling us why. They kept recounting that the Queen of England was celebrating her 41st birthday. As letters might be censored I won't try and tell you the gossip and speculation in this, but will send a message-tape with Ros. [I later received a letter from Thetis (the ikon expert with whom I had toured the island in May 1966), which had been opened and had a censor's stamp across it.] Besides, it is forbidden to discuss the situation and so I can't find out much about what the islanders think about it or discover their political allegiances. One of the cafenion owners did a little dance over the emergence of 'his' party.

There is also the worry about Ros getting back to Athens, because we aren't sure if there will be a boat this week, and she has to be in Athens for a flight at dawn on Wednesday 3rd May...

Figure 13   The sarcophagus near Kastelli

FIELDNOTES, ANAFI, MONDAY 24 APRIL 1967

Late awakening, wind from the south-west still, veering more southerly in the late afternoon, the waves making it unlikely that any dinghy would be able to go out to the steamer. I went up to the PO with my letter to parents and parcel to Susanna. Various people, including Vinzenzos, Yioryia Khalari and Rinakis, were waiting to put a calls through to Athens. When I got back Ros was washing her hair, and in the middle of it Efthimia appeared with a plate of wild greens, *khorta,* from her mother. The policemen were playing *tavli* on the balcony. At 1pm we heard on the radio from the Voice of Israel that King Constantine had been put under house arrest because he wouldn't put his signature to various enactments of the military junta.

A little later I went up to the Kiriakos café but only Maria was there. She said Kiriakos had gone out to Piryi 'to see what damage had been done by the wind', but I think it was really to get his gun to surrender to the police. Then the Santorinian meat merchant came in and wondered if he would be able to leave and at 3pm we heard on the shipping news that the 'Mirtidhiotissa' had left at midday and was coming via Naxos, so Ros would be able to leave to get to Athens in time for her plane.

Coming away from the post office we began to shop at Patiniotis's grocery. Theodoros Pelekis, the deaf old man who always wears a soldier's jacket, was there buying five kilos of loukoumi for Easter for distribution in commemoration of his dead wife, also a bottle of banana liqueur, totalling 120 drachmas. There were jokes by Patiniotis that Theodoros had killed his wife by falling too heavily on her and not being able to hear her cries because of his deafness. Then he asked: 'you are doing this for your wife, who will do it for you?' Katina Nikoli, who had come in, said to me 'his daughter'; he has one daughter here and one in Athens. Patiniotis then commented that the husband of the daughter living here (Pananos) was a good man and not to worry (did he mean that Pananos would allow money to be spent on the mnimosino, or allow his wife to make the arrangements?).

In the middle of this shopping I was called back to the post office as a call was going to come through from Susanna. While I was waiting I asked Nikos the postman whether Ros would be safe in Athens. Nikos replied that there were 55,000 tourists in Greece [implying that of course she would be safe]. Then I said: 'But with this new development...', and pointed to the picture of the King, and made a gesture of locking up. They asked what I meant and I said 'the army officers have shut the King up in his house, because he doesn't agree with what they want to do.' Had they heard this? Nikos said this was the first he had knew of it, and they all looked pretty dumbfounded, but I heard Nikos say to the others that this had been a speculation on Cairo radio that morning.

We went up to the Rinakis's house as Katina had told me that Vasiliki had made bread the day before and I needed fresh bread. We found Mrs R sifting flour. We admired the clean covers for Easter. Sarpakina [Mrs Rinakis's sister] came in; she had been at Milies, and asked if a family phone-call to Athens had gone through. Letters were not going to go on the boat but at the last moment Nikos said that they were after all. Mrs R took us into the saloni which was all decorated with white covers, gave us orange sweet and cherry-brandy-treated *tsikudhia*, and then brought us a loaf of bread. Vasiliki appeared after Sarpakina had gone, she said it was likely that she and Yiannis Khalaris, Yiorgos Birbilis and Anezini's son, would be engaged soon. He was staying on for Easter. She said she would call me to the ceremony. Just then Rinakis appeared, told his wife his phone call had got through and all was well. He came into the saloni and opened a table drawer. I could see various notebooks inside, possibly the cooperative records I've been trying to get hold of? We left and took the bread back home.

As we went down the street Kiriakos seemed to be waiting for me at the top of the steps so we began to talk in rather low voices and I asked if he had any new information, and when he said he had been out in the fields all day I said that the Voice of Israel had reported the King's house arrest. He hadn't heard this and said it was a very confused state of affairs. I turned the conversation to worries about Ros's departure and the state of the sea. Then Theodoros (his brother-in-law; Maria's sister's husband) called out from the courtyard of his house which was right behind us, and Kiriakos answered in terms of the weather and the possibility of leaving the island. [The implication in these notes seems to be that Kiriakos, well known for his left wing views, was even careful about what he said about the current situation in the hearing of his own brother-in-law.]

Then we took containers back to the Proedhrina and got the evening's milk. Nikolaos Nikolis their workman brought in a great pile of beetroot, and Maria said he was to take it to Patiniotis; on being asked, she told me that they let him sell produce from Ayio Yianni to Patiniotis for himself. When I asked her about Ros leaving because of the troubles in Athens she said that under military rule the situation is always quiet. She seemed unperturbed that the King had been put under house arrest, and when Granny Marusi came in they agreed that everything was all right. It was difficult to tell what they really thought, as they were ostensibly discussing the situation in terms of Ros's safety rather than the legality of the military rule now.

We went into the Kiriakos' café and noticed that Manolis Birbilis came in with two wrapped-up guns. I asked K if he had heard that what I had told him was true, and he said that he had heard since from the radio. Again there was discussion about Ros leaving. Only one station on the radio was working and it was relaying a church service on the radio. K lifted an eyebrow when the words 'oh ye hypocrites!' were transmitted. Rinakis walked out soon after we went in. Mikhalis the policeman was grinning.

Went into the Dhamighos café, Rinakis was talking to him in the kitchen of the café. Yianni four-finger was there, Manolis the olive-press owner, Lambros, Russetos of the forge ... Presumably these men are all supporters of the party Yiannis Dhamighos favours? He said he wasn't leaving for Athens after all: 'because of the weather'.

FIELDNOTES, ANAFI, TUESDAY 25 APRIL 1967

The wind dropped but the sea was still heavy, with tremendous waves. We went down to the harbour about 3am for Rosalind to catch the steamer back to Athens. Nikos Khalaris said that the Takhidhromos was leaving with about twenty baskets, with khorta and eggs inside, but most with vrasti, sent as gifts to various relatives. I asked if he took any to sell, but Nikos said that just before Easter there weren't any spare cheeses for sale, afterwards there would be. People were driving the shepherds mad with demands for vrasti to make melitera (cheese-cakes) for Easter.

There was a great argument when Patiniotis stormed into the harbour shed and showed a bag of cement which, he said, had been deliberately opened and some taken. Kostis came in and said 'what bad people there are in the world' in a mock-sympathetic voice, and most of those present seemed to be making a little fun at Patiniotis's rage. Manolis said to me 'what a stirred-up state of affairs'. 'Only on the sea?' I queried. 'Sea and dry land', he laughed, and later there seemed to be some discussion of the current situation, but more a pooling of information than an expression of opinion. I heard something about political detainees.

The Takhidhromos's baskets were coming down slowly ... one of them had been addressed to Margarita Tzuzuka, openly using a nickname (Granny Marusi's daughter). The steamer came about 4:40am. Manolis, Antonis, and Antonis Seklemis manned a dinghy with a motor which bucked over the waves. [Ros told me later that she had to jump from the dinghy and in through a cargo hold door, hitting her head in the process. She was later violently sick and wondered whether she had concussion. She slept all the way back to Athens, and seemed all right.] Anastasios Kollidhas was holding two sheep and a kid, and Damigos said that they wouldn't be allowed on the boat alive, because of some new law, so for the very last trip of the dinghy, Yiorgakis helped him kill the larger sheep and the goat. Blood poured out of the sheep's mouth and Yiorgakis washed his hands in the sea. Despite feeling sick about this, I asked about the Santorinian meat merchant who had left. Nikos said a caïque would be sent over to collect the animals; the meat-merchant had made his arrangements with the shepherds.

As we were walking back up to the village, a boy who had arrived on the steamer was asked about the disturbances in Athens and replied he had experienced one incident when trying to get to Omonia Square and was turned back. My news about the King was received with no comment. I had a rest and later phoned Susanna. She said it was not clear now whether or not the King was still under house arrest, and that one radio programme had suggested the new military government might try for a popular victory by attempting to regain Cyprus. The astinomos was also there; when I asked Nikos Ludharos what news, he stalled by saying that the battery on his radio had gone dead.

I then did my washing. The sea was still rippled with wind and waves, but very much calmer. Later in the afternoon I was preparing to go out for a walk, but Zabetti Ludharu [Niko postman's wife] came to my balcony with Apostollos to watch the arrival of the *landza* from Santorini with the four boys who go to high school there, including her son Manolis.

As the boys were walking up to the village, I set off on my walk, intending to gather flowers on the hill-terraces on the way to Ayios Andreas. I walked near the mill where Flora 'short sleeve' lives, sister of Markakis Dhamighos. By the mill were a large flock of sheep; also many young boys lying down on the hillside and talking. Probably these animals are being herded in wait for the caïque to transport them to Santorini for slaughter for Easter.

On the path I found Antonia, the wife of Makarios Arvanitis and mother of Iakomi the albino boy, watching a flock of sheep and goats, their own, about 40–50 animals. She said one of those which had been put with the flock for the meat-merchants' caïque had come back to its own herd from near the mill. So the herd I had seen where the boys were lying in the grass contained all the animals sold to the meat merchants. She asked me if I wanted to go with her to watch the vrasti being made.

She drove the mixed flock up into a pen of stone walls topped with bristly bushes. The goats went into one enclosure and the sheep into another; force of habit, she said. Goats were easier than sheep to milk, they had larger udders. There was whey from the morning's ordinary cheese already in the cauldron, and she added water and sea water in proportion to the milk. All the vessels have to be scrupulously washed every evening and rinsed in the morning; the cheese baskets also have to be cleaned. She gave me a plate of vrasti and talked of her hard life. There was an old mother to look after for 18 years who died aged 93; a sister who died and a brother who died aged at 30. She also offered to bring me wool when she next went to Vayia.

The fields were full of poppies. I went back on a tiny track, stopping to look at the flock by the mill which was looked after by tall young Mattheos. He said there were about 140–150 animals altogether. After I got home, it clouded over and began to rain.

I went up to the Kiriakos café about 7:30pm, it was full and I had to take a seat by the counter with my back to the door. Yianni bulbous nose was teasing the old soldier (Theodoros Pelekis) to give him grazing land, and offered him a 1,000 drachmas for it... Kiriakos said it was all a joke but I wonder if there is competition to get hold of the pasturage. K said that now was the time to see to the beehives, and said that the bees here were of a fiercer strain than elsewhere; they give more honey. One could regain one's outlay on beehives the first year, he said. i.e. two hives costing 1,000 drachmas would result in enough honey to cover the cost. Discussion seemed mostly agricultural, as usual. Kiriakos said that the animals would all go together down to the harbour for the Santorini caïque later in the week; half their price was paid in advance and the remainder afterwards.

Telegram To Parents, 26 April 1967

This telegram was sent, at my request, by Susanna, from Santorini. This was because the post-office clerks on Santorini were more familiar than Nikos with English orthography, and also because I didn't want to have to explain what it was about or why I was sending it. By now I could well understand how the islanders felt about their neighbours and local officials knowing all about their doings.

Can only tell you am safe and well love Margaret.

This choice of wording was intended to hint at the possibility of censorship, and to suggest caution in what they wrote and sent to me.

Fieldnotes, Anafi, Wednesday 26 April 1967

Went for milk to the Proedhrina. When I went there she asked me what I had heard on the news. I replied by asking her what she had heard and she said nothing new. I said that apparently the King didn't agree with the military government and she said Cairo radio also said that; she speculated that the King might not agree with the possible executions, political exiles, etc., and if so, they might force him to abdicate. She characterised him as acting from self-interest only, *poniros*.

Headache Margarita came in; they both took me to task for paying Nikos so much for the donkey trip to Kastelli. The Proedhrina said that Nikos's wife was a bad woman; she had asked Kalliopi to give her beetroot [Kalliopi's husband Nikolas was given beetroot from Ayio Yianni] and when Kallio said there were beetroots in the grocery, she replied 'but there I would have to pay 4 drachms per kilo', and they both clucked that she wanted them free. The Proedhrina went on to say that her husband, Mikhalis, who was in Athens, had forgotten to take his identity card with him and couldn't walk about in Athens without it; she had sent it with Manolis Takhidhromos.

I went into Kiriakos café for a glass of tea, Maria was finishing off a *roba* (button-through housedress), and shortening trousers. Lambros the barber and the Abbot were in the café. This time the Abbot asked me what news and I asked what news on the Greek radio stations. He said 'disturbed'. I said my piece about the king not agreeing with the army officers, and he nodded as if he had heard this, then the conversation turned to none of us understanding politics, and his view that no-one should be top, all men should be equal, each doing his own work according to his capabilities. I then did my washing, came up to the café area again and sat on the wall.

Suddenly a plane flew over and dropped leaflets, like fluttering birds or snow. Children rushed to collect them; they were a transcript of the new President's speech on the radio, and included a passage about regaining Cyprus. There was laughter as the plane flew over Pakhia to drop leaflets because there were only sheep and goats grazing there to read them.

I had a short talk with Nikos the astinomos in which he said he had a lot of worries, implying in the context of the conversation that he had to make up his mind about obeying the military government or following the rumour of the King's disagreement. Marulidhi and Theodoros [whose house is next to the Kiriakos café] were clearing up after whitewashing; Nikos mentioned something to them about guns, and Marulidhi said there was a very old broken gun at their holding. Nikos told them it would have to be fetched and handed in. He said to me that he could make a lot of troubles on Anafi if he wanted to – presumably closing cafenions, etc. When he had gone off for lunch Marulidhi asked me about Ros and gradually worked round to the state of the nation. She said they listened secretly to Moscow, Cairo, and Bulgaria which had broadcasts in Greek at certain hours, and also knew about the King. She said things had been better before and it was a bad thing that now there wouldn't be elections (whereas the Proedhrina thought things were always quieter and the country had a chance of improvement under military rule). Marulidhi also said that in Crete they wouldn't want to give up their guns.

I listened to the 1pm news on Voice of Israel. Nothing new, except that household heads have to report any strangers staying in their house, and gatherings of over five people are forbidden, as is the possession of amateur radio receivers and transmitters, and the spreading of rumours contrary to public order. On Anafi there seems to me to be a wait-and-see atmosphere, a suspension of tension, but a watchfulness. There is concern more for relatives in Athens and elsewhere than for the involvement of Anafi. The 6pm Voice of America news said that exiles had been sent to various Aegean islands, that troops had been withdrawn from certain parts of Athens, and that a spokesman had said that the king would chair a meeting of the new government in a few days.

I went up to the K's café for an ouzo. Although it was dusk he had not lit up as usual; he explained that he had to shut up the cafenion during the church service that evening. In the meantime he lit a small paraffin lamp with a wick. Men kept coming in and asking had the bell gone.

Eventually, about 8pm, he shut the cafenion and in fact when we went up to the church the service had already started. There were more people than usual – about 50 men and boys; almost all family heads. K had said that there had been a bell at 3:30pm for people to go and make their confessions, and that they would take Communion in the morning.

Just behind the candle-stand there was a small table draped in black with a white cross sewn on the front of it. Before four readings of Epistles and Gospels, this table was drawn forward (when Marusi Ghavalla came in she touched the ground in front of it three times) and the readings took place with the Abbot next to it. There was a sudden movement and men began to cluster round and when I asked, women told me that there was oil in a bowl on the table (inside some other bowl with something in it and three candles stuck in) which was blessed and forgave sins. The Abbot touched forehead, chin, the two cheeks, and the palms and backs of the hands. While this was going on various people got the giggles and the Abbot began to make funny remarks. I was led off by Eleftheria. She said this service was called *efkeleon*, unction. Oil, wine and bread are in a bowl which is inside another bowl, filled with *sitari* (wheat), into which three candles are put. This is said to heal the body and soul. There are seven gospels read at this service. After the service, the cafenions re-opened. It was about 10pm.

FIELDNOTES, ANAFI, THURSDAY 27 APRIL 1967

Up early, having heard the church bell at 6am. Waited for second bell in vain and as I was going up to the square I saw people coming from the church, and realised the service was over. So I went up to the café, where Maria was serving. Nikos Ludharos came in, bringing back a coffee cup. Maria wished that his father be forgiven his sins (presumably because he had saved her the trouble of going to get the cup). I asked whether there was a tax record here so I could investigate the economic position of each family; Nikos said there were none, and that everyone was the same here. I protested and said what about those with houses rented in Athens? He said, just the proedhros. Then

I went on to the need for cash and they agreed with my interpretation that wage labour here and in Athens comes from contact with a money economy.

FIELDNOTES, ANAFI, FRIDAY 29 APRIL 1967 [MEGALI PARASKEVI = GOOD FRIDAY]

Was up and ready by 8am, went up to the church. On the way, I met Katina Nikolis near the post office and when I asked her how she was she said she was annoyed because her period had started and now she couldn't take communion, or kiss the ikons, epitafios, etc., and all her preparatory fasting was wasted. In the church Nikos the teacher was fixing the lights on the *epitafios* [an ornately carved structure, rather like a domed stretcher, onto which the ikon of the dead Christ is placed, see later]. Children were there, but no-one else at that point. A little later Granny Marusi and Bella Arvaniti came in. Marusi said that the flowers put on the epitafios contain prayers, and would be put afterwards in the beehives. She thought this custom was a good one, but asked the Abbot about the custom of counting the 12 gospels with thread, which she thought was a sin. Margarita Dhendhrinu (the widow who is said to do her own ploughing) began helping to thread blossoms into chains. Eight women and lots of small girls were there. Manolis Nikolis and other boys were taking turns to toll the *nekrika* [the single bell strokes which announce a death].

Ariadhni said there weren't as many flowers as usual, due to frosts and rain. Last year the whole church was decorated with flowers. Margarita Sighalla, Lambros the barber's wife [they lived just behind the church, I think Lambros may have been sexton], was dusting, and putting black tulle around some of the ikons, replacing their white decorations. She also filled ikon lamps with oil, and seemed also to be changing the red glass holders to black. She and the Abbot dusted the wooden silhouette of Christ in the tomb which had been taken down from the altar screen. I noticed she carefully collected the dust from it. They then wrapped the figure in a sheet. This sheet is kept specially for the church, when it is washed, the water (like that for church vessels) is put down a special church drain. I think the wrapped figure was put on the altar to be brought out and put into the epitafios.

The Proedhrina put dust from the epitafios in her prayer-book for Good Friday, out of it fell a piece of cotton wool which she had used to wipe the *efkeleon* oil from her face and hands on a previous day. The Abbot came in to give directions. Two white embroidered cloths were put on the raised middle section of the epitafios, then a special cloth, dull red with a picture in black on white (like an old engraving) of the Descent from the Cross, or the Entombment. There were some crumbs on it of holy bread which the Abbot scooped up with the base of the chalice.

I went to record the bells, then went and sat on the wall outside the café and had a coffee. Men were waiting to go down to the harbour for the 'Marilena' [the name of the current weekly steamer]. Vinzenzos had slaughtered about four or five animals, and Patiniotis six (judging by the number of the skins drying on poles). Several men were sitting outside the café in the sun. One man told little Katina to ask the astinomos to give him his gun back, joking about the situation. It was the usual boat-day feeling…

I went back up to the church with my camera and asked the Abbot for permission to photograph from inside the church, he agreed. The service began about 11am; only seven men present at that point. Towards the end, around midday, Marulidhi, 'Liz Taylor', came in with her brother Antonis, and some other men. Then there was a ripple of interest as Maria Dhamighu, 'mad Maria', came in, wearing a fresh cotton dress, the sleeves lengthened with other material and trimmed with crochet. She had a patterned headscarf, and her hands were bare and her nails painted with pink polish. She laid a few flowers and fronds on top of the special cloth of the epitafios.

Granny Marusi pushed me forwards to see the Abbot taking the figure of Christ off the cross as he continued the words of the gospel. He had a white cloth over his shoulder, pushed out the nails from the hand of the wooden figure on the cross, shouldered the figure and went into the sanctuary. He then came out with the figure which had earlier been wrapped in a sheet, holding it horizontally across his forehead, and laid it on the bier. Later he brought out the Gospel and laid it at the feet; insisted that people kiss the Gospel as well as the Christ figure when the service was over.

After the service I walked along the path with Marusi, who pulled me along to her house; she gave me a loaf of island bread and of Athenian white bread, and six melitera, and pressed me to eat with her. We had fava, tarama (plain and salty, not made into salata because she would have had to use oil), and she opened a tin of squid (this, octopus, and snails, don't have blood, she said, so can be eaten on fast days). She served it all without oil, although she offered me some. She said she didn't feel full without oil.

By the time Anna Kollidha, the lame girl came in (her god-daughter), she had switched on the radio and was exclaiming how wonderfully well it was giving the answer to the 'Communists on Radio Cairo'. She said that the radio said that there had been no disturbances, that the Communist Manolis ? who had been rumoured to have been sentenced to death was not … she said they had all been saved from a Communist plot. She then made me a candle to take to church to 'take light' for Easter. She said she would make one for the astinomos and anyone else who would otherwise not have a candle made for them.

People were passing so I went up to church about 7:45pm. Within half an hour almost the whole village was there; people I had never seen in church before like Meraklis and Barba Kosta came in. Yiannis four-finger was attending to the candles. There was a collection for Lambros, presumably to do with him acting as the sexton, taken by the teacher. Men kept going out, standing in the yard with the children. The Abbot sprinkled the epitafios and the congregation (amid giggles because of a few deliberate aims on his part, for example at Lambros), using cologne in a milky glass bottle. Stella said that the ikons were streaked with the last year's cologne, its spirit burnt off the paint. Two of the chanters, Nikos Ludharos and the village secretary, stood by the epitafios for the last verse of the anthem. The aghrofilakas helped Dhamighos and the astinomos. The epitafios was taken around the village; down the main street and round behind the kastro, with lights and candles. On its return (a few people like the midwife left the procession when it reached their houses), the Abbot carried the enshrouded form from the bier to the sanctuary and walked round the altar three times with it against his forehead. After three readings, the Abbot left the church.

Then a woman began to sing the Panayia's *miroloi*, a lament. It was Anezini, sister of Evangelio the midwife and of Yianni four-finger. Someone told me later she has a kind of vow to sing it because of a brother of hers who died. This miroloi was an account of Mary searching for her Son and finding him on the cross. I recorded most of it. Other women and children sang too, a few men joined in, but it was mainly a woman's affair.

FIELDNOTES, ANAFI, SATURDAY 29 APRIL 1967

Wrote about Good Friday's events and then read until 4am. Hence was still asleep when there was a knock on the courtyard door. Marulidhi, wife of Theodoros Dhamighos, had come to measure my head for a palm-fibre hat. As I was preparing a very late breakfast, Yiannula and Poppi Nikoli (Kostis and Katina's daughters) came in and played about. Yiannula said her father was out at Vayia near her godmother Polidhoru's cottage, attending to the bees. They had slaughtered their Easter kid that morning in the courtyard (do they sell the skins? I saw lots drying on sticks on Polidhoru's terrace above the grocery). Katina was busy baking *tiropittes*, cheese pies.

Hearing a bell late in the afternoon I went up to investigate; it was for confessions, so that people could take communion. The Proedhrina was there, also Manolis Arvanitis who owns the olive-press. I called in at the post office on the way back; Rinakis was there and I overheard him say that Vasiliki was getting engaged on Sunday evening. I asked Nikos about this as I haven't seen an engagement, and he said I could only go if invited.

Later I went into the Dhamighos café; he stood me an ouzo because yesterday his son's wife had given birth to a daughter (possibly to be named Margarita). Lambros came in to cut hair. Yianni said that in former years after the epitafios had encircled the village it was held up in front of the church doorway, and people re-entered church by going underneath it. But the custom had stopped, possibly through a priest who didn't agree with it, or possibly the Bishop of Santorini, who had stopped customary practices at the Monastery festival.

The bell went about 11pm, there were lots of people in the church courtyard waiting to go in, but the church was locked and there was no key. It was eventually fetched. I noticed that all the men went in the main door, and none of the women, but later a few (like 'Liz Taylor' and some others) did come in this way. All the men had candles (household heads, widows' sons for their mothers, I was told), none of the women. There was a lot of fuss working out the timing … finally all the candles were blown out, the pressure lamp was taken down and the Abbot came forward into the altar screen doorway, which had a candle stuck into a holder with an ikon of the Resurrection fixed to the front of it. As he said 'come, take light', the chanters lent forward to be first, others rushed up, those further away lit their candles from other people's candles. Then there was a movement outside.

Because of the wind, the lectern was set up in the courtyard instead of in the square. So only a few people could get out of the church. Others came up the stone steps round from the back door. The Gospel was read, there was a pause, more consulting of watches to get exactly midnight. Finally, '*Khristos anesti*', and Evangeli, son of Mikhalis the policeman ran into the square with what seemed to be fireworks sparkling. Later I found out this was pan-wire, scouring pads, lit with matches and whirled round on a length of string. He capered around the war memorial and around the mill. The astinomos and Mikhalis jumped when someone lit a banger, or was it dynamite? Shooting off guns, and explosive fireworks, have been forbidden by the Junta, and Mikhalis went off angrily to see if it had been Evangeli. Some people left the church then, but a lot stayed, trickling out slowly, the men shielding their candle-flames and relighting from other candles when they blew out. A number of people said that they 'didn't understand' that it was Easter without a lot of bangs. [It was 1988 before I witnessed another Easter on Anafi.]

Stella invited me to go and eat with them, and we left as the liturgy was beginning, when people kiss the Bible. The offering which is made just before is for the souls of the dead she said, which is the reason why girls don't go up, or young men, only family heads, widows, married women. The teacher had put their roast in Yiannis Nikolis's furnace. It was sealed with cement and made me think of parallels with Christ's tomb, and the lamb imagery.

It seems groups of neighbours put their roasts in together, and as the seal has to be broken to take them out, they all have to assemble together, or the householder takes them all out when he takes his own. After eating with them, I went back up to church to see if anything was still going on, but it was over, about 2:30am.

FIELDNOTES, ANAFI, SUNDAY 30 APRIL 1967, PASKHA (EASTER SUNDAY)

Bells all morning. When I went out, Spiridhula Dhendhrinu and other girls were swinging in Pliti Peleki's courtyard and singing 'Samiotissa'; young men were up on the kastro and there were occasional bangs, firearms or fireworks, or even dynamite. Groups of prettily dressed little girls were walking up towards the kastro. Dhimitris Nikolis and another boy came giggling to watch the swings (and the underwear) but hurried away when they saw me. As I was walking back home, Efthimia was coming out of her aunt Marulidhi's house with a garland for the first of May.

The bell went at 3pm for the 'Second Resurrection', an afternoon Easter service. I went up to the square, on the way stopping at Marulidhi and Manolis's to see the swing hung on chains and the seat made of sacking. Boys were ringing the bells, again waiting for the Abbot. Men and boys sat on one side of the square on the wall above the Proedhros's house, women on the ledge below the church. Mereklis came rolling drunkenly into the square from the northern mill side and shouted 'are you all waiting for me?' and boldly went up and shook hands with the Abbot who had just appeared.

Men relit their Paschal candles inside informally, the service started with lots of antiphonal speaking before breaking into song. Lots of children seemed to be holding baptism candles. Men kept walking outside. Eventually the ikons were taken out, and the procession went round the village; Nikos Khalaris carried the Resurrection ikon, Kostis Nikolis had a smaller one.

Back in church, the teacher read what he told me later was two years' ago's Easter message from the Bishop of Santorini because this year's message hadn't arrived in time, then everyone rushed outside. This was because of a mnimosino distribution for the souls of the recently dead, who are said to be freed now from purgatory for the fifty days until Pentecost. There was a scramble for loukoumia and the choicer tidbits. Mereklis had a plate of cheese (who for?), the man nicknamed the 'wild beast' (Tzortzis Dhrossos) gave out *poto* (liqueur), for Barba Tassos (on behalf of Ariadhni), Nikos Ludharos had loukoumi for his father who died a year ago, Khristos had poto for Petros Allafuzos (on behalf of Eleftheria); Lambros Birbilis had loukoumi (who for?), Mattheos Nikolis also had loukoumi. One lot of loukoumi and poto was presumably the batch Theodoros Pelekis had been buying in Patiniotis's grocery.

Figure 14 Easter Day mnimosino distribution, 1967

Lots of good wishes all round. Vasiliki asked me to her engagement party (did Nikos drop a hint?), and when the square was clearing, Katina Nikoli and some children jumped down into the courtyard of the teacher's former house, rented from Papakhristos, to gather geraniums for the First of May. They said the garlands would be hung over the door in the early morning.

Went into Kiriakos's café, full of men in their best suits looking bored and playing cards; I noticed lame Michael playing with Theodoros Dhamighos, and Antonis the village secretary, and another lad. Efthemia Ludharu whistled me out of the café as I had arranged to tape-record some songs. Four other girls came with her to my room [to sing, to hear other tapes and to taste some of the birthday cake which my mother had sent me]. They sang me 'Samiotissa' and other songs to tape record. I went along to Nikos and Stella's to take them some cake, and we went along to the engagement party together.

LETTER 65, ANAFI, MONDAY 1 MAY 1967

I got your telegram on the 27th, in the afternoon, and so know you must have got mine, which Susanna sent from Santorini. I'm still not sure how much I can say, none of my incoming overseas mail appears to have been opened although some of Susanna's letters have been, but I expect your knowledge of the situation is better than mine: the Cretan American air base has made no reference at all to the crisis, but I get some news from the Voice of America from Rhodes, the Voice of Israel from Israel, and other fleeting newscasts in English, heavily obscured by static, including Radio Prague which is magnificently biased in the other direction. None of my Manchester Guardian Weeklies has come. Anafi seems completely outside the stream of events, only affected by the various directives which come by telegram; I keep wondering whether we will get a batch of exiles. This morning was rather ridiculous, people were finally allowed to take back their guns and were carrying them home from the police station when a contrary message came through and they had to give them back again.

Everyone baked on Thursday, and I went and watched at several houses and had interesting chats with some women; I decided to concentrate on these good relationships rather than try to spread myself across the whole population. Margarita Khalari and her husband apparently cheated me over the price of some cakes she made me and for the donkey ride to the old city. I am hearing lots of gossip about meanness and cheating, so you could say that even the bad experiences have their compensations!

Thursday evening was the service of the Twelve Gospels, in the middle of which the wooden effigy of Christ on the cross is brought out and set up, and a garland of flowers laid at its feet. I went up to the balcony with the old women and children, I could see better and lent on the railing so my feet didn't hurt as much as usual from the long hours of standing. The chandelier caught the flickering prismatic candle flames and I was entranced.

On Friday morning I helped decorate the epitafios *(the bier of Christ) with flowers. It is a wooden contraption, rather like a stretcher. There is a removable top part which is a sort of shrine, with a domed top (with little lights inside worked by batteries), carved posts supporting the top, and a raised section in the centre of the base, where the wooden effigy of Christ is laid, representing the Entombment. This elaborately carved epitafios was a gift from the Proedhros' wife's brother in Athens... It seems to me that the women, who are the most frequent churchgoers, are also repositories of older traditions, like the wailing, which the men, and organised religion, have no place for.*

I wrote fieldnotes about this Good Friday service until 4am on Saturday morning and got up at midday; there was a smell of blood and shit, people were cleaning the intestines of slaughtered animals to make into a sort of soup, which is eaten after church on Saturday-Sunday night, because of the weak state of the stomach after fasting. My stomach turns to think of eating it. By late afternoon people were putting their roasts in the furnace, and sealing the door. Usually guns are let off and dynamite flashes, but this was forbidden this year; the Anafiots say they haven't been able to realise that it is Easter or to enjoy it this year without the usual noise and uproar.

The post office man and his family came down to my room and I lit the candles on my birthday cake and sang 'Happy Birthday' and we all sampled it, and they decided it was 'exceptional.' They sent you lots of good wishes and hoped I would live to be 100...

There's a christening this afternoon, it's the first of May, there are garlands on the doors, and crosses are marked with honey. I am terribly busy and tired and muddle-headed so if this letter is incoherent, blame fieldwork.

CHAPTER NINE

'My last letter from Anafi'

And what happened later

＊

Although the routines of everyday and seasonal activities carried on as usual, life on Anafi was affected in various ways in the aftermath of the Colonels' coup. Political topics were now difficult to discuss in the cafés, but my friendships with a number of people resulted in private conversations in which opinions were voiced. Through these I gained some idea of the range of political views. I remember, for example, that in May 1967, when walking to the Monastery with Stella and her schoolmaster husband, for the festival of the Virgin of the Life-Giving Spring (see Chapter Six), Stella referred to an Athenian Anafiot whom she imagined must be in prison. The name she mentioned was Petros Khalaris, a man I remembered as a summer visitor in the previous August. Why would he be in prison now? I asked. Because of what he had done during the Occupation, said Stella, but did not elaborate. I was left to assume that he was regarded by the new regime as dangerously left-wing. More than twenty years later the same Petros Khalaris told me about his activities during the German Occupation, when his nickname was *to yeraki tis Athinas*, the falcon of Athens. It was clear to me that he held left-wing views, and he referred to what his wife and her father had done for the political exiles on the island in the thirties and forties. I began to realise the implications for people in the sixties of what they had done in previous decades, and the reputations they had then created for themselves, whether or not justified, which resulted in their arrest, imprisonment, exile, torture, and in some cases, death, under the Junta.

For me the months following the coup were dominated by the pressure to bring my research to some sort of conclusion, and by the overwhelming desire to go home. Because of this, I did not extend my fieldwork in space or time by embarking on an investigation of the Anafiot migrants in Athens. To begin city-based research in the current political climate did not seem to me to be a good idea, even though I had now established a number of very useful contacts among the migrant community. My picture of the migrants remained one based on an island point of view until I was able to carry out further research in Athens seven years later.

LETTER 74, ANAFI, WEDNESDAY 9 AUGUST 1967

My room looks very bare with all the maps and posters and collages of newspaper photos and postcards and Tom's drawings taken down; a few clothes are hanging up and there's a gradually filling rucsac, for as I finish each task I label and pack it, just leaving my fieldnotes and dictionaries on the table. I feel a corresponding emptiness in myself. My time here is finished, my emotional involvement exhausted; I shall be glad to leave. In fact there is a knot of tension growing in my stomach about the actual departure because I shall have to respond to so many people's farewells (and demands to be given my bottled-gas stove!) that I really will be exhausted... and so I end my last letter from Anafi, but with the same love, always, Margaret.

Reverse 'culture-shock'

It took me some time to get used to being back in Britain. My independent life on Anafi and in Athens made it difficult for me to slip back into the role of dependent daughter. The habits I had adopted on Anafi stayed with me for several months: when my mother told me about the death of an old family friend, I found that my right hand automatically shot up to my forehead to begin to make the sign of the cross. I had to get used again to flushing the lavatory after use, to letting washing-up water run down the plug-hole instead of throwing it out the back door. When I returned to Canterbury, I found that my circle of friends at the University of Kent had changed; the first intake of undergraduates whom I had known from October 1965 to May 1966 were now in their final year, and there were two years of new faces around with whom I felt I had no connection. There was a great sense of camaraderie between the returning fieldworkers (Mick and Nancy back from Mani via western Greece and Italy; Marie and John returned from Ronda in Spain) which compensated for the isolation we each experienced when trying to 'write up', the phrase used to describe the process of making coherent sense of fieldnotes, and in our case, organising a text for presentation as a doctoral thesis.

Although I felt I had the thread of argument for my thesis (the interconnections between naming, rights to property, and obligations to carry out the rituals for the soul), I struggled to set this out in the conventional form of chapters, presenting the logic of the argument to the reader, using the academic style I was used to reading in which the author hardly appeared in the text at all, except perhaps in an introductory chapter listing methods and sources. As well as writing the thesis, and by doing so attempting to turn my experience into an acceptable anthropological form, and myself into a professional anthropologist, I was also trying to make sense of what I had done and what I had become as a person while in Greece. I didn't really know how to be the new me now that I was back in England.

I made very slow progress with writing up, partly because each time I tried to make a generalisation such as: 'women tend to marry at the age of twenty-two, the groom usually being about five years older', all the exceptions and counter-examples would spring to mind. I would refer back to the index cards on which I had copied the village register entries, get side-tracked by trying to establish a previously unsuspected connection between two families, hunt through my fieldnotes for relevant references, and then find that several hours had gone by. Much later, when my friend Rosalind returned from her fieldwork in Burundi and began work on her own doctoral thesis, she wrote to me that when she woke up each morning she saw her olive-green portable typewriter sitting 'like a malevolent toad' on the desk and knew that another day of frustration lay ahead. Although I never cast my grey-blue Olivetti in such a hateful role, my problems were similar.

I was surprised to find how difficult it was to get outside Anafi, to view it objectively and make clear to a reader all the taken for granted assumptions about the islanders' lives, having felt when I was there that I had never been able to get inside them. I felt great nostalgia for the place and the people at the same time as remembering how much I had longed to get away. Certain pieces of music provoked these fits of nostalgia: Miles Davies's 'Kind of Blue' and Stan Getz's 'Focus' album took me back to Mani, sitting on the terrace with Mick and Nancy, listening to the crickets chirping; the Mamas and the Papas singing 'California Dreamin'' brought back Santorini in the summer of 1966 when I had visited the bank there when I ran short of money on Anafi; Theodorakis's *Sto periyiali to krifo*, 'On the hidden shore', reminded me of sitting in the Pulakis's taverna after the coup, listening to the record being played very quietly on the jukebox before it was taken off and hidden away, all Theodorakis's music having been banned. The sight and taste of *taramasalata*, smoked roe dip, vividly recreated Stella and Nikos the schoolmaster's kitchen in their newly built house in the village, with Stella pounding the smoked roe and fine breadcrumbs together, and dribbling in olive oil, drop by drop; *tzatziki*, cucumber, garlic and yoghourt dip, reminded me of Thanasis Vafiadhis, urging me to try it, telling me that his recipe came from *tin poli*, the city: 'Oh, from Athens?'; 'No, from The City – Constantinople'.

At other times, I thought only of all the unpleasant and uncomfortable aspects of the experience: sweating in long sleeves to avoid painful sunburn when I had run out of sunscreen and shivering in the clammy chill of the winter months when I often went to bed in the clothes I'd worn all day rather than getting colder by undressing. Expressions of envy from those who imagined fieldwork on a Greek island must be idyllic brought to mind scratching flea bites or the prickly rash from horse-hair sofas, soothing the bruises from café chairs and wooden donkey saddles and sneezing continually from hay-fever at threshing time. I remembered painful cramps from period pains during long church services, changing the plasters on split and bleeding feet, blinking from eye-strain after reading and typing by paraffin lamplight, and treating blisters from pulling up buckets of water every day.

Within a year of the return from Greece, there were more changes. Mick Lineton was appointed to a lecturing post at Bristol. He and Nancy, with Tom and Ben and baby Zoe, set off again in the Volkswagen Microbus, which eventually rusted to pieces in their back garden. I applied for the post of Assistant Lecturer in the Department of Sociology and Anthropology at Swansea and by October 1968 was living in a converted coal-cellar with a view of people's feet walking along the Mumbles Road. Thesis writing had to take second place to preparing lectures and tutorials. Later there were further adjustments required when I was married in the autumn of 1970. My thesis, typed by my mother, was finished in the summer of 1971, and rushed to Canterbury by car (stopping overnight in Bristol to collect Mick's) to meet the deadline. Mick's thesis was prefaced by a common Greek phrase, expressed as a question, but often used as a fatalistic acknowledgement of the impossibility of altering circumstances: *Ti na kanume?*, 'What can we do?'. My own thesis used as its motto a verse from a Bob Dylan song, 'Ballad of a Thin Man', which to me encapsulated all the puzzles and anxieties of fieldwork:

> You walk into the room
> With your pencil in your hand
> You see somebody naked
> And you say 'Who is that man?'
> You try so hard but you don't understand
> Just what you will say when you get home
> Because something is happening here
> And you don't know what it is,
> Do you, Mr Jones?

Worried that a reference to Bob Dylan might be thought to imply lack of seriousness, I attributed the verse to Robert Zimmerman (Dylan's original name). Neither the internal examiner (my supervisor) nor the external (Ernest Gellner) commented on it during the viva. In the United States this examination, following the reading of a thesis by a number of examiners, is known as 'the thesis defence'; but mine was hardly an ordeal of the kind I had anticipated. I had been expecting to have to explain the change of topic from my original research proposal (inter-island links), and to argue a case for my interpretation of what I had put forward as the key principles which structured island social life. Instead, as the viva ended, I was the one to ask what the examiners thought of the main argument of the thesis, and was then asked to summarise it while as the celebratory sherry was being poured. The anti-climax of a rite of passage which hadn't really tested my credentials for a new status has stayed with me; I felt the same seven years later after participating in Natural Childbirth classes and then having to undergo delivery by Caesarian section.

Urban research in the seventies

After obtaining my doctorate I began to think about a return visit to Greece, particularly to visit members of the Anafiot migrant community in Athens to carry out the research that I had not attempted at the end of my period of fieldwork. I am sorry to say that the thought that I might be seen as in any way condoning the Colonels' regime by visiting Greece simply did not occur to me. I successfully applied to the Social Anthropology Committee of the Social Sciences Research Council for a grant to fund travel and other expenses during the university long vacation, the summer of 1973. I carried out nearly two months' research in Athens with the help of a Greek undergraduate student, Dina Mikhu, and was joined by my husband Chris for the last few weeks.

AFFLUENT MIGRANT WORKERS

Dina and I paid several visits to the hiring café, 'Arkadia', in one of the Athenian suburbs. While talking to contractors and subcontractors at tables in the tree-shaded square across the road from the café, we noted that their potential workforce sat in and around the café itself. The younger, mostly unskilled and more recent, migrants stayed inside playing with the table-football machines; older, more skilled men sat outside. When the phone rang with a message for one of the contractors, the café proprietor walked over to call him to the phone, and the contractor would then go round the café recruiting a team for the job.

The Anafiot building workers were doing well financially, particularly those with skills such as tiling and cementing. Every workman's aim was to become a contractor in his own right, so as not to have to take orders from

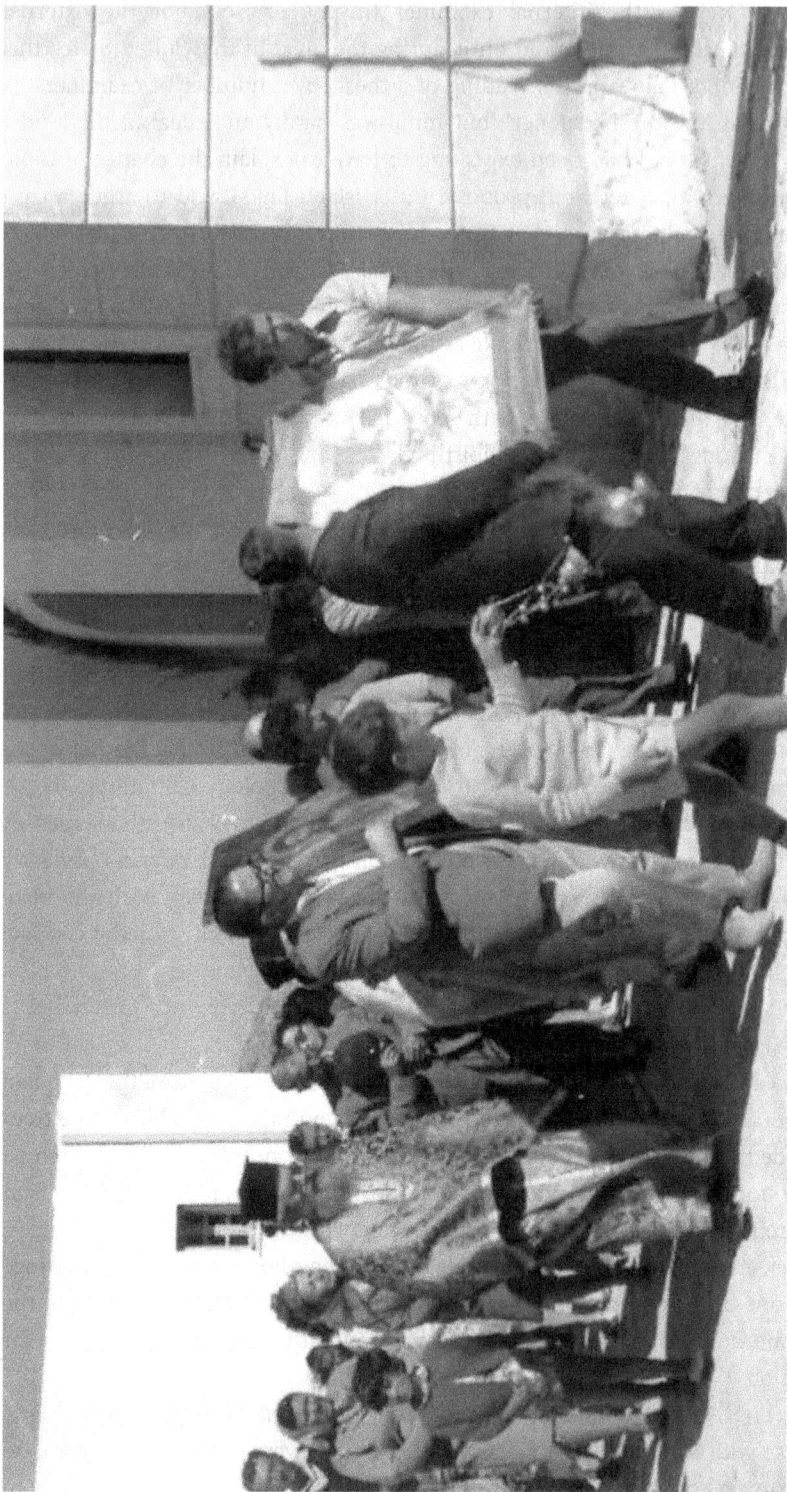

Figure 15   Anafi in the 70s: the Monastery festival, September 1973

anyone else, just like the island agricultural workers. Savings were invested in building plots or suburban blocks of flats. I wondered whether migrant labourers might be used by contractors in undercutting unionised labour in the city, but this was far too sensitive a topic to broach without spending a lot more time establishing trust with workmen and contractors.

The income of unskilled and skilled building workers, and of contractors and sub-contractors, had outstripped that of white collar workers and the high status professions and was producing a *nouveau riche* stratum within Greek society and upsetting earlier assumptions about manual and non-manual jobs, income, and status. Within the Anafiot Migrants' Association the earlier generation of members was criticized by the more moneyed recent migrants who were actively making moves to take over at the next Association elections. Fifteen years later, when these people were in secure positions on the committee, they were themselves being challenged by the next generation of activists among members; what I had thought to be the factionalism of a particular moment seems now to be an instance of a recurring phenomenon.

A few days after my arrival in Athens at the beginning of July 1973, the Migrants' Association held its last social event before the summer break: a coach outing to the beach near Marathon. It was an ideal opportunity for me to meet members of the Association, many of whom were people I knew from the summers of 1966 and 1967 on Anafi, or from visits to Athens, and some were villagers who had migrated in the meantime. Among them was my friend Katina and her husband Kostis Nikolis, who were now working in a market garden near Marathon. I was able to collect names, addresses and telephone numbers from many people at whose homes I met more migrants and old acquaintances.

These visits enabled me to see much more of the range of variation between migrants than events run by the Migrants' Association to which, on the whole, only the successful and prosperous turned up. I sat in the scruffy back kitchen of a flat rented by a group of brothers whose sister had come from Anafi to cook, wash and clean for them while also working. 'It's hard work Margarita, but it's better than being stuck on Anafi a hundred years behind the rest of the world', she said to me. 'But I won't be going "down" [to the island] for the festival in September; I would have to take a shirt for my father, a gift for my mother, something for my godchild, and I just can't afford those extra things. Next year perhaps'.

From another kitchen I looked down into the yard, and saw there Efthimia, the village girl who had begged me to take her photo after her hair had been permed. I had known her then as the niece of Maria, the dressmaker (wife of Kiriakos, the café proprietor). Now married, with small children, Efthimia claimed her husband was an *ergholavos* (contractor). This was most likely an exaggeration, understandable in the context of our comparing lives in the past seven years. Her husband was Antonis Karamalengkhos, son of Kiriakos's sister, and hence a kind of cousin by marriage. I later nicknamed him in my fieldnotes 'the Cowboy', not because of his building skills but because of the stetson-style hat he habitually wore in the summer. Fifteen years later Efthimia and I talked in the kitchen of the restaurant which 'the Cowboy' had built at Klisidhi beach. There were several rooms to rent on a lower floor; their teenage daughter had spent the whole summer helping make beds and clean rooms, and waiting at table. When they got back to Athens at the end of the summer there would be examinations for which she had been unable to study because of the pressure of work in the family business. Efthimia had made a vow to walk *ksepoliti ke munyi*, in stockinged feet and without speaking, from Klisidhi to the Monastery to intercede with Panayia Kalamiotissa on her festival day for help with those exams. However, in the summer of 1973, the financial success of the future family business catering for tourists to Anafi was completely unforeseen.

At a committee meeting in the Association's offices later that July, I was standing with the President of the Association (son of the old woman I had nicknamed 'Granny Glasses', Marusi Ghavalla), when I was embraced warmly by Zabella, wife of a building contractor named Manolis Ludharos. Manolis was one of those opposing the 'old guard' on the committee. He told me that he felt the Association should stop holding receptions and dinner-dances in central Athens hotels and put on more popular and informal gatherings in suburban tavernas.

I had first got to know Manolis and Zabella in the summer of 1966 through my friendship with their niece Rita (Margarita), daughter of Manolis's brother, Petros *foksakis*. Rita, who had been 17 when I first met her, was now in her mid-twenties, and married to a hairdresser. Manolis also had a daughter named Rita (after his and Petros's mother), still a teenager in 1973. Fifteen years later, she was running a fast-food shop at Klisidhi with her husband. Her mother, Zabella, had inherited land there, and was herself renting out cabin-style rooms to tourists. During my first fieldwork that land yielded only a small amount of cheese rent from the shepherds whose flocks grazed the abandoned hill terraces overlooking the beach. In the spring of 1988 I investigated the Anafiot land sale records which were stored in a lawyer's office on Santorini, and found out that building plots at Klisidhi were being sold at hundreds of thousands of drachmas, sums that were piffling by Athenian standards, but huge in terms of the inflation of traditional Anafiot land values.

The Migrants' Association's social events, and the use of their register of members, gave me a very particular kind of sample: the migrants who needed each other to confirm their success, to recognize the extent to which their move to the city had been justified by consequent changes in their lives. These changes were perhaps not very extraordinary by the criteria of other Athenians, but by Anafiot standards they counted. Only those from the same place of origin could judge how far they had come. Meeting migrants who were not members of the Association was a matter of luck: visits to the homes of people I already knew often brought me into contact with fellow migrant neighbours. The only category of migrant it was impossible to investigate systematically was that of Anafiot migrants who had dropped their contacts with their place of origin and with other migrants. This was a methodological problem there seemed to be no solution for!

If I had been able to stay longer than eight weeks in Athens I would have tried to rent a place in one of the suburbs where Anafiot migrants lived, to get some impression of everyday interaction between them. The Taverna Pulakis no longer let rooms on its first floor, but I was lucky enough to find a one-roomed flat to rent in the Plaka. Living in that neighbourhood allowed me to explore the area on the lower slopes around the Akropolis where the first Anafiot migrants were said to have lived. Walking around the winding maze of steps and narrow paths called Anafiotika I was able to locate a few of the last Anafiots to live there. One old woman (Irini Sirighu) I recognised as a summer visitor I had met in my first months on Anafi who had told me stories of the miraculous powers of Panayia Kalamiotissa. Through her I met another woman (Vasso Ghavalla) who told me that she was on the organising committee of a chapel nearby which was 'ours' (i.e. Anafiot), the chapel of Saint Simeon. When I went to look through its locked courtyard gates I saw over the doorway a plaque recording that Anafiot migrants had placed there an ikon of Panayia Kalamiotissa in 1847. That confirmed the oral histories and the Great Greek Encyclopedia account of an Anafiot presence in central Athens in the mid-nineteenth century (see Chapter Seven).

As I walked around I also came across handwritten notices on walls and lamp-posts protesting at proposals to knock down parts of Anafiotika for archaeological excavations and the reconstruction of the ancient Sacred Way. One poster referred to an exhibition about Anafi and Anafiotika, and gave a phone number through which I made contact with architecture students who had formed a pressure group to draw public attention to the plans for the destruction of 'this stinking shanty-town' (as one official had called it). People living in the area had been told to vacate their houses, hand in their keys and await information about government compensation. I was told stories about people foolish enough to do this who then found their family houses taken over as clubs. Irini Sirighu declared that she would have to be carried out feet first rather than leave her two-roomed house, and Vasso Ghavalla told me that she had lived long enough to have heard all this before, and nothing had come of it. In the event, a few old houses were knocked down, but many were restored and refurbished, and no large scale excavations or road building operations were undertaken after all.

RETURN TO ANAFI

After more than six weeks research in and around the centre and suburbs of Athens in July and August, Chris joined me and we travelled to the island in the company of a large number of migrants to attend the Festival of Panayia Kalamiotissa. The steamer arrived at dawn, just as the sun rose over the peak of Mount Kalamos. One of the migrants gripped my forearm and whispered in a voice choked with emotion: *I Anafi mas, Margarita!*, 'our Anafi', and I found myself similarly moved.

Our early morning arrival in the village was not auspicious. I was wearing the jeans into which I had changed the previous night when it got windy on deck, Chris, his beard needing trimming, was in shorts. As we came up the main street we saw the usual boat-day cluster of observers outside Kiriakos's café watching the stream of visitors coming up from the harbour on foot or on donkeys. Taking his yellowed cigarette-holder out of his nicotine-stained beard, the Abbot dryly observed: *Poli anapodha mas yirises, Margarita...*, 'You've returned to us totally the wrong way round, Margarita; you're wearing the trousers and you've brought us a husband who's a priest in shorts.'

Thanasis Vafiadhis was waiting to put us up, as previously arranged. We had phoned from Athens to tell him that we were bringing fresh fruit and vegetables with us. Chris spent his first morning in the village helping Thanasis cut up tomatoes, aubergines, onions and courgettes for a ratatouille. One of the migrant holiday-makers, on hearing about this cheerful involvement in preparing and cooking meals exclaimed: *Margarita, o andhras su ine lukumi!*, 'your husband's a real sweetie.'

Possibly because of our arrival on the pre-Festival steamer, together with so many migrant visitors, we were not as much a focus of attention as my earlier experiences had led me to fear. But there were other factors at work too. As we had landed from the dinghy onto the jetty, I noticed some obviously non-Greek men and women sitting outside one of the harbour sheds which had been converted into a café. There were perhaps ten or fifteen tourists, mostly sleeping on the beach and eating at this new harbour café. It had been set up by Margarita Vafiadhu's step-brother, Tzortzis Russos, and his wife Popi (Kalliopi), whose dowry flat I had visited in Athens (see Chapter Five). There was a complicated story to explain why Tzortzis had left Athens; one of those tales which ends '...best thing that ever happened to me. Otherwise I would still be driving a *trikiklo* (three-wheeled small delivery truck) round the suburbs.' Ten years later the harbour-shed café had been replaced by a large restaurant with six rooms to rent above it; fifteen years later a steamer ticket agency, run by Tzortzis's son Iakovos, had been built on, and a small super-market next to that. Twenty years later Iakovos had become *proedhros* (president of the village council).

During the first few days of the visit in summer 1973 I called on all my old friends and acquaintances and caught up with the news. Any feelings of self-congratulation I might have had about being 'immediately accepted back into the community' were dispelled when I was talking to a woman living near the village church. Her son, in his late teens, came out of the house and listened in to our conversation. 'I don't believe you are a "professor" [the Greek word *kathiyitis* can mean a high-school teacher or anyone teaching at a university]', he interrupted. 'Professors don't talk to peasants.' Maria the dressmaker, wife of Kiriakos, chided me for not wearing a gold watch now that I worked in a university and was a married woman. And wasn't I still using the same camera as I had six years before? Other women friends told me they were worried that I was much thinner than I had been during the first fieldwork. The word for thin, *adhinati*, also means weak; what was wrong? Was married life, particularly its physical side, not satisfying? was my husband making me unhappy? why hadn't I had a child after three years of marriage? My weight loss was puzzling in a culture where married women's bodies are expected to 'open' after marriage, to gain weight, to produce children, to become matronly. I was urged to make a pilgrimage to the miracle-working ikon of Panayia Kalamiotissa to set all these things right, and was told many stories of cures, rescues, interventions, and other demonstrations of her power.

One of the main reasons for the timing of our visit to Anafi was to attend the Monastery Festival to see it from the migrants' point of view. Migrants and islanders with dead relatives to commemorate held memorial services at the village church in the days before the festival, when there were capacity congregations. Migrants had brought with them city-made cakes and imported confectionery for the distribution following the services, and, in one case, packets for *kolliva* printed with the name of the deceased. I noticed that Athenian styles in the construction of family vaults in the cemetery had been introduced.

THE MONASTERY FESTIVAL, 1973

Dina, Chris and I made the journey to the eastern end of the island at dawn on the morning of the Eve of the festival. We found Yianni four-finger at work butchering animals from the Monastery's flocks for the pilgrims' meal that evening. The Abbot was entertaining important older members of the Migrants' Association committee (such as Yiannis Ghavallas who had a menswear shop in central Athens, whom I had met in 1966). All the cells were taken and the Abbot said he couldn't find us anywhere for the night. News of this travelled fast; on our return to the village Thanasis commented ironically: 'I hear the Abbot made you coffee when you got there and allowed you to use his suite of rooms'. Delayed by the attempt to find somewhere to sleep, we had a sweaty climb in the mid-day heat to the Upper Monastery, with views down to the Lower Monastery, showing clearly its location inside the ancient temple groundplan. At the saddle leading to the chapel of Panayia Kalamiotissa on the peak of the mountain, the rock sloped sheer down to the sea on either side of the path. How could I have forgotten how terrifying this last section of the climb was? What if the wind blew strongly as we were crossing the place where there seemed to be only one foot's width to stand? I went across on my hands and knees.

Seven years before when I had seen it for the first time, the dome of the chapel was badly cracked and holed, and the walls crumbling after the Santorini earthquake of 1956. Now, as a result of the Migrants Association's fund-raising efforts, the whole chapel structure, and several monks' cells nearby, had been repaired, renovated and repainted. From up there we could see along the south coast of the island to where the houses of the village were gleaming in the sunshine, like a sprinkling of snow on the hill above the harbour.

When we arrived back at the Lower Monastery a café had been set up inside part of the ancient buildings by Kiriakos and Maria. People, mostly men, sat around on blocks of marble talking and watching others arrive. Some came as pilgrims, in stockinged feet with bamboo staves, going immediately into the church to venerate the ikon of Panayia Kalamiotissa before greeting friends and searching for a place in a cell to spend the night. Some arrived by motor-boat from the harbour. Men had been out shooting wild birds and we were offered appetisers of tiny larks, spitted on twigs and roasted over an open fire.

After the communal evening meal Vespers began in the church, while outside the Monastery walls, on a flat area of ground, younger people were preparing to dance to cassette players. One tape being used had been recorded in a village café during the previous week when Barba Kostas and other local musicians had played. After watching for a while, we went off to lie down on a sleeping-bag stretched out on the dining-room floor. Just before dawn, finding the Monastery's latrine unusable, we went outside to search for secluded places among the rocks. From there could be heard the weekly steamer's siren sounding from the harbour; soon those who had travelled on it, together with people from the village and from the holiday houses at Klisidhi, were arriving by small boat and on foot. Kiriakos and Maria were busy making coffee for the early risers and new arrivals, the church was already full as many pilgrims had kept vigil there all night long. I was dizzy from lack of sleep and too tired to be able to take much notice of who was greeting whom, and whether important members of the local and migrant communities had better vantage points than any one else. Eventually the procession of ikons, led by Panayia Kalamiotissa, pushed its way out of the church. Outside the temporary cafenion, people were standing on blocks of marble, some with cameras, to get a glimpse of their patron saint's representation as it came through the church door opposite. Just as he had seven years previously, Yianni four-finger was carrying the ikon, but this time with the help of his now teenaged son.

Although it only lasted three months, this piece of research not only provided a great deal of information about island migrants in the city, and the role of the Migrants' Association, it made me look back at the earlier fieldwork with an altered perspective. I realized that I had accepted too readily the islanders' catch phrase about being 'far from God'. There were many close and complex ties which bound them to the urban migrant community. Had these ties existed before and I just hadn't seen them? or had they multiplied in the intervening years with the increasing prosperity of the migrants?

The difference in reactions to me now that I was known to be a university teacher and a married woman enabled me to recognize how in the sixties I had fitted in with other people's views of who and what I was. I had felt myself to be inexperienced and uninfluential and I had views about self-presentation with which I was unwilling to compromise. I did not feel comfortable 'dressing up', wearing clothes appropriate to a higher status than I felt I was entitled to. When people had asked me how much my father earned, or what my political views were, I had told them. I had assumptions about politeness, sincerity and respect for privacy which were at odds with Greek, and particularly Anafiot, notions about information as a valued resource, knowledge as power, and prevarication as a social skill. Had public expression of political views which I thought to be uncontroversial (at least by student standards in the sixties) prevented the access I had so desperately tried to gain to village council and agricultural co-operative records? Later still, however, it seemed that some of the opinions I had voiced in the sixties resulted in the eighties in confidences about left-wing views, and in being shown an archive of glass negatives from the commune of political exiles on Anafi in the thirties.

A few months after leaving Greece I read of the events at the Athens Polytechnic which, together with the Turkish invasion of Cyprus, eventually brought about the downfall of the Colonels' regime. News of friends and acquaintances continued to reach me in occasional letters and Christmas cards. It was thus I learnt that Thanasis Vafiadhis had died, still only in his sixties. Grieving for my old friend, I also castigated myself for not having taken the opportunity to talk more with him during the visit about his experiences as an exile, and about his long association with the island.

Anafi in the Eighties

I was next able to visit Anafi in the spring of 1983 during the university Easter vacation. An electricity generator had been built at the harbour and most houses now had electric light, refrigerators, and even television sets. The long promised harbour repairs and improvements had begun with the construction of a harbour mole. A number of signs at the harbour and in the village advertised rooms to rent and it was clear that considerable numbers of both foreign and Greek tourists, as well as migrant holiday-makers, were coming to the island between May and September.

This visit was made not only with Chris, but with our four-year-old son, Peter, who had been born when I was thirty-seven after several years' treatment for infertility. My island women friends were thrilled that I had not only had a child, but a son, and Maria and Kiriakos (who was now *proedhros* after years as leader of the opposition on the village council) offered Peter a piece of loukoumi every time he went into their café. Also travelling with us were Chris's parents. Nikos the schoolteacher invited Chris's mother, a former primary schoolteacher, to visit the village school; his wife Stella invited us all to a lunchtime meal at Ayio Yianni, her late father's estate. Stella was curious: why on earth had I agreed to travel with *ta petherika*, in-laws? Greek women do not get on with their husband's mother, she told me. In her own case, she claimed to pay as few visits as politely possible to Nikos's mother when, in widow's black with a black jersey pull-on hat instead of a black headscarf, she stayed in the family house, a square, nineteen-thirties structure built on a knoll halfway between the village and the harbour.

The lunch at Ayio Yianni was arranged as a result of me asking if it would be appropriate to take a votive thank-offering to the ikon of Panayia Kalamiotissa at the Lower Monastery. I felt that I now had a greater understanding than during my first fieldwork of the connection which the Greek Orthodox Christian tradition perceives between outer form and inner meaning and that my action would not be interpreted as hypocritical. I wanted to express my personal feelings of thankfulness and my respect for island customs.

We set out very early in the morning with Stella, walked together as far as Ayio Yianni, where she turned off to prepare a meal for us on our return from the Monastery. We continued along the south coast of the island to the Monastery. Following island custom, I walked barefoot up the rocky path and in through the gateway framed with inscriptions from Apollo's temple. I found the Abbot to get from him the key to the church and to ask him whether I would be permitted, as a non-Orthodox believer, to hang on the ikon the *tama* I had bought in Athens, a luggage-label shaped piece of metal stamped with the imprint of a swaddled baby. As an 'agnostic ritualist', convinced of the significance and power of ritual but with profound religious doubts, I was not prepared for the extraordinary feeling of achievement and completion which came over me as I left the church. Tears were pouring down my face before I was even aware I was about to cry.

The next visit to Greece was in late August of 1986 when I was invited, along with many other scholars who had researched in Greece, to the inauguration of the first anthropology department at a Greek university at the University of the Aegean on Mytilene (Lesvos). Time constraints and the steamer schedule did not allow me to visit Anafi but on my return to Athens from Mytilene, I was able to attend Vespers on the Eve of the September festival in the chapel of Saint Simeon on the side of the Akropolis used by the migrants. At first I recognized only a few faces, but then the familiar features of Nikos *teleghrafitis* beamed at me. He was now retired and a grandfather. We reminisced over the legendary night that the cistern in my kitchen had overflowed and I had struggled out in the dark and rain to ask for his help. Word got round that I was there and soon old friends and acquaintances were crowding around. Had I heard the news from Anafi? 'Oh yes', I said, 'Improvements to the harbour and electricity..', 'Not that', was the reply, 'about the tragedy'. That was how I learnt that my Anafiot neighbour Eleftheria's husband Antonis, together with his newly married son Yiannis, had been killed by prematurely exploding dynamite charges while fishing a few weeks before.

I used the information I collected on these two brief visits in the eighties to apply to the Economic and Social Research Council for a grant to return to Greece for a longer period of time. I wanted to look in greater depth at the interconnections between the islanders and migrants particularly with respect to the involvement of migrants in the tourism development of the island. The research grant I was awarded was for nine months which allowed me to take unpaid leave of absence from the university coupled with three months' sabbatical leave so that I could spend a whole year in Greece. The plan was for the research to begin at the end of the academic year in late June 1987. It was to start with a six-week stay on the island in the summer, observing the relationships between islanders, migrants and tourists during the height of the season. The middle period would be spent in Athens from autumn 1987 to spring 1988 investigating the lives of urban migrants and the activities of the Association. At the end there would be several weeks on the island in July 1988 to compare with the previous summer and to consult records to which I hoped by then to have access. Preparing for the visit, I used photographs taken during my previous researches to make a forty-minute documentary video recording aspects of life on Anafi and in Athens which I hoped I would be able to show when I visited people and which would elicit useful comments on the past, recent changes, plans for the future, and so on.

FIELDWORK IN THE EIGHTIES

Just before I left for the year away in July 1987, with Chris and eight-year-old Peter, the university published a list of research grants awarded and the title of my project caught the eye of a local reporter. As a result of an article in a Swansea paper, the national press took up the story with captions such as 'Just the Job!', asking why public money was being used to pay for someone to lie on a Greek beach and interview sunbathing nudists. A *Times* 'Fourth Leader' ironically wondered where the end of the queue was so that everyone 'could dip their bread in such succulent gravy'. This unpromising start to the research was continued by arrival in Athens to find the city suffocating in the *nefos*, the cloud of air pollution, and sweltering in exceptionally high temperatures. Leaving most of our luggage in a basement flat in the suburb of Pangrati, we took a steamer to Anafi, arriving with hundreds of other travellers.

The harbour now had a deep-water jetty so that steamers and car ferries could disembark passengers and cargo direct onto the quayside. Deep freezers, heavy machinery, and all manner of consumer goods could now be imported but still had to be transported to the village by donkey. However, some young islanders had motor-bikes and scooters which bounced along the old stepped path between harbour and village, and many holidaying migrants brought summer supplies by car, driven from the ferry and left at the harbour for the length of the stay. Greek and foreign holiday-makers were staying in rooms to rent at Klisidhi, the harbour and the village, and many others were camping on the beaches along the south coast between the harbour and the Monastery. The Migrants' Association had put up signs reminding tourists that nudism was forbidden, but they found it difficult to persuade the local police to enforce the law strictly enough to satisfy the migrants with holiday-houses at Klisidhi. Makarios Arvanitis, secretary of the Association, exposulated 'This is a family place, Margarita, but we see here scenes better suited to the bedroom than the beach!'

Stables and outhouses in the village had been converted into rooms to rent and into souvenir shops selling sunhats, t-shirts, decorative plates, disposable cigarette lighters, all with 'Anafi' printed on them. 'The season's supposed to be May to September, but it's really only July and August', I was told, 'We have to make enough money then to last all year'. How did the islanders survive? Hardly anyone now could be hired for agricultural labour, people said, as men preferred to find employment building holiday-homes and renovating buildings. It was almost impossible to get teams of women to pick olives, however much oil was offered in payment. Everyone had turned to tourism as a source of income. Even my former neighbour Eleftheria, whose wardrobe mirror and television-screen were still concealed with cloths in mourning for the deaths of her husband Antonis and son Yianni, seemed constantly to be

Figure 16   Anafi in the 80s: tourists at the steamer ticket office, August 1987

washing sheets for visitors to the purpose-built rooms she was renting. One of the ruined windmills near the cemetery had been converted into a bar and disco with a flashing blue light on its roof, reminding me of the police phone-box concealing the Tardis in 'Doctor Who'. Rubbish had become a major problem and the village now had street-corner collecting skips. The council employed a collector to empty these weekly into a pit dug outside the village. On the south coast beaches, rubbish of all kinds was accumulating, from syringes and used toilet paper to plastic sandals and empty suntan-oil bottles. Oil-drums were set up as collecting points but there were no funds to employ anyone to empty them. Sewage disposal had yet to be tackled.

The Migrants' Association had commissioned a set of twelve island views from a professional photographer which provided a wide selection of scenic postcards, and a poster had been designed with the sketch map of the island inside a heart shape. These were sold in aid of the Association's funds and there was talk of publishing a brief history and guide-book to the island as a further source of income. Used to the pace of village life during my first fieldwork, I was bewildered by the speed of change.

Once again we attended the island's festival at the Monastery. This time there were squabbles over the allocation of eighty foam mattresses provided by the Migrants' Association for pilgrims' use, with allegations of favouritism and preferential treatment of relatives. Dancing after the pilgrims' meal in the Monastery dining-hall took place on a large concrete dance-floor built by the Migrants' Association just outside the Monastery walls, illuminated by generator-powered spotlights and with loudspeakers to relay music. Pilgrims who had come over from Santorini, particularly groups of young people, seemed set on competitive displays of dancing and there were many foreign tourists watching and attempting to join in. The next morning, the procession of ikons after the Liturgy made only one circuit of the church, and many of those watching were pushed aside by those with camcorders and cameras wanting unimpeded lines of sight to record the event.

We left a few days later so that Peter could start school and for the urban-based section of the research to begin while summer contacts with migrants were still fresh. I attended most of the events put on by the Migrants' Association; its programme began with elections for the officers and committee members in November followed by a Christmas dinner dance. Then came the cutting of the New Year cake (*vasilopitta*) and singing of seasonal songs to the island bagpipes and drum in January; joint involvement in preparing the festivities at the patron saint's festival at the chapel of Ayios Simeon in Anafiotika in February; a pre-Lent Carnival party; and a dinner and dance at Easter. The dinner dance included a special display of traditional Cycladic island dances by the newly formed dance troupe, consisting of mostly teenage girls, some of whom were obliged to wear male costumes and dance the male parts in order to make up the numbers. The Association's programme of events concluded with a coach trip or outing in July before everyone left for summer holidays.

During the winter months I was asked to talk about my research at one of the archaeological schools which offers facilities for visiting scholars. I was able to invite some of my migrant friends to a talk in the chandeliered reception rooms in which a selection of the photographs taken during the summer was on display and during which I mentioned the video-documentary. This had unexpected repercussions. The news soon went round that research about Anafi was known in the scholarly community and I was asked to show the video first at a meeting of the Migrants' Association in January, and later, during an Easter visit to Anafi, to the island's recently established Cultural Society (founded by returned migrants to 'retain and restore traditional island customs'). This gave an opportunity to try to summarise and explain the various pieces of research I had carried out to the people most intimately concerned. If the making of the video and its showing in Athens and on the island had been a carefully thought out strategy, it could not have been more successful. Soon, everyone in the island and migrant communities had heard about it and wanted a copy. People were now anxious to talk to me and give me information to supplement the original studies and to aid the current project.

Every Sunday during the winter months the Migrants' Association football team played matches against other Associations' teams in stadiums all over the suburbs. The teams were not always made up of Anafiot migrants but frequently included in-laws, friends and neighbours. I was often the only spectator in the stands but found I could collect a great deal of information from these players about attitudes towards the committee's plans for events in the city and for improvements on the island. Also of interest to me were the various explanations given of my research by the Anafiot members of the team to their non-Anafiot team-mates. Parallels were made with investigative journalism and I was surprised at the young players' apparent familiarity with the idea of social research.

I also made short visits to the island outside the tourist season, and went over to Santorini to the local office of the Ministry of the Environment to consult the records of applications for building permits and to assess the amount of historical material stored in a lawyer's office there dating back a century: land sales, dowry agreements, wills, deeds of gift, etc. These comings and goings of mine were more characteristic of a member of the migrant community than of an outsider, and villagers seemed to take me much more for granted with each return trip. My frequent brief stays and re-appearances provided useful markers by which family heirlooms were looked out to show me, and old books of records tracked down. I brought enlargements of photographs to give to people, and showings of the Anafi video prompted others to invite me to watch professional and amateur films of weddings and christenings.

When we paid our last visit to the island in July 1988, work had started on a road from the harbour to the village via Klisidhi. Dynamiting was under way, and fresh water springs were blocked as portions of hillside were blasted out. Would there be funds for the road to be continued as far as the Monastery? Would there be a regular steamer schedule outside the tourist season? In the meantime, a helicopter pad had been built near the cemetery on a reasonably flat piece of ground and any medical emergencies could be rapidly transferred to hospital on Santorini or Athens. An Athenian cardiologist had bought land on the south coast from which a small jetty was immediately built so as to land a mechanical digger. Village men had a long period of employment constructing this holiday-home (finished in 1992). Returned migrants with seats on the village council were anxious to make plans and get funds for a piped water system, and a pressure group was forming to establish two museums: one to conserve the archaeological remains at Kastelli, the other for items of traditional island folk culture. Some of my old friends in the village spoke bitterly about these returned migrants and their plans for the village which seemed to have curious connections to the land plots they owned or the businesses they were running. 'You spent a winter with us, Margarita, I can remember [the story of the night the well overflowed in my kitchen]... whereas these people say they know what's best for the island when they haven't a notion what it's like here in November or February...'

In the last weeks of July 1988 Thanasis's widow, Margarita, asked me to set aside a morning to come and look at some *enthimia*, mementoes. Her younger daughter, Maria, whom I had first met during the sixties when she was eleven, was now married with two sons, and took charge of the unpacking of the items Margarita wanted me to see. She set a number of wooden boxes on the table in what used to be my room. One contained Thanasis's shadow puppets, made from cardboard pieces jointed with pieces cut and hammered out of sardine tins. I recognized from Thanasis's puppet show ten years earlier the trickster Karayeoryi and his son Kollitiri (a name which means 'stuck-together', that is, thin to the point of emaciation); Alexander the Great; and the dragon called *Therio*, the wild beast or monster. During his exile Thanasis had given a show in the village school, and when the audience had called out the dragon's name, one of the villagers, whose nickname this was, took offense, and stormed out. 'And he hasn't come into my café from that day to this', Thanasis had told me. The puppet of the Pasha's beautiful daughter had patterns cut in her harem trousers, over which coloured sweet wrappers had been stuck to show through onto the screen. There was a magazine photo of the Taj Mahal, which Thanasis had copied for scenery. As we lifted out the pieces, Maria and I, and her eldest son Minas, exclaimed at the care and ingenuity with which they had been constructed.

'And now', she said, 'Maybe you would like to see a few photographs'. With that, she opened the other boxes and revealed an archive of glass and celluloid negatives showing the life on Anafi of a commune of political exiles in the nineteen thirties and forties. There were one hundred and sixty of them, the remains of a larger collection which had been hidden in one of the houses which the political exiles had rented and which had been left when they were all shipped to Athens during the Occupation.

That moment determined the next decade of research for me: I knew I had to find out more about the political detainees during the Metaxas regime (1936–41) and to ensure that the photo-archive was preserved and published.

Anafi in the Nineties

A decade went by before I visited the island again, for a week, in the spring of 1998. From the Migrants' Association newspaper I knew that a road linking the harbour and village, via Klisidhi, had been completed, and that there was now a bus meeting the thrice-weekly steamers. Nikos Ladhikos, the village schoolteacher at the time of my first research, and now retired, was leader of the village council, *proedhros*. The front page story of the Migrants' newspaper at the end of summer 1997 was not, as I had expected, devoted to a description of the Monastery Festival. I was startled to see a headline reading: Anafi on fire, *kaïke i Anafi*. In early July, possibly as a consequence of the smoke-devices used by bee-keepers setting fire to brushwood, one third of the island, mostly inland along the south coast, went up in flames. None of the inhabitants, or tourists, was injured, but buildings, trees, and bee-hives were completely destroyed and the antiquities on Kastelli were badly damaged. Because most of the villagers now use bottled gas or electricity, very few people gather brushwood for fuel any longer. Once this caught alight, dry as tinder in the scorching summer, and with no firebreaks in between, the hillsides blazed for nearly a day. Fire-fighting planes were sent from the mainland, and soldiers on duty on Santorini were brought over to prevent the fire reaching the village.

My return visit occured right at the beginning of March 1998. I arrived on Apokreas Sunday, the last day of Carnival before Lent begins on Clean Monday, *Kathari Dheftera*. In the dark of an early March day, after a twelve-hour over-night journey, I walked out through the car door of the ferry onto the jetty and saw Manolis the fisherman, now grey-haired and rather stout, securing a rope to a capstan. 'You're back again, Margarita' he remarked, seemingly unsurprised. I lifted my rucsac up the steps into the back of the bus drawn up outside Popi's restaurant, noting the number of cars and trucks also parked there. The bus driver was Tzortzis Dhamigos (three years old at the time of my first fieldwork), the son-in-law of my old neighbour Eleftheria. I later watched him and his wife Aghapia busily refitting a bar in the room above Eleftheria's house which had previously been Yianni Dhamigos's café and more recently rented by Athenian Greeks as a café-bar. With a few passengers on board, including Manolis, the bus rattled up the new road, overtaken by the cars and motor-bikes of those who had been waiting for relatives, or supplies from Athens, and by a large lorry with the Rinakis surname painted on it. When the bus pulled up, Manolis helped me with my bags and showed me which way to go. 'I'll come and see your wife later, when I've had a lie-down', I promised.

The room in which I had arranged to stay was below the village square, with a view eastwards to Mount Kalamos, and westwards towards Santorini. It was in a two-storey block of holiday rooms run by Kalliopi (Popi) the eldest daughter of Tzortzis *mavros* (she had been six years old at the time of my first fieldwork). She was now married to Panayiotis, son of Manolis *birbilis*, the bagpipe player. They and their three children lived in part of the block; one of their own rooms was just above the one I was renting. As she showed me around, Popi told me how busy she was in the summer. The steamer arrival times often meant that she had to clean rooms and make beds in the middle of the night after one lot of tourists left and before the next ones arrived.

Panayiotis ran one of the few café-restaurants which operated all year round (like Popi Russu's at the harbour), and had been in business now for over ten years. Just off the old path down to the harbour, the restaurant had expanded from the one barrel-vaulted room and courtyard I remembered from 1987. The courtyard wall of the adjoining house had been knocked down to make a larger area for setting out tables for summer patrons and the other house was currently used to store tables and chairs. Outside the tourist season the original building was used on weekday evenings as a cafenion for village men and at the weekends there was a small clientele for evening meals, mostly schoolteachers from the local primary and secondary schools.

Fringing the terrace outside the room I was renting from Popi and Panayiotis was a little vegetable and flower garden, watered by a hose attached to a tap in the wall. This called my attention to other gardens, and vegetables, planted in old paraffin tubs and broken waterjars, outside village houses. There seemed to be more than I remembered even from ten years ago, let alone from the sixties, when water had to be hauled up from the cistern with a bucket and rope (except for those few who had domestic pumps). The installation of piped water had made a small but important difference to everyday life.

After a couple of hours sleep, I went up to the village square to wait until the Sunday service was over so as to greet old friends. Next to an electricity supply pole on one side of the square was a card-phone, next to it a motor-bike was parked, one handle-bar leaning against a large old fridge tied up with rope (waiting to be taken away for repair?). I could hear snatches of the liturgy through the open door of the church, but the sound was drowned out by the roar of a concrete mixer and the shouts of workmen. A two-storey house was being built beside the smaller chapel next to the church, on the site where Antonis the fisherman used to have a flour mill, and concrete was being poured. I soon found out that this house was being built for Antonis's daughter, Margarita, and her policeman husband, for use in the summer, and that bad weather had delayed building work which now had to be finished in a hurry. I remembered being chastised on a Sunday in the sixties for sewing up a skirt hem; a woman could embroider, I was told, but no 'work' could be done. Times had certainly changed.

When the service finished, and the congregation began to come out of church, I was greeted with a cry of delight by Eleftheria, who introduced me to her current tenant, one of the schoolteachers, a widow from Crete. Also in the crowd coming out of church was the village secretary, Antonis Kollidhas, son of 'honey Anna', who had been such a help to me ten years before. He couldn't see me next day, he said, as it was a public holiday, and there would be a civil servants' strike later in the week over pension rights. As I digested the implications of this, my hand was seized by Zabetti Rinaki, younger sister of my friend Vasiliki. Zabetti was now married to one of the island's two priests, and in the summer they ran a restaurant near the beach below her family's garden lands at Rukuna. 'Come and have coffee' she urged, and I found her house full of people, a large proportion of the congregation. Maybe the other half of the congregation was having coffee in the house of Papa Nikolaos and his wife Anna (sister of Tzortzis the bus-driver)?

This invitation gave me the opportunity not only to meet old friends, and hear their news (usually of the death of other acquaintances and gruesome tales of operations and painful illnesses) but also to meet some of the primary and secondary level teachers at the village school. When they heard about my past researches, and that I had brought photographs from the sixties with me (from the final draft of this book), I was invited to come and talk to the pupils when school re-opened on Tuesday. This was a useful bonus, as the children told their parents what I had said in the talk, and about the photos, and I found myself sought out during the remainder of my stay. The text of the book was examined, and the photos searched for familiar faces. From their comments and observations, I learnt a lot more about people and places and the past.

I watched Zabetti serve the crowd in her house with coffee, home-distilled grape-brandy which she had flavoured with clove and cinnamon, and bitter-orange spoon-sweets she had made herself. I remembered her as a fourteen year old, eagerly showing me the pottery beehives at Stavros in January 1967, and helping her mother at Vasiliki's engagement party. It seemed that outside the tourist season she was just as busy as she was at Rukuna.

Afterwards, I accompanied Eleftheria and the Cretan schoolteacher down as far as the Patiniotis's grocery. It didn't seem to have as large and varied a stock as in the past. Maybe the mini-markets with their deep-freezers and chilled drinks cabinets offered too much competition? But Rembelia told me that her daughter Flori, wintering in Athens, who had been running a mini-market down at the harbour ten years ago, now had both a 'market' and a café-snack bar at the harbour which she ran with the help of the wife of her brother Evangeli. The main mini-market in the village, which I visited later, was run by Rembelia's niece Yiannula and her husband Iakovos, Popi Russu's son. Now that all their children were married or independent, Rembelia and Yianni kept the grocery on 'because we're used to it' rather than for the income. Talking about Easter celebrations in the past, Rembelia painted a picture of a united community, observing traditional customs, and happy to be good neighbours. As she talked, she searched through a plastic bag full of photographs. 'Here it is', she exclaimed 'Flori was asking me to send it to her so that she could have it copied'. She pulled out my old photo of her husband Yianni in his Carnival costume in March 1967, with stocking mask, fez, high boots, apron, and wooden phallus.

Walking on through the village from west to east, I felt that it had doubled in size. The new road, winding up from the harbour via the edge of the holiday houses at Klisidhi, curving round the back of the kastro and leading up to the edge of the village square, had provided new opportunities for building as well as tripling land values. New houses stretched further down the southern slopes overlooking the harbour, but the majority of recent building was concentrated at the eastern end of the village. Old houses on the kastro rock had been renovated, and the donkey-stables and storehouses on the northern side of the kastro had almost all been replaced by houses and blocks of rooms to rent to summer visitors. Nearly everywhere in the village I could see building work, renovation, or reconstruction, in progress, with many buildings using modern versions of the traditional barrel vaulted roof. Where building was near the road, cement-mixers, trucks, lorries, and other heavy equipment was on site. I could see how difficult it must be to work on the houses in the middle of the village where the lanes were still stepped and narrow.

All the houses in the village had enjoyed piped running water since 1993; the majority of them, and the rooms to rent, now had solar-panel water

Figure 17   Anafi in the 90s: the village in March 1998

heaters on their roofs. As I reached the eastern end of the village I met Sofia, the widow of Antonis Kollidhas (nicknamed *seklemis*), fisherman and olive-press owner. Sofia was one of the daughters of Anezini, the woman who had sung the Virgin's lament on Good Friday 1967. I had watched and helped in Antonis's olive-press in November 1966, and also remembered him as one of the boatmen, rowing out to the steamer in a dinghy. In the summer of 1987 he had gone out in his boat to help a tourist yacht which had got into difficulties when its engine failed, and the grateful passengers had given a party in his honour at Popi's restaurant, where Sofia was working as a kitchen helper. Antonis had been drowned in August 1996 when his fishing-boat overturned. Sofia, in black, was sitting by the side of the path near the door of the press. I joined her and gave her my condolences and we exchanged tearful reminiscences. People were 'better' then, said Sofia, and the village was 'one'. I was fortunate to have known Anafi thirty years ago, she said. Our conversation then turned to the island's dependency on tourism.

My arrival coincided with the Carnival celebrations which mark the beginning of Lent (Apokreas). At a dinner-dance sponsored by the Parents' and Guardians' Association of the Primary and High School, I talked to some old friends, and caught up with more news. I was sitting opposite Kostas, son of Manolis the fisherman, who, as a little boy aged two, had sat on my knee to play 'Down the road away went Polly', and now had two children of his own. Plates of chicken were served, and plastic bottles which had previously contained lemonade or cola and were now filled with wine were brought to every table. As at dinner dances held by the Migrants' Association in Athens, raffle tickets were sold, and prizes distributed later in the evening. Near the door was a table where the young unmarried men were sitting, many in fashionable leather bomber-jackets. At another table sat the primary and secondary school teachers, supporting the Parents' Association fund-raising efforts. Across the room I could see Zabetti Rinaki, sitting with her husband the priest and a teenage son. When tape-recorded music was switched on, her husband danced with obvious enjoyment, tucking up his robes so as not to trip over them. Children in costume were also dancing, spraying each other with foam string, and tossing paper streamers about.

At another table sat Manolis Loudharos, nephew of Nikos who had been the postmaster in the sixties. Manolis was now in charge of the post-office himself, providing a travellers' cheque changing service in the summer, and also directing tourists to the rooms run by his wife at the eastern end of the village. Apart from these, there were very few other people there I recognized; this was a dance patronised mostly by younger couples or by middle-aged people with teenage children, people whom I might have known when they themselves were children but whom I needed to get to know now as adults.

I left the dance in the early hours, but was told afterwards that the dancing went on until after 4am. The village was certainly very quiet for most of the next day, Clean Monday, *Kathari Dheftera*. The only person up and busy was the baker, Maria Nikoli. She was married to Dhimitris, Rembelia's youngest brother (one of the sons of Mattheos 'the cat'). She was making *laghadhes*, flat bread heavily indented with finger-marks, traditionally eaten on this day. Pleased to have some company, she made me coffee and talked to me while she worked. 'In the summer I get up at 3am, to make bread for the restaurants and cafés which serve breakfasts, but getting enough sleep is difficult because of the noise. I make 400–500 kilos of bread a day in the summer; this time of year about 150 kilos every other day.' When I asked her what the most important change there had been in island life, she said that piped water had certainly made the greatest difference to her work load, particularly with respect to clothes washing.

I walked down to the harbour by the new road noticing the children's playground which had been built at the edge of the eastern end of the village, and a number of new buildings with painted boards advertising breakfasts, fast food, cold drinks, suntan oil, film. At the harbour I went into Popi's restaurant to say hello and to catch up with her news. Her work load in the summer was overwhelming, she said. The numbers of tourists were constantly increasing and there were now Flying Dolphin day-trip tour-boats from other islands as well as the steamers. On one particular day there had been four boats during daylight hours and she had made up her mind she would not put herself under so much strain again this summer. I walked back up to the village by the old road.

Next day, and until the civil servant's strike, I was able to talk over my impressions with the village secretary, Antonis Kollidhas. I remembered him getting married in the summer of 1987 (the first wedding on Anafi I had ever attended, and the double wedding of two sisters at that). Afterwards he had phoned up a senior colleague in the administrative hierarchy to ask whether, as village secretary, he could lawfully record his own marriage (he could).

He told me that all the rooms to rent (nearly 130 in the village and at Klisidhi) had their own bathrooms and small fridges; some had modest cooking facilities as well. The summer population was six times that in the winter, with returning migrant Anafiots coming for holidays or to run businesses, other Greek holiday-makers and foreign tourists. Camping (illegal except at recognised sites) on the beaches was still a problem. However, the greater number of cafés along the south coast beaches, and the frequently running water-taxis linking the beaches with the harbour where there was a mini-market for supplies and provisions, now meant that campers and nudists tended to use the beaches beyond Klisidhi.

During the rest of the week I continued to explore the village and the harbour noting the changes which had taken place, and talking to old acquaintances and new friends. Much of what I was seeing and hearing about was already familiar from accounts of the impact of tourism on small communities: some locals trying to make enough during the tourist season to live on for the whole of the year while others tried to diversify; disruption of the routines of daily life by tourists' late-night partying and early morning departures; changes in the work patterns of men and women and in the relationships of parents and children. The Anafi I had known in the sixties seemed now almost to belong to another century, to have been 'a hundred years behind the rest of the world', *ekato khronia piso ap' to kosmo*, as the villagers used to say. Even though some of my old friends' reminiscences of the experiences we had shared seemed to me to be overly tinged with pink, I also felt a pang of nostalgia for the past, or maybe just for my past self.

What is the future of an out-of-the-way Greek island like Anafi? Given the vagaries of fashions in holidays, will tourism continue to be a main source of income? Could agricultural production revive with the use of machinery and the encouragement of government grants? I have seen radical changes in the islanders' lives in the three decades since I first arrived on Anafi. I hope to be around to see what happens in the next thirty years.

CHAPTER TEN

'An honorary citizen of the island'

Research in the twenty-first century

∗

I visited Greece three times in the first decade of the new millennium (2002, 2003, 2006), while still employed at Swansea University (I retired in September 2008). The first two of these visits were during the spring vacation, so as not to interrupt teaching. The third, in 2006, was in a three-month study leave. These visits also enabled me, while in Athens, to carry out further research on political exiles and, most importantly, on the Anafi exiles' handwritten newspapers.

During the 2002 visit I was able to give one copy of *Greek Island Life* to the Migrants Association and another one to the mayor (*proedhros*) to place in the community office. As the book was in English, most people, both in Athens and on the island, were interested in the illustrations rather than the text, in identifying themselves and their relatives when younger, and in noting the changes that had taken place in the village and the countryside in the intervening decades. When they looked at the book I had written (*The Social Organisation of Exile*) about the political exiles who had lived on the island during the Metaxas regime, 1936–41, illustrated with images from an archive of glass and celluloid negatives, they were mainly interested in those photographs which showed village scenes featuring local people (a wedding, a funeral, a saint's day celebration), or identifiable parts of the landscape (the harbour, hill terraces, parts of the village).

I am able to give an almost contemporary account of those three visits by quoting from the annual newsletter that we include with Christmas and New Year cards to friends and relatives.

FROM THE NEWSLETTER AT THE END OF 2002: ATHENS AND ANAFI IN APRIL AND MAY

I arrived in Greece just after my 60th birthday to renew acquaintance with, and collect information about, migrants and resident islanders from Anafi since my last visit (1998). By good luck, I had arrived just in time to attend the two-yearly elections for the Association's committee and was able to meet old friends, show them the books, tell them about the negotiations for Greek translations, and make contacts for my projected visit to the island. I also went to the Benaki Museum photo-archive (whose curator comes from an Anafiot family), where negotiations have begun to lodge my photographs and slides. [The photo-archive was at that time located at the top of a building overlooking Kolonaki Square.]

Chris joined me after three weeks and we then took a ferry to Anafi, arriving just as preparations for Easter started. The changes to the island since my previous visit four years earlier are very striking, particularly the asphalted roads between harbour, beach and village, to the monastery at the eastern end of the island and to a heliport. There is also an extensive network of wide dirt tracks (usually called agricultural roads in Greek) to nearly all parts of the island. We hired a scooter and made a day tour of the island, seeing more of it in a few hours than in the previous 36 years. These roads make for much easier access and many agricultural areas are being opened up again, particularly for domestic subsistence, but also so that renovated field cottages can be used, and rented out, as holiday homes.

FROM THE NEWSLETTER AT THE END OF 2003

I had an amazing time in Athens in April when I went to the Greek Communist Party's headquarters in Perissos, a suburb of Athens, to look at what I thought would be perhaps ten or so handwritten newspapers from the Anafi political exiles' commune (discovered after a flood at the headquarters, and featured in a newspaper article which I was sent). There turned out to be over forty, with seven different titles (from Antifascist to Arts News), and there was precious little time before the Orthodox Easter to make notes on them all and then to begin to transcribe them. Chris came out to join me, but there wasn't enough time to get to Anafi and back again before returning to the UK.

In 2004 Swansea University decided to close down the School of Social Sciences and International Development and to 'disinvest' the subjects of Anthropology, Development Studies and Sociology (and also Chemistry and Philosophy), meaning that these subjects could no longer be taught to new undergraduate or postgraduate students. Many younger staff left for posts elsewhere, some older staff took early retirement or negotiated a slightly later one. Eventually the remaining staff became part of a new School of

Environment and Society and joined the Department of Geography in that School. The university had the obligation to provide teaching for the remaining students who had to be seen through to their degrees or postgraduate awards. In November of that year I was invited to give a special lecture at the Centre for Hellenic Tradition of the University of Manitoba in Winnipeg, Canada, and one of the audience came up to tell me that his mother was from Anafi and that it was his grandfather's windmill, on the eastern edge of the village, that featured in a large number of the photos (it is now a bar and disco).

As the fortieth anniversary of my first arrival on the island was coming up, I applied for funding to carry out research in the spring of 2006 and was fortunate to be awarded a Small Grant by the ESRC (Economic and Social Research Council) for three months on the topic 'the transformation of a peripheral community: a pilot study'. My hope was to use this initial investigation to provide material for a much larger-scale full-time study covering a year (rather like the one in 1987–8, in which I would move between the island and migrant communities). The hoped for larger-scale project was not funded. The report on this research in 2006, some of which is excerpted below, can be found on the ESRC website: www.esrc.ac.uk/my-esrc/grants/ RES-000-22-1641/read

FROM THE NEWSLETTER AT THE END OF 2006

At the end of February we set off for twelve weeks in Greece, divided between Athens and Anafi, in a kind of sandwich: three weeks in Athens (mostly working in the library at the British School at Athens and making contacts), then six weeks on Anafi which included the Eastern Orthodox Christian Easter, and then three further weeks in Athens. While in Athens I visited the Folklore Centre of the Academy of Athens, which has its base in a neo-classical building in Plaka, and was shown in the archives a notebook dating from the summer of 1965 which contained notes taken on a research visit to Santorini and Anafi by one of the centre's researchers. The idea was planted that the section of the notebook about Anafi could be published, illustrated with my photos from 1966–7. [I later had time to read through the Anafi part of the notebook (about 90 handwritten pages) and found that all but one of those who had given information were still alive when I reached the island and that I had photographs of them which could be used.]

FROM THE REPORT TO THE ESRC

The main method of investigation used, both on the island and in Athens, was traditional anthropological participant-observation fieldwork. Conversations with the majority of informants in Athens and on Anafi were with people whom I had known for years, and in some cases, decades. Some of them had known me for forty years, since my first visit to the island, many of them were personal friends, although a few were as suspicious of my activities and motives now as they had been then. Given that one of the major themes that emerged from this research is the issue of simferon *(self-interest, personal advantage), it may be significant that I heard at second-hand that the research itself was being defined by some islanders and some migrants as an example of simferon, rather than of 'genuine' involvement with the island. I was also told that those who supported and cooperated with the research had responded by saying that one visit might be an example of simferon in order to acquire some desired qualification (as with my doctoral research in 1966–7), but that continued association and involvement over forty years surely indicated my sincerity.*

On most days on the island I walked around the village, talked to people in their houses and shops, and in cafes. On other occasions I made rented scooter or quad-bike trips to various parts of the island, taking a large number of digital photographs to record changes in buildings and in use of land. I was particularly interested in the expansion and development of residential and agricultural locations outside the village, and in the repair and renovation of field chapels and family vaults and bone depositories. I discussed my observations with villagers, as well as with the school teachers who were intrigued by my work and association with the island. Many of them took the opportunity of using computers in the schools to google my name and find out about my research and publications. This 'immediacy of verification' was a novelty in the research process for me.

I was particularly struck that frequent reference was made to the greater prevalence of simferon nowadays compared with the past, with people calculating what was to their personal advantage rather than for the common good. What was interpreted as the loss of community was bewailed by people who claimed that twenty or thirty years ago the islanders 'were all one'. I felt that this was a rose-tinted view of the past, particularly when looking at records of my first fieldwork in 1966–7, when people said that the then present was a shadow of the communal values of the past.

I wrote up fieldnotes every day, finding that a laptop allowed revision and interpolation of forgotten material [as well as the incorporation of Greek in the text by toggling to a Greek keyboard]. An unexpected discovery was that the use by island shopkeepers of tills which recorded time of day as well as the date on receipts allowed a more detailed reconstruction of a day's activities than memory alone (unless, of course, the till was mis-programmed, or had not been adjusted when the hour changed). Indeed, the impact of new technology on myself and my own working methods (a digital camera, a laptop, internet access, a mobile phone) and the impact of some of these items on the social lives of islanders and migrants deserves discussion in its own right.

I found it much more difficult in Athens than in the past to arrange to meet members of the migrant community, all of whom had busy, active lives, often with several jobs. The greater involvement of women in paid employment meant that I was not able to pay visits to households in the late afternoon (a traditional time for women's visits) to talk to women, and their school-age children. The transport network in Athens (metro, bendy buses, trams) has greatly improved, so that I did not have to make as much use as planned of taxis to reach, and return from, suburban destinations. The use of a mobile phone (now that few kiosks have pay-phones any more) to liaise with migrants in paying visits, was a bonus, and also meant that I could phone for directions when lost in a maze of streets.

FROM THE NEWSLETTER OF 2006
Shortly after arriving on Anafi, I celebrated my 64th birthday by giving a talk at the village secondary school about my forty years of research. The highlight of the visit for me was a ceremony in the village council's offices, when I was presented with a letter announcing the unanimous decision of the council to make me an honorary citizen of the island to mark forty years since I first went there – and they gave me a medal to mark the occasion (left over from the previous summer's swimming competition). I was also on Anafi when I was sent an email to tell me that I had been promoted to Professor.

After my return to Swansea, I was given permission by the university to shift all my teaching into the first term of the academic year (2006–7) so as to be able to take up the post of Visiting Fellow at the British School at Athens from February to May of 2007. However, that and all further plans for research and travel were put on hold when I received a diagnosis of breast cancer in December 2006; I spent most of 2007 undergoing surgery, chemotherapy and radiotherapy, and then recovering from 'chemo-brain' and dealing with newly growing hair. This was followed by a five-year-long medication regime. When I recounted all this to my Greek friends, partly to explain why I hadn't visited Greece, the thing which impressed them most was that under the National Health Service in Wales *'kai i perouka tsampa'* (even the wig was free). I retired at the end of the academic year 2007–8, after forty years at Swansea University.

FROM THE NEWSLETTER AT THE END OF 2008
Shortly before the end of September, my last month in post, I was amused to receive a letter from someone in the university administration asking me when, in the forthcoming year, I would like to give my professorial inaugural lecture. My reply, suggesting a valedictory lecture in the light of my retirement and the

Figure 18   'An honorary citizen of the island': with the mayor in April 2006

disinvestment and disestablishment of my department, remained unanswered.
I have had great fun composing a text called Valedictory Villanelles which will,
I think, use lines from two villanelles – Dylan Thomas's famous 'Do not go
gentle into that good night', and Auden's 'Time will say nothing but I told you so'.

Retirement enabled me to read, think, and write more than I had been able to
do for many years, without any time pressures or too many conflicting calls
on my time. My husband Chris was working, with other scholars, on a history

of Oxford University Press, so I was able to accompany him to Oxford, and to work in what I thought of as the Modern Greek Library in Wellington Square, five minutes' walk from 'Clarendon College' (the OUP building) where Chris was working. During this time, by a lucky chance – another Visiting Fellow could not take up the position – I was offered the position at the British School for early 2009 and after passing the January check-up flew off to Athens for three months, joined by Chris at the end of February.

FROM THE NEWSLETTER AT THE END OF 2009

The Visiting Fellow position at the School gave free accommodation with bedroom, study, and bathroom, in return for which I was to give one public lecture and one seminar. I was also expected to be 'involved' with the students at the School (of all ages, mostly archaeologists and classicists, but also including students of modern Greek history and modern Greek cultural studies), and 'play a part in the life of the School' (which entailed attending some committee meetings, deciding on the award of Bursaries, and giving a talk to the Friends of the School and to a Classics Teachers' course). I also gave a seminar for the Greek Society for Ethnology on 'Ossuaries on Anafi: their construction and significance'. The audience – which included some of the Anafiot migrants in Athens – seemed to like it, and joined in with comments and explanations, and later the members of the Committee elected me an Honorary Member (only the fourth in its history).

Recent Greek history and customs also came to the forefront at a three-day conference I went to, which celebrated the centenary of the Greek Folklore Society. One speaker chastized some of his colleagues for failing to deal with the written and oral testimonies of people during the time of the Greek Civil War and the subsequent periods of exile and of 're-education'. 'They are the 'folk' as much as people in the countryside' was his point – and this was reinforced by a paper about supermarkets! So Greek folklore studies is not the rather old-fashioned and ahistorical pursuit that it once was – or rather, that I thought it to be, because it seems that there has always been this strong undercurrent of interest in urban life, migrants, the development of new customs, and traditions which are redesigned for new environments.

After my three months as Visiting Fellow were up, we set off on the 'Prevelis' (a ferry from Piraeus that takes a circular route to Santorini, Anafi, islands in the Dodecanese, Crete, and back again) for a few days on Anafi. There, having expected that we would once again hire a scooter to explore the island, we were loaned a car, which made travel more comfortable, but a little less adventurous – no bumping over rutted tracks to remote chapels.

During this visit we stayed in the house where I had rented a room during my first fieldwork. There were several days of constant rain, and we had to keep an eye on the cistern to make sure it did not overflow – there were now electric cables which could have been shorted out by any flooding in the kitchen. I was asked once again to give a talk at the High School, and luckily had stored on my laptop a set of PowerPoint images I had used for a seminar at the British School. Once again the photos of people and places were the main talking point, as members of the audience shouted out identifications, or exchanged comments. There was hardly any need for me to have prepared a talk at all.

From the newsletter at the end of 2010

In June I heard that an application I had made to the Leverhulme Foundation for a grant had been successful. These grants are designed for retired academics to complete a project and mine [mentioned earlier] was to collect details of names and places so as to annotate all the fieldwork photographs I had taken on Anafi and among the Anafiot migrants in Athens since 1966, so that they could be donated with as much information as possible, to the photographic archive of the Benaki Museum in Athens. I had met the Director of the archive many years earlier, when it was little more than a cupboard in a backroom of the museum, and she had asked me to promise that I would give my photos to the archive – not surprisingly, she turned out to come from an Anafiot family.

The grant funded two visits to Greece: one for two months – one on Anafi, one in Athens – and the other for one month next year (which I now realize will be much too short).

In the months before the first visit I put in order the photos taken during my research on Anafi and in Athens in 1966 and 1967, and for three months in 1973, scanned all the negatives, prints and slides. Annotating them required searching through fieldnotes and diaries, and letters I had written to my parents, so that I could date events and identify individuals. But there were many gaps and I had to consult islanders and migrants to fill in the missing information. These were donated to the Benaki Museum photographic archive in 2010. The report to the Leverhulme Foundation at the end of this research can be found on their website: www.leverhulme.ac.uk/sites/default/files/imported_pdfs/eliciting%20memories-%20%20photos%20of%20long-term%20fieldwork%20in%20greec%20(kenna).pdf

I timed the visit to Anafi so that I could attend the main festival day on the island, on 8th September, which celebrates the Birth of the Virgin Mary (who as Panayia Kalamiotissa, the All Holy One, the Virgin of the Reed, is the patron saint of the Anafiots) and is held at the Lower Monastery.

The miracle-working ikon of Panayia Kalamiotissa had been brought down to the church of this Monastery from the chapel on the peak of Mount Kalamos, where it had been found after a lightning strike in 1887. I had not been at this festival since 1987, when five of us slept overnight on the floor of the Lower Monastery dining room, lying across a single foam mattress. As anyone might expect, many things had changed in the intervening decades, not least the construction of a paved road to the Lower Monastery, and the island's acquisition of a bus – so no more sleeping there overnight (except for pilgrims from the neighbouring islands).

There was some controversy about the 'improvements' carried out (at the cost of hundreds of thousands of euros, it was said) by the Abbot of a monastery on Santorini who was now in charge of the monastery on Anafi. Some people felt that the festival was no longer the island's own, while others felt that things were now properly managed. Anafiots, both islanders and migrants, were divided over the Santorini Abbot's decision that, as the venue of the festival was a monastery (even if with no monks), monastic rules, particularly about food, would be observed. His view was that if the festival fell on a day when monks would not have eaten meat, then the pilgrims would not be served it. It used to be the custom that sheep and goats from the monastery flocks would be slaughtered for a meat stew served with spaghetti, and pilgrims would also eat other produce from the monastery lands: cheese, honey, vegetables, and bread made from its wheat fields. All that had changed anyway, as no one on the island could find agricultural workers, and there was only one small flock of sheep and goats left (there had been 5,000 of them in the 1960s when I first went to the island). The controversy seems likely to continue, and I hope to find out more when we go back in the spring.

In the event, the spring visit to Greece in 2011 had to be cancelled because of a medical emergency involving Chris (the Leverhulme Foundation were extremely helpful and sympathetic about extending the time limit for research and the resulting report). We did not return until September 2012, taking with us a suitcase weighing nearly 17 kilos containing all the photos from the 1980s to donate to the Benaki Photographic Archive. We spent time in Athens, then on Anafi, and back to Athens for a conference at which Chris was presenting a paper (one of a series run by the Greek Parliament Foundation).

FROM THE END-OF-GRANT REPORT TO THE LEVERHULME FOUNDATION AT THE END OF 2012

The project centred on a large collection of photographs, dating from 1966 until the present day, recording life on a small Greek island and among the migrants in Athens with whom I have carried out anthropological research over five decades. It is a unique archive covering ten fieldwork visits to the island and to Athens from 1966 to 2009.

The photographs were scanned and annotated before being donated to a photographic archive in Athens, which has state-of-the-art facilities for conserving and storing them, and would allow scholars and other interested parties access to them. A beginning had already been made when the project started, but the scanning and annotation took much longer than anticipated; for one decade (1980s) there were over 1,500 images to catalogue. The plan was to show these photographs to islanders and migrants and to collect specific information about the identity of the individuals and locations shown, and also to elicit detailed comments on them through different kinds of question. The comments were expected to be about the past which these photographs capture, the individual histories and subsequent fate of the people and places, and the wider perspective of the past fifty years' history of Greece.

As things turned out, events in Greece overtook all these plans and expectations – it was much more difficult to visit people and to talk to them than had been thought. People were only free at weekends because of the length of the working weekday, or (particularly in 2012) they were unwilling to have visits when they were out of work. Comments made on the photos, particularly the oldest ones (in 'documentary' black and white), had current events as their immediate context: life on the island in the 1960s (subsistence agriculture and livestock raising) was described frequently as 'simple' and 'pure', in contrast to the complexities and difficulties of city life in the present. Islanders were somewhat more insulated from urban problems by tourism, but apart from full bookings for July and August, the season started later and ended sooner than usual, and tourists were looking for less expensive accommodation and food, so takings were down. Improvements to roads on the island meant that more people were going out to family fields and growing their own food.

Apart from seeing the past through the lens of the present (an unsurprising finding, very well known to media specialists, but very fresh for me), viewers were much more interested in identifying people and places than in describing what was being done (harvesting with sickles, for example). What the people in the photos were doing seemed to be secondary to the importance of correctly securing the name of the person and the location. To some extent, this fits in with the focus on remembering the deceased in the cycle of ceremonies following their death, and the importance of having a namesake descendant. The volume of overlapping comments made it almost impossible to make a record of what was said. On two occasions, images were shown on a large screen to audiences of about fifty people; when smaller numbers of people were looking at images on the laptop, they tended to jab the screen with their fingers, chatting with each other and ignoring questions. The proposed methods of 'photo elicitation' and plans for the recording of comments had to be abandoned.

ANOTHER PERSPECTIVE ON THE 2012 VISIT, FROM THE NEWSLETTER AT THE END OF 2012, FROM FIELDNOTES, AND FROM LETTERS TO FAMILY MEMBERS

There were two trips per week to Anafi by the Prevelis (ANEK Lines, a Cretan firm). We took the boat that left Piraeus on Friday at 6 pm, due to arrive at Anafi about 5 am Saturday. After a very smooth journey, we left the boat in the dark, and besides a small group of tourists disembarking, I noticed the only surviving son of the woman who had been my next-door neighbour in the village and used to pass eggs and vegetables across the fence to me. Her husband and one son had been killed while fishing in the mid-1980s, and another son died in his sleep. She had died suddenly three years earlier while cleaning horta (wild greens) in her courtyard. As it turned out, the reason for the son's visit was his mother's ektafi (exhumation).

We were met at the harbour by a friend who drove us to the village-square end of the periferiakos dromos (the road which now surrounds the village, previously a dirt road but now asphalted all the way around) so that we could walk downhill along the village street to 'our' house [the one where I had lived during my first fieldwork]. At the edge of the square we found huge hollow bollards had been set up to prevent cars and trucks from entering the square, but this clearly didn't work (they must be moveable) as on a later Sunday a small fork-lift-truck-sized dumper truck had clearly been driven through the square and down the main path from the church and was parked near the old post office to be used for loading rubble from building repair work. Halfway through the church service the truck could be heard rumbling across the square to dump one load and return to the site.

The weather while we were there was almost entirely wonderful, sunny and very hot, sometimes too hot. On most evenings we could sit out on our terrace and watch the sunset colours over the offshore islands and on the slopes of Mount Kalamos. And on one occasion we went up to the square, which faces west, to watch the vivid sunset over Santorini. I got the opportunity to talk to two women also there to watch the sunset, going over the story of the ill-fated mill which used to stand where a ruined house, equally ill-fated, stands today. The story is about a local girl and a monk, whom she said she would only accept as a lover if he shaved off his beard and cut his long hair. When he did so, and they met at the mill, she laughed at him and he cursed the spot, which ever since has brought bad luck on mill-owners or house-builders [this story was also told to the folklorist who visited the island in 1965 and is recorded in his notebook].

One of the main reasons to be on Anafi was for me to get agreement from the demarchos (Anafi has just been made a deme, a higher administrative unit than before; he was formerly proedhros = mayor) to approve of and possibly financially assist in the publication of a book about the folklore and customs of Anafi. This is based on notes found at the Folklore Centre in Athens (part of the Academy of Athens). The notes were made in 1965 by the then young folklorist Stephanos Imellos, who is now an academician (an athanatos *= 'immortal' as they say in Greece, as in France). To my amazement this was all decided very quickly (thanks to a phone call from Imellos, whom I imagined opening the conversation by saying 'I am the immortal academician for Folklore...'). The President of the Anafiot Migrants Association was also keen to be involved.*

The other reason to be on the island was to tell the islanders once again about my donation to the photographic archive of the Benaki Museum of all the photos I've taken on the island and among the migrants in Athens since 1966. The ones from the 1960s and 1970s were handed over two years ago, and the ones from the 1980s were donated on our arrival. I still have the last two decades (1990s, 2000s) to do! This has been funded by a grant from the Leverhulme Foundation. Also to my amazement, arrangements were very quickly made, with the co-operation of the high-school headmaster, for me to give a talk there, illustrated by PowerPoint slides I very luckily had with me. The headmaster had also worked on the island of Ai Strati (Ayios Efstratios, used as a place of exile), and had an interest in exile islands and knew the book I had written about the Anafi exiles, which had been donated to the school.

The village supposedly has a wi-fi network, but some spots are hotter than others and most restaurants and cafés have their own boosters because, of the eight masts set up around the village, only two work. We usually went to the former community office, an old barrel-vaulted room, which had at one time been the village ksenona *– guest house – where the visiting meat-merchants used to stay when they came to buy sheep and goats before Easter. This building now houses KEP, Kentro Exiperitisi Politon, Centre for the Service of Citizens, a one-stop shop where the knots of Greek bureaucratic red tape can be untied. It formerly had computers for the use of villagers and tourists, but now just has a table at which one can use a laptop (or when it's closed, sit on the bench outside, surrounded by parked motorbikes). This means that any citizen who comes in has their business overheard by anyone else in the room... In the meantime, the former KEP office has become the Demarchion, partly, it seems, because it has three rooms, so degrees of status can be marked out, and maybe because doors can be shut to keep conversations more or less confidential.*

On the first Sunday I went to church to find that a table had been set up for the celebration of two mnimosina (memorial services). One of these was for a recently dead woman and was the six-month memorial, early on in the cycle of ceremonies which occur at longer and longer intervals after the death. The other was the final memorial, after which the deceased's bones are exhumed from the village cemetery and put in a box to be placed either in the communal ossuary next to the cemetery chapel, or in a family vault, or in a chapel or ossuary outside the village, on family fields. At the end of the service (at which the hymn 'Aionia i mnimi' – Eternal Memory – was sung) the families of the dead offer the congregation a mixture of boiled wheat mixed with pomegranate seeds, sugar, dried fruit and other things. When I first went to the island, this was heaped up on a large tray, usually set up on one of the church gateposts, and people just took scoops of the mixture (called kolliva*). Nowadays it is handed out from a table in the church courtyard in sealed packets (bought from specialists in Athens), sometimes with the name of the deceased printed on them. Little cakes and buns are also offered. This is to elicit the prayer/wish that the deceased's sins will be forgiven. Previously a flask of flavoured liqueur was also offered outside in the square, with one little glass for everyone to use. Now the congregation goes to a café where coffee and a strong drink are served, and the members of the family are wished a long life to remember the dead person.*

After this, a few people set off for the cemetery where the exhumation of my former neighbour took place. The assumption is that after the full cycle of memorial services (and all those prayers for forgiveness), the soul is now free from a lifetime of sins, and ready for a positive outcome at the Last Judgment. On Anafi the coffin is (now – some people say this is a post-war development) put in a cement-lined trench in the ground, and sealed in by two large square blocks of cement with rings in them, cemented on top of the trench. In other words, there isn't any soil around the coffin, just air. So the cement seal was broken with pickaxes and chisels, and then the sealing stones raised. Adverse comments were made by some that as non-natural materials had been used for the coffin and the shroud (laminated wood, polyester cloth), natural processes hadn't operated. The bones were taken out and put in a large plastic bowl, and the skull was washed in wine and wrapped in a cloth. One of the women chanters in the church did most of the work, but the dead woman's daughter and son-in-law were standing by with wine, cloths and a large box. Most people stayed well back, although the son who had been on the ferry and another man were overwhelmed by tears and had to retreat to the cemetery wall to deal with their grief. It was an extraordinary feeling to see the skull of the woman who had been such a good neighbour to me, and yet it was also acceptable – this is the inevitable cycle.

We tried to patronize the two existing groceries equally. One is very near 'our' house and thus more convenient, the other at the eastern end of the village. This was once the poorer and more run-down end of the village, but the road up from the harbour has made it a major place for tourists to get off the bus and look for accommodation, cafés, restaurants and shops. This is where the new demarchion, and KEP, are located, so the whole centre of power has shifted, from the four cafés in the street above our house which were the centre of political (and men's) life even into the 1990s.

We were invited to visit old friends at their properties outside the village. On one of these occasions I was shown on a laptop a video which was taken from a documentary about the island made in the late 1970 by a Danish film-maker. I was startled at my own reactions to it. The village had electric light, but still no motor road to the harbour. A sick woman had to be carried down to the harbour on a stretcher, a fridge had to be brought up to the village on a donkey. Passengers and cargo still had to get off the steamer into small dinghies to get ashore. To me, houses and walls looked grubby, furniture was old and worn or broken, faces looked lined and worried. If this was what Anafi had looked like in the late 1970s, what had it looked like a decade earlier when I was carrying out my fieldwork? Was I looking back, as others did when they looked at my photographs taken then (and describing life then as 'pure and simple'), and seeing things in a kinder light than was really the case? I hadn't thought so until I experienced such a strong reaction to this film. Other viewers of the video called out the names of those they recognized, some of whom I had known, or the names of children, now adults, whom I would not have recognized. Some arguments ensued about the names of places where scenes were filmed. All very useful for the Leverhulme project final report.

Back in Athens, arrangements for the assembling of the Imellos book typescript began. Both Imellos and I want to situate our research in the context of folklore and anthropology in the 1960s, and it is important to write something about the way in which folklore, social history and anthropology have grown together and overlap now, instead of vigorously defending their disciplinary borders. Audio-tapes recorded by Imellos and by me will be turned into a CD of traditional Anafiot music. I prepared two pieces for the Anafiot Migrants Association newspaper to give information about this project, and also about the donation of the photos to the Benaki photo-archive.

Chris's conference on British-Greek links in trade and education in the nineteenth and twentieth centuries went well. Along with other conference participants, he was invited to a dinner at the residence of the British Ambassador, and also to a dinner at what I thought was the Greek Flat-Earth Society's clubhouse. This turned out to be a faulty interpretation of anti-sfairisis, *which I thought must mean 'against the sphere' (objecting to the view that the earth was that shape), and actually means 'lawn tennis' ('sphere', i.e. 'ball' as in* podho-sfairo, *football) going to and fro.*

Many shops in Athens were closed, employees were being laid off, those kept on taking home reduced pay, the Benaki museum staff on half-pay (and the 'ladies who lunch' in the restaurant there, with the wonderful view of the Acropolis choosing cheaper dishes); fuel prices were increasing, some people could no longer afford to drive to work, and if they lived in places with poor public transport now found themselves in great difficulties. Parish priests and voluntary organizations were running free-meal dining rooms, and not only for their parishioners or church-goers, or 'real Greeks'. Most apartment block tenants voted not to have the communal central heating on in autumn and winter, which would have put their communal maintenance costs up. Almost each week had its strikes, but many could not afford to go to the proposed demonstrations. The situation on Anafi, and I suspect, on other islands, was rather different. The summer season had been shorter, but still there were no free rooms in July and August. There were EU grants in place for road-clearing and maintenance. However, the local bus only ran to take people to and from the ferries – so the bus driver was being paid much less than in the summer – and villagers were making extra efforts to plant and care for vegetable gardens, as imported foodstuffs were increasing in price. The city-island contrast was in some ways reminiscent of the early days of the German Occupation – the later days were characterized by people dying of hunger in the city, while those in the countryside were being raided by the occupiers for their food stores – this is when the Oxford Committee for Famine Relief was founded, specifically to help the Greeks, an organization later to become Oxfam.

FROM THE NEWSLETTER AT THE END OF 2013

In late September we flew to Greece. This trip had two purposes. The first was to take all the Anafi photos and negatives from the 1990s (all annotated during the previous months) to join those from previous decades in the Benaki Museum photo-archive. This purpose was realized (only the ones from 2002 remain to be donated – it was after that date that I acquired a digital camera). The other purpose was to finalize the arrangements for the publication of the Stephanos Imellos notebook (his folkloric record of Anafi in summer 1965, to be illustrated with my photos from May 1966 to August 1967). Imellos, now an Academician, hadn't completed his editing of the notebook, so we weren't able to finalize anything, but hope to do so after Easter next year. It was another sandwich visit, with Athens at the beginning and end, and ten days on Anafi in early October in the middle. I was able to swim from Klisidhi beach, and just as Chris took a photo of me to prove it, two kayakers paddled round the rocks. They come every year, and have even circumnavigated the island on calm days. I hope they will donate any photos they have of the north-east and north-west coast to the Benaki as well.

We found Athens both uplifting and depressing – on the benches near the Evangelismos Hospital, people had taken over wooden benches as their homes,

Figure 19   Some things never change... a memorial service in October 2015

Figure 20   And some do. The 'not' has been erased in both the Greek and English versions of the sign, October 2015.

adorning them with plastic flowers and photographs; one man had brooms and brushes and a pail of water to wash the pavement around his bench. We were able to meet up with old friends on the island as well as in Athens, and to enjoy our stay at the British School there, which included the formal opening of the Catling Terrace (built with donations to commemorate a long-serving Director of the School, Hector Catling, and his wife Elizabeth), with a built-in barbecue section. The building of the terrace necessitated the sacrifice of the washing lines, where, in older days, women students were told not to hang their underwear in case it 'inflamed the gardeners' (this may be an apocryphal story).

FROM THE NEWSLETTER AT THE END OF 2014
In late September we flew to Greece, for our usual 'sandwich' visit (Athens-Anafi-Athens). This time the final batch of prints and negatives of images of Greece (dating from 2002) was handed over to the Benaki Museum photo-archive (after that I got a digital camera). What was supposedly the final meeting with Professor Stefanos Imellos about the publication of his notebook about Anafi folklore, dating from July 1965, to be illustrated with my photos from 1966–7, did not go quite according to plan. On previous occasions (actually, over several years) he had 'not quite completed' the editing of the notebook; this time he had done so, not only adding comparative material to his original text but also finding unknown manuscripts by linguistic scholars who had collected dialect words on the island, material which would be incorporated in the book. However, he now insisted that the few pages I had written, as originally agreed, should be expanded to thirty or fifty, so that 'now we are waiting for you!'

Well, the additional pages have now been written and so my contribution to the book will be appear both in English and in Greek. Plans for publication, sponsored by the Academy of Athens (of which the National Folklore Centre is part), supported by the *deme* of Anafi and by the Anafiot Migrants Association, are well advanced. [The book was published in 2015.]

Conclusion to the Second Edition
Anyone who now wants to know about Anafi has a wealth of resources to consult. Not only does the island have a website, but many island enterprises (restaurants, cafés, rooms to rent, shops) have their own as well as Facebook pages. Many Anafiots and migrants post photos and film clips on social-media sites, as do visitors and tourists. Some of these clips link to TV programmes and newspaper and magazine articles, as well as to documentary films about the island. Most of my publications have been uploaded to the website academia.edu and islanders and migrants are able to read in Greek, as well as in English, what I have written over the course of many decades. Fifty years

have passed since I first set foot on the island (18 May 1966), and there have been more than twenty visits over every decade since. I hope to continue this long association (equivalent now to a golden-wedding anniversary) for many years to come.

BIBLIOGRAPHY

Apollonios Rhodios, trans. R.C. Seaton, 1912. *Argonautica* (London: Heinemann, Loeb Classical Library).

Bent, James Theodore, 1885. *The Cyclades: or, Life among the Insular Greeks* (London: Longmans, Green).

Bendtsen, Margit, 1993. *Sketches and Measurings: Danish Architects in Greece 1818-1862* (Copenhagen: Skrifter udgivet af Kunstakademiets Bibliotek).

Birtles, Bert, 1938. *Exiles in the Aegean: a Personal Narrative of Greek Politics and Travel* (London: Victor Gollancz for the Left Book Club).

Bourdieu, Pierre, 1976. "Le sens pratique", *Actes de la recherche en sciences sociales* 1 (Février): 43-86.

Campbell, John K., 1964. *Honour, family and Patronage: moral values in a Mountain community* (Oxford: Clarendon Press).

Fermor, Patrick Leigh, 1958. *Mani: Travels in the Southern Peloponnese* (London: John Murray).

Friedl, Ernestine, 1965. *Vasilika: a village in Modern Greece* (New York: Holt, Rinehart and Winston).

Greger, Sonia, 1985. *Village on the Plateau* (Studely, Warwickshire: Brewin Books).

Kenna, Margaret E, 2001. *The Social Organization of Exile: Greek Political Detainees in the 1930s.* (Amsterdam: Harwood Academic Publishers).

Kininmonth, Christopher, 1949. *The Children of Thetis: a study of islands and islanders in the Aegean* (London: John Lehmann).

Mazower, Mark, 1993. *Inside Hitler's Greece: the experience of Occupation, 1941-1944* (New Haven and London: Yale University Press.

McNeal, R.A., 1967. "Anaphe: home of the Strangford Apollo", *Archaeology* 20: 254-263.

Naval Intelligence Division, 1919. *Greece.* (3 vols).Geographical Handbook Series (Naval Intelligence Division).

Naval Intelligence Division 1944, 1945 (revised version of 1919 edition). *Greece: vol I Physical Geography, History, Administration and peoples; vol II Economic Geography, Ports and Communications; vol III Regional Geography.* Geographical Handbook Series (Naval Intelligence Division).

O'Connor, Vincent Clarence Scott, 1929. *Isles of the Aegean* (London: Hutchinson).

INDEX